D0001321

STRESS AND ANXIETY

THE SERIES IN CLINICAL PSYCHOLOGY

CHARLES D. SPIELBERGER
and IRWIN G. SARASON   · Consulting Editors

BECKER · *Depression: Theory and Research*

FRIEDMAN and KATZ · *The Psychology of Depression:*
Contemporary Theory and Research

KLOPFER and REED · *Problems in Psychotherapy: An Eclectic*
Approach

REITAN and DAVISON · *Clinical Neuropsychology: Current Status*
and Applications

SPIELBERGER and SARASON · *Stress and Anxiety*, Volume 1

SARASON and SPIELBERGER · *Stress and Anxiety*, Volume 2

STRESS AND ANXIETY
Volume 1

EDITED BY

CHARLES D. SPIELBERGER
University of South Florida

IRWIN G. SARASON
University of Washington

HEMISPHERE PUBLISHING CORPORATION
Washington, D.C.

A HALSTED PRESS BOOK

JOHN WILEY & SONS
New York   London   Sydney   Toronto

Hemisphere Publishing Corporation
1025 Vermont Ave., N.W., Washington, D.C. 20005

Distributed solely by Halsted Press, a Division of John Wiley & Sons, Inc., New York.

Library of Congress Cataloging in Publication Data

Advanced Study Institute on Stress and Anxiety in
  Modern Life, Murnau, Ger. (Kreis Wilheim) 1973.
  Stress and anxiety.

  (The Series in clinical psychology)
  "Sponsored by the Scientific Affairs Division of the
North Atlantic Treaty Organization."
  Includes indexes.
  1. Stress (Psychology)—Congresses. 2. Anxiety—
Congresses. I. Spielberger, Charles Donald, 1927-
ed. II. Sarason, Irwin G., ed. III. North Atlantic
Treaty Organization. Division of Scientific Affairs.
IV. Title. [DNLM: 1. Anxiety. 2. Stress,
Psychological. WM172 S755a]

BF575.S75A38 1973   616.8'522   74-28292
ISBN 0-470-81605-8

Printed in the United States of America

CONTENTS

II EXPERIMENTAL RESEARCH ON
ANXIETY AND FEAR

CONTRIBUTORS

J. Bastiaans, Professor of Psychobiological Research, Psychiatrische Kliniek, Rijksuniversiteit Leiden, The Netherlands

Norman S. Endler, Professor and Chairman, Department of Psychology, York University, Toronto, Ontario, Canada

H. J. Eysenck, Professor of Psychology, Department of Psychology, Institute of Psychiatry, The Maudsley Hospital, University of London, London, England

J. J. Groen, Professor of Psychobiological Research, Psychiatrische Kliniek, Rijksuniversiteit Leiden, The Netherlands

H. D. Kimmel, Professor of Psychology, Department of Psychology, University of South Florida, Tampa, Florida, United States

Malcolm Lader, Member of External Scientific Staff, British Medical Research Council, Institute of Psychiatry, The Maudsley Hospital, University of London, London, England

Isaac Marks, Senior Lecturer and Consulting Psychiatrist, Institute of Psychiatry, The Maudsley Hospital, University of London, London, England

Donald Meichenbaum, Associate Professor of Psychology, Department of Psychology, University of Waterloo, Ontario, Canada

R. W. Ramsay, Lecturer in Experimental Clinical Psychology, Psychologisch Laboratorium, Universiteit van Amsterdam, The Netherlands

Irwin G. Sarason, Professor of Psychology, Center for Psychological Services and Research, University of Washington, Seattle, Washington, United States

Charles D. Spielberger, Professor and Director, Doctoral Program in Clinical and Community Psychology, University of South Florida, Tampa, Florida, United States

PREFACE

In modern technological societies, stress and anxiety have become a part of the fabric of daily life, and there is general concern about their adverse effects on human behavior. These problems are obviously complex and not limited by national boundaries, thus requiring the combined efforts of scientists from many countries and various academic disciplines for their solution. During the past two decades, advances in the behavioral and medical sciences have enhanced our understanding of stress and anxiety, and dissemination of this knowledge can contribute importantly to the survival of civilized society.

This volume reports the proceedings of an international Advanced Study Institute on *Stress and Anxiety in Modern Life* that was sponsored by the Scientific Affairs Division of the North Atlantic Treaty Organization. The Institute was held in Murnau-am-Staffelsee, West Germany, in June, 1973. The goals of the Institute were to provide an opportunity for the dissemination of available knowledge on stress and anxiety, to facilitate the exchange of information among behavioral and medical scientists from different countries who were presently working in these areas, and to stimulate new and collaborative research efforts.

The chapters in this volume are based on the major lectures that were presented at the Advanced Study Institute. The lecture-seminar format of the Institute was designed to facilitate give-and-take critical discussion of theory and research on stress and anxiety. The scientific content of the lectures was concerned with an analysis of historical trends, the evaluation of recent theoretical developments and a review of the burgeoning empirical literature.

The topics considered in this volume relate to three general areas. The chapters in Part I are concerned with the effects of psychosocial stress and biological dispositions on clinical anxiety, and on the development of psychoneurotic and psychosomatic emotional disorders. The chapters in Part II report the results of experimental studies of stress, fear, and anxiety under more carefully controlled laboratory conditions. In Part III, recent developments in the management of stress and in the treatment of anxiety are considered. In addition to the major lecture-seminar presentations, informal reports on a variety of related topics were given by a number of participants at the Institute. Abstracts of these informal presentations are included in Appendix A.

We would like to express our gratitude to Professor H. J. Eysenck, who served as a member of the Institute Planning Committee, and to Dr. J. C. Brengelmann, for his work on arrangements for the Institute in the host country. The consultation and guidance of Dr. Tilo Kester of the NATO Scientific Affairs Division is also gratefully acknowledged. For technical and clerical assistance in processing the manuscripts for this volume, we are indebted to Benjamin Algaze, Robert P. Archer, Florence Frain, and Mrs. Diane L. Ludington.

Charles D. Spielberger
Irwin G. Sarason

STRESS,
CLINICAL ANXIETY,
AND EMOTIONAL DISORDER

1

THE NATURE OF
CLINICAL ANXIETY
IN MODERN SOCIETY

Malcolm Lader
Institute of Psychiatry
University of London
London, England

Not being an epidemiologist, I am not qualified to give an exhaustive, critical review of epidemiological surveys of neuroses in general and anxiety states in particular. The main purpose of this presentation is to emphasize the difficulties of defining, either in clinical or in operational terms, "neurosis" and "anxiety." A second goal is to point out the deficiencies of any of the commonly used models of illness when studies of a broadly based population are carried out. The data outlined later give some ideas of the magnitude of the problem in terms of human suffering; this is what concerns members of the so-called "caring professions"—doctors, clinical psychologists, social workers, clergy, and so forth.

The relevance of epidemiological information for laboratory scientists is much greater than might appear at first sight. One of the prime objects of scientific research is to establish rules or laws by which a mass of data can be parsimoniously reduced, that have a useful degree of predictive generalization, and are susceptible to experimental disproof. In other words, there should be a high probability that people outside the original sample studied, or even outside the population from which that sample was drawn, will display phenomena of the type predicted by the putative laws. The laboratory scientist, when dealing with a clinical sample, is usually fully aware that he is dealing with a highly selected sample. What should concern him is how biased that sample is, so that he can say with a reasonable degree of precision how far his findings apply to the generality of patients who display in some degree the phenomenon of interest.

The second and more important reason for attempting to assess morbidity in the community is to provide information for health authorities in order that adequate treatment services can be set up. This is a realistic aim where major illnesses are concerned. For example, schizophrenia in its acute form presents problems of medical management and treatment which are most efficiently solved by admitting the patient to hospital, be it to the psychiatric wards of a general hospital, a specialised university clinic, or a large area mental hospital. Similarly, chronic schizophrenia results in grave social difficulties in the spheres of accommodation, employment, and social contacts. Community social services must be instituted and vigorously maintained and may take various forms such as day hospitals, day centres, sheltered workshops, hostels, special flatlets, etc. Whether the health authorities use the available information is a political and not a scientific matter.

When minor or minimal psychiatric disabilities are assessed and epidemiological data amassed, the choice of "cutoff" point between the "ill" and the "not ill" is crucial. With too high a cutoff point, persons who would genuinely welcome and benefit from medical and social help will not be cared for; too low a cutoff point and the gibe can be made that mentally healthy people are merely those who have not yet had the misfortune to encounter a psychiatrist. As will be seen later, astonishingly high prevalences of mental illness have been claimed in some studies. The influence of psychoanalysis is also an important one here, because many schools emphasize the inevitability of maldevelopment of some part or other of the "psychic structure."

Medicine has had its greatest successes in developing prophylactic rather than curative measures. This is often forgotten, especially by the layman, who is much more impressed by a heart transplant operation which prolongs life by a few months in one individual than by the eradication of malaria from a whole province, saving hundreds of lives and improving the general health of thousands. Indeed, it is repeatedly pointed out that a developing country with limited medical resources can do much more, on a cost-effective basis, by concentrating entirely on prophylactic measures than by setting up a few hospitals.

The prevention of mental ill health is much more difficult because there is so little known about the aetiological factors governing the onset and maintenance of such conditions. In particular, no necessary aetiological factors, the removal of which form the quintessence of the public health prophylactic approach, are apparent. For example, smallpox epidemics, although often associated with unsanitary conditions, overcrowding, etc., can be abruptly terminated by vaccinating all the population so that the virus can no longer find susceptible hosts. There is no equivalent situation in psychiatry; therefore, many more nonspecific measures, such as a general improvement in living and working conditions, must be resorted to. This is especially true in the attempted prophylaxis of minor psychiatric conditions such as anxiety states. Nevertheless, accretion of data regarding the prevalence of such conditions in the community might yield pointers towards aetiological factors.

The next section of this presentation is concerned with the crucial problem of the definition of anxiety states. The prevalence and incidence of such conditions in psychiatric hospital practice, in general hospital clinics, in general practice, and in the community at large is discussed in succession. I will concentrate on a few important studies which illustrate a particular point rather than attempting a comprehensive review (Lader & Marks, 1971).

THE DEFINITION OF
ANXIETY STATES

It is not my purpose to become sidetracked into a long discussion of what is meant by "clinical anxiety." Definitions of illness are unsatisfactory whether they are in biological (Scadding, 1967), behavioural (Mechanic, 1968), or social terms (Taylor, 1971). What concerns us here is the extent of "dis-ease" in the community, how these people come to our attention and how health services deal with them. Accordingly, we can resort to a simplistic, subjective notion of clinical anxiety. It is a patient's suffering from his symptoms of anxiety which leads him to answer questionnaire items positively, to badger his general practitioner for tranquilizers, to require long-term supportive psychotherapy, to end up with his frontal lobes surgically mutilated. Apart from questionnaire responses, the other behavioural consequences follow from the patient's concern regarding his suffering and from his wish for help.

Are such people normal? The concept of abnormality is complex, and can be regarded as absolute or relative. In the first case the deviation is from some Utopian criterion of perfection; in the second the deviation is from some norm, either the population norm or the patient's own previous norm. If the deviation is from the population norm, then the subject is concerned with symptoms which he regards as unusual in the general population but from which he may have suffered for a very long time. This is a personality abnormality, to be more specific in the case of anxiety, the abnormally anxious or neurotic personality. If the symptoms of the subject are regarded by him as a change in his usual status, then this is an abnormality according to individual standards. Such a condition, the clinical anxiety state, fits the medical model of illness.

An interactive model is often proposed with respect to anxiety—life stresses raising the anxiety levels of a moderately anxiety-prone individual to intolerable levels. As will be seen later, this type of syndrome is less common than one might expect although such patients do tend to filter through to the psychiatrist to bias his sample.

To define anxiety is even more difficult. Here one is dealing with an amalgam of overt behavioural characteristics that can be studied scientifically, and introspective feelings that are epistemologically inaccessible. Nevertheless, in the latter case we rely on verbal reports and on their more formalised equivalents, questionnaire responses. Anxiety can be a mood, a feeling, an emotional response, a symptom, a syndrome, or an illness with course, prognosis, etc. What is common is its generally unpleasant nature, its projection to the future, its similarity to fear, and its lack of referents.

There are undoubted deficiencies in many of the studies I shall cite with respect to criteria for neurosis, anxiety states, etc. In several studies the unstandardized definitions of individual general practitioners have been used, and the results sometimes throw more light on the variability of doctors' views than on the prevalence of anxiety. Nevertheless, if a pragmatic view is taken, what is important is the extent of the problem as patients, general practitioners, and psychiatrists view it, not the absolute scientific rigour with which cases are identified. Our purpose as members of the "caring professions" is to help sufferers, not to judge them.

ANXIETY STATES IN PSYCHIATRIC PRACTICE

The problem of clinical anxiety as seen by the psychiatrist is not an important one. In many countries, hospital psychiatry developed in the context of large, isolated mental hospital practice in which the bulk of the patients were psychotics, often with a poor prognosis. Psychoanalysts provided great impetus for the study of neurosis. Indeed, Freud (1894) first delineated anxiety neurosis as a separate disease.

Among psychiatric outpatients, anxiety states are diagnosed in about 6%-27% of all cases, but other related conditions like phobic disorders swell some of these percentages (see Table 1-1). The figure of 8% for Maudsley Hospital outpatients (Hare, 1968) excluded phobics and has remained constant over the past 9 years.

In patients with cardiovascular symptoms seen in a cardiology practice, anxiety states were diagnosed in 10%-14% of cases (White & Jones, 1928; Wood, 1941).

NEUROSIS AND WORK FACTORS

A study by Russell Fraser (1947) is worth citing in detail despite the fact that it was carried out over 30 years ago. In the early years

Table 1-1

Prevalence of Anxiety States in Outpatient Psychiatric Practice

Area	Source	Percentage
Oslo	Eitinger, 1955	6
Teheran	Davidian, 1969	7
London	Hare, 1968	8
Kuala Lumpur	Tan, 1969	15
Hong Kong	Yap, 1969	16
Chicago	Carmichael & Masserman, 1939	20
London	Garmany, 1956	25
Boston	Cobb, 1943	27

of the 1939–45 War, it became apparent that neurotic illnesses were responsible for a considerable amount of absence from work. Because it seemed apparent that the further stresses of war would increase this incidence and thereby prove a serious threat to the industrial efficiency upon which the survival of Great Britain depended, it was decided by the Industrial Health Research Board of the Medical Research Council that an appropriate study be instituted as a matter of urgency. What was required was an objective estimate of the true incidence of neurosis among factory workers and its effects on production and an appraisal of the factors predisposing to such illness.

A random sample of 3,083 was drawn from over 30,000 workers in light or medium engineering factories. Diagnosis was based on the clinical appraisal of any recent illnesses brought to light by examination or careful enquiry. Intelligence tests, an interview by a social worker, and a full psychiatric assessment were carried out, together with appropriate special investigations and a physical examination where necessary.

The term "neurosis" was used to cover mental illnesses such as anxiety states, mild depressive states, obsessional states, and hysteria. A second grouping consisted of "minor neurosis" and included mild personality disorders and cases of psychosomatic illnesses such as migraine, "functional" dysmenorrhoea, peptic ulcer, and dyspepsia. "Definite neuroses" had caused absence from work in most cases, whereas "minor neurosis" had tended not to do so.

During the 6-month period of the survey, 10% (9.1% of the men and 13.0% of the women) had suffered from definite and disabling neurotic illness. A further 20% (19.2% men and 23.0% women) had experienced episodes of minor neurosis. Neurotic illness caused between a quarter and a third of all absence from work due to illness and represented an annual loss of 3 working days in men and 6 in women. Although the data were not broken down by specific psychiatric diagnoses, anxiety states must be presumed to form an appreciable proportion of this morbidity.

Although the survey was made in wartime, factors peculiar to a wartime situation were not especially prominent at the time it was carried out. There were few bombing attacks, and though the hours of work were generally long, wages were high and there was no fear of redundancy.

Russell Fraser lists circumstances associated with a lower or higher incidence of neurosis. In the former category were workers with normal domestic responsibilities as well as their work duties, workers with above-average social contacts, and workers who found their employment congenial. Of course, no cause and effect relationship can be postulated. These circumstances need not necessarily protect the individual against neurosis but may merely reflect the non-neurotic person's ability to adapt to the situation by, for example, increasing his social contacts.

The list of circumstances associated with an increased incidence of neurosis is much longer:

1. Working over 75 hours of industrial work per week.
2. Taking a relatively inadequate diet.
3. Restricted social contacts, recreation, or leisure interests.
4. Widowhood or separation.
5. Demanding, atypical responsibilities associated with illness or death in the family, or special shopping, housing, financial, or transport difficulties.
6. Work found boring, or disliked.
7. Very light or sedentary work.
8. Work requiring skills inappropriate to the worker's intelligence. This could be either workers of low intelligence doing highly skilled work or workers of high intelligence doing unskilled work.[1]
9. Assembly, bench, inspection, or toolroom work, especially if this required constant attention but with little scope for initiative or responsibility.
10. Work programmes offering little variety.
11. Tasks for which the lighting was unsatisfactory.

Although many of these factors could have been products of the neurotic predisposition in the individuals, others, e.g., number 11, are very probably true aetiological factors. There was a definite relationship between unsatisfactory social relationships outside the

---

[1] The majority of women were on jobs of low skill, and this might account for the excess of neurosis found among women of average or high intelligence as compared with those of low intelligence.

factory, work dissatisfaction in the factory, and neurotic illness. Good welfare and social work, detailed assessment of the worker's potentialities and work preferences, and continual monitoring of the worker's attitudes and performance would all be advantageous in lessening the incidence of neurotic illness.

NEUROSIS IN GENERAL PRACTICE

It has long been recognised that nervous disorders are common afflictions among the general population of Great Britain. This is exemplified by the following quotation from Cheyne's treatise (1733) engagingly entitled: "The English malady: or a treatise of nervous disorders of all kinds, as spleen, vapours, lowness of spirits, hypochondriacal and hysterical distempers, etc." He opines:

> The Moisture of our Air, the Variableness of our Weather (from our situation amidst the Ocean) the Rankness and Fertility of our Soil, the Richness and Heaviness of our Food, the Wealth and Abundance of the Inhabitants (from their universal Trade) the Inactivity and sedentary Occupations of the better Sort (among whom this Evil mostly rages) and the Humour of living in great, populous and consequently unhealthy Towns, have brought forth a Class and Set of Distempers, with atrocious and frightful Symptoms, scarce known to our Ancestors, and never rising to such fatal Heights, nor afflicting such Numbers in any other known Nations. These nervous Disorders being computed to make almost one third of the Complaints of the People of Condition in England.

Shepherd, Cooper, Brown, and Kalton (1966) point out that Cheyne expressed some pervading notions about mental illness which have persisted to this day: that mental disorders are increasing as a result of our decadent, sedentary, unhealthy mode of life; that they are associated with dampness, the climate and overcrowding; that they are more common in England than elsewhere; and that they are much more common than they were. Even his estimate of prevalence has a modern ring to it; it is similar to that suggested by a working party of the College of General Practitioners (1958).

Subsequent opinions have not all been based, like Cheyne's, on personal conjecture and prejudice. Perhaps the earliest comprehensive survey was that carried out by Bremer during World War II (Bremer, 1951). He had been posted to a remote rural district in the north of Norway and was isolated there for 5 years of the German occupation. He came to know everyone of the 1,000-strong community "at very close quarters, knew their joys and, in particular, their sorrows and worries." Bremer reported that a quarter of the population showed gross psychological abnormality at some time during the 5-year period. This included psychoneuroses, "war neuroses," and milder forms of depression. Bremer was not only in a position to be able to suspect mental illness but he could also undertake a psychiatric interview to confirm or refute his suspicion.

Other studies vary enormously in their estimate of psychiatric illness in the community. A 1-year morbidity study by eight doctors scattered throughout the United Kingdom revealed that psychiatric illness was responsible for less than 4% of all consultations (Logan, 1953). However, a group of six practitioners working in collaboration with a psychiatrist reported that about one-fifth of patients seen in any 1 day in an urban practice were suffering from stress disorders (Finlay, Gillison, Hart, Mason, Mond, Page, & O'Neill, 1954). Quite obviously such figures depend enormously on the definition of mental illness. In this regard, Kessel's (1960) figures from one London general practice are very revealing. Using criteria based on the International Classification of Diseases (ICD), a prevalence rate for psychiatric morbidity of 50/1,000 of the population was obtained. If the criteria were loosened to embrace all patients who showed "conspicuous psychiatric morbidity" (i.e., overt psychological disturbance regardless of diagnosis), the prevalence rate rose to 90/1,000. If patients with physical symptoms for which no organic cause was detectable were included, the figure became 380/1,000. If all patients with psychosomatic disorders such as peptic ulcer and asthma were added, the final prevalence reached 520/1,000.

A careful and extensive study was carried out by Shepherd et al. (1966). They used general practitioners in London as their sources and sampled every eighth case envelope from the practitioners' medical records. The prevalence rate over 1 year for adults who sought help for psychiatric problems was the main statistic of interest. Problems arose both from the difficulties of defining psychiatric illness as seen in general practice and from differences among practitioners in their criteria for diagnosing such illnesses.

Furthermore, because the practices studied covered a wide range of socioeconomic circumstances, real differences in prevalence rates were to be expected. To assess these factors independently and as objectively as possible, the Cornell Medical Index Health Questionnaire (CMI) (Brodman, Erdmann, Lorge, Wolff, & Broadbent, 1949; Culpan, Davies, & Oppenheim, 1960) was administered in a proportion of practices. An attitude questionnaire regarding psychiatric illnesses was given to all the doctors taking part.

Shepherd found that psychiatric morbidity was one of the commoner reasons for consultation: among female patients it came second to respiratory conditions; among males, it ranked fourth after respiratory illnesses, orthopaedic and traumatic conditions, and gastrointestinal morbidity. In this study psychiatric morbidity referred only to conditions with a psychiatric diagnosis—"formal psychiatric illness"; "psychiatric associated conditions," which included organic illnesses in which the practitioner recognized psychological and emotional disturbance as playing an important role, constituted a further source of morbidity of about half the

Table 1-2

Patient Consulting Rates per 1,000 at Risk for Psychiatric Morbidity, by Sex and Diagnostic Group

Diagnostic group	Male	Female	Both sexes
Formal psychiatric illness:			
Psychoses	2.7	8.6	5.9
Mental subnormality	1.6	2.9	2.3
Dementia	1.2	1.6	1.4
Neurosis	55.7	116.6	88.5
Personality disorder	7.2	4.0	5.5
Total[a]	67.2	131.9	102.1
Psychiatric-associated conditions:			
Psychosomatic conditions	24.5	34.5	29.9
Organic illness with psychiatric overlay	13.1	16.6	15.0
Psychosocial problems	4.6	10.0	7.5
Total[a]	38.6	57.2	48.6
Total psychiatric morbidity[a]	97.9	175.0	139.4
Number of patients at risk	6,783	7,914	14,697

[a]These totals cannot be obtained by adding the rates for the relevant diagnostic groups because while a patient may be included in more than one diagnostic group, he will be included only once in the total.

Table 1-3

Distribution of the Main Psychiatric Categories: Comparison of
the Shepherd et al. Survey with Hospital Statistics

Category	Shepherd's survey[a]	Maudsley Hospital outpatients 1956-58[b]	Mental hospital first admissions, England and Wales, 1957[c]
Psychoses	4.2%	24.5%	72.3%
Neuroses	63.4	43.6	18.1
Character disorders	3.9	23.2	5.0
Miscellaneous	28.5	8.9	4.6
Total	100.0	100.0	100.0
Total number of cases	2,049	6,752	48,266

[a]Shepherd, Cooper, Brown, & Kalton, 1966.
[b]Hare, 1962.
[c]Registrar General, 1957-58.

formal psychiatric illness rate. The data by diagnosis and sex are shown in Table 1-2.

It can be seen that the great majority of patients in the category of suffering from formal psychiatric illness were diagnosed as neurotic whereas the psychoses accounted for less than 1 in 20 of this group. Shepherd et al. compared their data with those of Maudsley Hospital outpatients (Hare, 1962) and of mental hospital first admissions (Registrar General, 1957-58). The enormous differences in diagnostic composition are apparent (Table 1-3).

There were wide differences in the psychiatric morbidity reported ranging from a consultation rate of 25/1,000 at risk to 300/1,000; the mode was 125/1,000. True differences in prevalence related to social class and mobility were discerned but differences in attitude of the general practitioner were very important, practitioners sympathetic to emotional problems having a high prevalence rate. Nevertheless, much of the variation in consultation rate between doctors remained unaccounted for.

The data derived from the Cornell Medical Index (CMI) throw some light on the main topic of this paper, i.e., anxiety. It was administered to 979 patients in the study of whom 798 were diagnosed as suffering from nonpsychiatric conditions and 181 were diagnosed as having psychiatric complaints. These data were

Table 1-4

Distribution of Cornell Medical Index Health Questionnaire Responses among Survey Patients and Psychiatric Outpatients

Code	Item	Sex	Percentage of affirmative responses		
			Survey patients		Psychiatric outpatients
			Nonpsychiatric	Psychiatric	
153	Is it always hard for you to make up your mind?	M	9.6	24.9	43.3
		F	22.9	28.6	42.2
163	Does worrying continually get you down?	M	7.5	29.8	59.3
		F	16.8	35.7	62.0
194	Do you often become suddenly scared for no good reason?	M	2.0	11.6	34.8
		F	7.3	15.5	30.6
31	Are you often bothered by thumping of the heart?	M	9.0	17.1	39.0
		F	14.2	22.6	38.1
182	Do little annoyances get on your nerves and irritate you?	M	26.4	45.3	54.7
		F	35.5	43.8	53.0
108	Do you often get spells of complete exhaustion and fatigue?	M	10.7	20.4	49.8
		F	18.0	36.2	49.9

Source: Shepherd et al., 1966.

compared to a 10% sample of new cases presenting at the Maudsley Hospital outpatient clinics. For some of the more pertinent CMI questions, the percentage of affirmative replies for the three samples were broken down by sex. These percentages are shown in Table 1-4. The high proportion of responders among the hospital and psychiatric patients is to be expected, but Table 1-4 illustrates the high morbidity rate among nonpsychiatric patients in general practice, especially the women. If we examine responses to question 163 we should get some idea of the prevalence of mild anxiety; 16.8% of the female nonpsychiatric patients, a third of the female general practice psychiatric patients, and nearly two-thirds of the outpatients answered positively.

A most interesting and meticulous study, which emanated from the General Practice Research Unit of the University of London Institute of Psychiatry, was carried out by Goldberg (1972). The aim of the study was "to devise a self-administered questionnaire that would identify respondents with a non-psychotic psychiatric illness, by assessing the severity of their psychiatric disturbance." During the course of the development of this "General Health Questionnaire," a series of items was given to three groups of people: (a) 100 "severely ill" psychiatric patients—inpatients on the disturbed admission ward of a mental hospital who were rated by their psychiatrist as severely ill; (b) 100 "mildly ill" psychiatric patients attending Maudsley Hospital as outpatients and rated as mildly ill; and (c) 100 "normals," selected by interviewers of an opinion poll organisation following a structured interview. It is interesting that obtaining the last group of 100 necessitated interviewing 162 subjects in a door-to-door survey. Among the reasons for exclusion were health problems which were present in 25 (15.4%) of the sample.

Questions with a particular bearing on anxiety are reported in Table 1-5, with the number of the subjects in each group responding positively. Some responses obviously reflect social conditions, e.g., "worrying over money." However, about 5% of a normal population, from which subjects with overt physical or psychological problems have already been excluded, admit to symptoms characteristic of anxiety states, e.g., "afraid something awful is going to happen," and "feeling nervous and strung up all the time." Of the original 142 items, 93 were selected on the basis of their ability to discriminate between the groups and were subjected to a principal components factor analysis. The first factor extracted accounted for 45.6% of the

Table 1-5

Item Analysis of General Health Questionnaire

Code	Item	Number of positive responders		
		Normal	Mild	Severe
C9	Restless and unable to relax?	6	52	72
C14	Difficulty getting to sleep?	5	32	62
E4	What is going to happen to . . . ?	22	52	71
F18	Scared and panicky . . . no reason?	1	36	61
F20	Worry over money?	19	34	38
F21	Everything on top of you?	5	49	72
F22	Easily upset over things?	15	52	70
G2	Losing confidence in yourself?	7	44	78
G7	Worrying unduly?	6	38	56
G9	Afraid something awful is going to happen?	4	35	60
G11	Feeling nervous and strung up all the time?	6	48	72
G16	Thoughts going round and round certain things?	11	56	83

Source: Goldberg, 1972.

total variance and was interpreted as reflecting "severity of psychiatric illness." The nine items with the highest saturations on this factor are shown in Table 1-6. It can be seen that many of these items are relevant to anxiety, although it must be emphasized that

Table 1-6

The General Factor, "Severity of Psychiatric Illness," Showing the 9 Items with Highest Saturations

Excerpt from item	Factor loading
Dreading things you have to do	0.808
Felt constantly under strain	0.806
Felt unable to face your problems	0.802
Couldn't do anything because your nerves were too bad	0.802
Less capable of making decisions	0.786
Felt scared and panicky for no good reason	0.783
Felt you couldn't overcome your difficulties	0.779
Felt life entirely hopeless	0.775
Felt nervous and strung up all the time	0.772

Source: Goldberg, 1972.

other psychiatric states, especially mild depressive illnesses, could also underlie positive responses to such items.

The project that best exemplifies the method of using trained psychiatrists as identifiers of psychiatric cases in the community is that at Lund, a rural area in the south of Sweden with a total population of 2,500. Every member of the community was interviewed by Essen-Möller or one of his three colleagues (Essen-Möller, 1956). Persons were not classified into psychiatric categories but were arrayed on a continuum which ranged from definite psychiatric illness through personality disorders to complete normality. The lifetime prevalence for psychosis was found to be 1.7%, and for neurosis 5.2%. Because many of the population were regarded as personality variants, only 39.6% of the men and 32.8% of the women fell in the normal range.

A follow-up study was carried out by Hagnell (1959, 1968) who asked more pointedly psychiatric questions. The figure for psychosis remained at 1.7% but that for neurosis was reestimated at 13.1%. Hagnell also calculated the risk of developing a mental illness over a 10-year period. This was 11.3% for men and 20.4% for women. The estimated cumulative lifetime risk up to the age of 60 years was 43.4% for men and 73.0% for women. These are alarmingly high figures, but it should be noted that the risk of contracting a mental illness associated with *severe* impairment of function was only 7.9% for men and 15.4% for women. A substantial proportion of this morbidity related to neurosis.

ANXIETY IN THE COMMUNITY

In total prevalence studies carried out in the United States, the wider the criteria and the more intensive the methods used for ascertaining cases, the larger the proportion of the population regarded as "ill" or needing help of some sort. In a survey in Stirling County, (Leighton, Harding, Macklin, Hughes, and Leighton, 1963), trained research assistants administered a long, structured interview to over 1,000 heads of households or their wives. The completed schedules were assessed by psychiatrists. A prevalence rate of 577/1,000 was obtained for subjects judged as being "genuine psychiatric cases." The Midtown Manhattan Study (Srole, Langner, Michael, Opler, & Rennie (1962) suggested that 23% of the population could be regarded as suffering from serious psychiatric symptoms and some degree of impaired functioning. In both studies it appeared that less than 20% of the population studied were devoid of symptoms of emotional disturbance, an astonishingly low figure for "normality." However, this reflects the wide nature of the criteria used, far beyond the bounds of usual psychiatric diagnosis.

If more conservative criteria are used, lower figures are, of course, obtained; but, again, there is wide variation, ranging from 60.5/1,000 in the Eastern Health District of Baltimore (Lemkau, Tietze, & Cooper, 1941; 1942; 1943), through a figure of 93.4/1,000 also for Baltimore (Pasamanick, Roberts, Lemkau, & Krueger, 1959), to 138.0/1,000 for New Jersey (Trussell & Elinson, 1959). Although this variation probably reflects methodological differences, it is still possible that some genuine variation exists from place to place and from time to time.

A large-scale study, which is perhaps one of the most germane to an examination of anxiety in the community, is that of Taylor and Chave (1964). It involved recording the prevalence of various types of mental illness in the community at large, in general practice, and in hospital practice in a satellite New Town, and comparing these data with those for a residential suburb and for a decaying area of London. The New Town (dubbed "Newton") was a socially planned community with full local work opportunities; the dormitory housing estate ("Outlands") had good living accommodation but poor social planning and no local work places; the old area ("Oldfield") had poor housing usually with shared bathrooms, multiple occupancy and a somewhat above-average number of elderly women. Data from the general population were also available.

The purpose of the survey was to delineate the influence of environment on mental health. Does a "good community" promote mental well being or are the influences of genetic and constitutional factors more important? In the field survey, a 1 in 14 random sample of households in Newton was selected, and 1,422 interviews were obtained. In Outlands a survey had been carried out a few years before in which 1,485 people were interviewed. In Oldfield, a pilot study was carried out on 218 people. A great deal of data was amassed, but the salient points with regard to anxiety and anxiety states are presented in Table 1-7. It may be noted that nervous symptoms were reported by about one-third of the subjects, this figure being approximately the same for the three samples. These findings are especially impressive when one considers the fact that

Table 1-7

Nervous Symptoms

Symptom	Percentage of adults reporting		
	Newton	Outlands	Oldfield
"Nerves"	18	22	24
Depression	17	17	12
Sleeplessness	10	12	10
Undue irritability	13	11	8
At least one of the above	33	35	31

Source: Taylor & Chave, 1964.

different interviewing teams were involved. The data strongly suggest that long-standing or constitutional factors are of more importance in this respect than the environment.

The percentage of females reporting neurotic symptoms in the Taylor-Chave study was about twice that of the males. The percentage increased with age in the males but hardly altered in the women. There was also a tendency for the percentage of positive respondents to be highest in the lowest social class. This group of respondents was regarded by Taylor and Chave as suffering from what they called the "sub-clinical neurosis syndrome." These subjects were more concerned about their health, and were actually more ill, both psychologically and physically. Hire-purchase commitments (time payments for credit) and short term working were particular sources of anxiety. Nearly 20% of both men and women described themselves as life-long "natural worriers."

All the doctors in Newton took part in a survey of general practice, and their data could be compared with data from Outlands and the general population. The ICD was used, in which Group V comprises "Mental, psychoneurotic and personality disorders." The 1-year-period prevalence rates for these conditions taken together for Newton and Outlands respectively were 81.0/1,000 and 85.9/1,000. The figure for the general population of the United Kingdom is only 60.3/1,000; but for London and the South-East (from which region the populations of both Newton and Outlands had been drawn), the figure is a third higher. Accordingly, there were no differences between the various London samples. The bulk of this group V comprised the neuroses, the prevalence rates per thousand being 74.7 for Newton, 81.0 for Outlands, and 56.6 for the general population.

Of particular interest is the breakdown of these 1-year-period prevalence rates by diagnostic category. The prime finding is that formally diagnosed anxiety states constitute at least half the psychoneurotic conditions (Table 1-8). Neurasthenia seems to be overdiagnosed in Outlands, but otherwise the prevalences are relatively similar. The conclusions of the authors with respect to the general practice survey was that "between 7 and 8 percent of adults in the new town were treated for neurosis during the year, and this took the form mainly of anxiety and tension states." Anxiety states were more prevalent in women than in men, and in the over-45's than the younger groups. In women aged 45–65, the 1-year prevalence rate was 83/1,000.

Along with the formally diagnosed psychoneuroses, milder conditions were classified by the general practitioners among the group of psychiatric symptomatic conditions. In general, however, the more a practitioner was prepared to make a formal diagnosis, the lower was the figure for psychiatric symptoms, and vice-versa. Only 4% of the patients with neuroses were referred to a consulting psychiatrist.

What is overwhelmingly apparent is the high prevalence rate for mental ill health, with anxiety being an important component.

Table 1-8

Prevalence Rates for Psychoneuroses in Newton, Outlands, and the General Population

ICD code[a]	Psychoneurotic disorder	1-year prevalence rate per 1,000		
		Newton	Outlands	General population
310	Anxiety state	45.6	38.1	28.8
311	Hysterical reaction	1.4	2.7	1.9
312–13	Obsessional state	3.9	(b)	(b)
314	Neurotic depression	6.7	4.0	1.8
318.45	Psychoneurosis (unspecified)	15.2	14.6	8.7
318.3	Neurasthenia	3.5	20.4	7.2
315–17	Psychoneurosis with somatic symptoms	9.9	8.0	8.7

Source: Taylor & Chave, 1964.
[a]ICD = International Classification of Diseases.
[b]Not available.

Taylor and Chave were themselves astonished that the incidence of subclinical neurosis "would be virtually the same in a decaying London borough, in an out-county estate without local work or social life, and in a planned new town." About a third of the population show this syndrome; it is not related to length of residence or to income. It is age and sex linked. This minor disease entity must presumably stem from the constitutional factors in the individual, "in the sense that it represents a deeply embedded pattern within the nervous system." The step from this subclinical syndrome to overt neurosis occurs when the patient takes note of the subjective symptoms and consults a doctor. This overt neurotic group varies in size according to the quantity and quality of general practice and specialist psychiatric services available.

Before accepting these and further implications of the data from Taylor and Chave's study, it must be emphasized that one survey may have been subject to bias, special conditions may have been prevailing, or the results could have been wide of the true figures due to a statistical freak. A very recent study with equally startling results, however, has now become available.

Salkind (1973), dissatisfied with currently available rating scales for anxiety, painstakingly developed his Morbid Anxiety Inventory (MAI). The instrument eventually took the form of a multiple-choice questionnaire, 21 questions dealing with various aspects of anxiety. Items included self-assessments of worry, shaking of the hands, headache, sweating, etc. The MAI was validated in several ways including against physiological concomitants of anxiety: it proved to correlate highly with measures of palmar sweat-gland activity previously shown to reflect overt anxiety (Lader & Wing, 1966). The inventory was shown to be sensitive to changes in anxiety level and to be an effective instrument in screening subjects for anxiety.

Clinical validation studies suggested that a score of 14 afforded an adequate separation between nonanxious and anxious subjects. The range 14–17 is a twilight zone in which there is difficulty in deciding whether an individual is anxious or not. Above 17 there is less difficulty; the misdiagnoses are almost all false negatives, due to denial of symptoms by anxious patients, so diagnosed by a psychiatrist.

Armed with these clinical data, Salkind organized a quota sample of the population of Great Britain carried out by Gallup Poll Organization, who are well known to psephologists. The Registrar

General's 12 Demographic Regions were studied; and representative samples with respect to age, sex, social class, and employment were obtained. Forty-four interviewers obtained full data on 420 people. Subjects were directly questioned regarding treatment for "worry, depression or any other nervous complaint": 29% answered positively, and about half of this group had received treatment in the past year. Hospital treatment accounted for a quarter.

Taking an MAI score of 14 as the criterion, no less than 44% of the adult population were anxious. If one uses the more conservative criterion of 17, then 31% fall into the anxious group, a figure close to that of Taylor and Chave for "sub-clinical neurosis." Women tended to have higher MAI scores than men, with means of 15.05 and 12.67, respectively. Scores increased with advancing age and in the lower social groups. There was no difference between the anxiety levels of the urban and the rural population samples; but baffling regional variations were found, the highest values being obtained from East Anglia, West Midlands, and South Wales.

CONCLUSIONS

Do 10 million adults in Great Britain have symptoms of anxiety, insufficient to cause them to seek medical aid yet great enough to cause them discomfort, distress, and suffering? The evidence from both Taylor and Chave's study and Salkind's survey is too consistent to ignore. What hospital psychiatrists are seeing is the tip of an iceberg; what general practitioners see is similarly but a fraction of human "dis-ease." How should such data influence the specialist psychiatrist in his view of neurosis in general and anxiety states in particular?

It seems that about a third of the adult population suffer constantly from nervous complaints, especially anxiety. This proportion is lower in males and the young, higher in females and the elderly. This condition appears to be a product of a constitutional substrate. Some of these subjects develop overt anxiety states, but the conditions that govern this step are not clear. To label these conditions "stress" is tautologous. Probably, attitudes toward neurosis on the part of the general practitioner and of the general public are the most important factors in determining the incidence of overt neurosis. A kind, sympathetic doctor with time to listen will find many of his patients with a subclinical anxiety state developing overt symptoms. When this happens he will no longer have time to listen; and some rough and ready regulation takes place.

A subgroup of anxiety states comprises those with lifelong anxiety of an almost entirely constitutional nature. This is present in about 5% of the population. The symptoms may vary but are rarely absent, and the prognosis is poor. Another subgroup is those patients who have no predisposition toward anxiety but who have developed neurotic reactions to overwhelming environmental factors. The extreme examples of this syndrome are the traumatic neuroses occurring in war conditions and following natural disasters. The prognosis is good. It is interesting that most animal models of neurosis seem analogous to these less common traumatic anxiety states rather than to the bulk of syndromes seen in humans.

The implications of the number of persons with subclinical anxiety or neurotic symptoms are frightening. The case load of psychiatrists and, particularly, of general practitioners could expand almost indefinitely. In the United Kingdom the average general practitioner would have about 500 subclinical anxious patients on his list, for whom he would be contractually obliged to provide treatment. If they all insisted on their rights and were each allocated only 15 minutes per week for a supportive psychotherapeutic interview, the general practitioner would be working 125 hours per week with this one condition. Patients are becoming more demanding and expect effective medical treatment not only for major acute illnesses but for minor chronic conditions as well. The potential for overloading the health delivery services is only too plain to see. At present, patients who come to their general practitioners with vague somatic complaints such as "nervousness" and "worry" sometimes receive sympathetic support; more often, because of the limitations of time, they are treated symptomatically with anxiety-allaying drugs such as the benzodiazepines (e.g., diazepam, Valium). In the United Kingdom in 1971, the National Health Service paid out 15 million pounds for this category of drugs. Though these drugs are fairly effective in alleviating anxiety and are safe in use, nevertheless, in view of the constitutional nature of the condition, long-term psychological dependence on these drugs occurs frequently. The moral implications of this are complex, but it could be argued that the situation is similar to but much less serious than that of the insulin-dependent diabetic.

I have stressed the constitutional nature of excess anxiety. One body of influential albeit nonscientific opinion, namely the various schools of psychoanalysis, would claim that the roots of such anxiety lay in childhood experiences of one sort or another. That a third of the populace is affected is no evidence against this argument. However, genetic studies, including twin studies, twins brought up apart, adoptive studies, and family surveys show that anxiety states and anxious personalities are strongly determined by hereditary factors. Indeed, in all the flurry of interest in the genetics of schizophrenia and manic-depressive psychosis, it appears that it has been forgotten that the genetic loading in anxiety states is the most pronounced for any functional condition (Slater & Shields, 1969).

I shall conclude on an optimistic note. Despite the Jeremiahs in our midst who believe that anxiety is a product of our time, there is no evidence that we are more anxiety prone than were our forebears. And it may be that anxiety, on balance, is more beneficial than harmful, providing an essential spur to human creativity, invention, and achievement.

REFERENCES

Bremer, J. Social psychiatric investigation of a small community in Northern Norway. *Acta Psychiatrica Neurologica Scandinavica, Suppl.*, 1951, 62, 1-66.

Brodman, K., Erdmann, A. I., Lorge, I., Wolff, H. G., & Broadbent, T. H. The Cornell Medical Index: an adjunct to medical interview. *Journal of the American Medical Association*, 1949, 140, 530-534.

Carmichael, H. T., & Masserman, J. H. Results of treatment in a psychiatric outpatient department: A follow-up study of 166 cases. *Journal of the American Medical Association*, 1939, 113, 2292-2298.

Cheyne, G. *The English malady: Or a treatise of nervous diseases of all kinds, as spleen, vapours, lowness of spirits, hypochondriacal and hysterical distempers, etc.*, London: G. Strahand & J. Leake, 1733.

Cobb, S. *Borderlands of psychiatry*. Cambridge: Harvard University Press, 1943.

College of General Practitioners. Psychological medicine in general practice. *British Medical Journal*, 1958, 2, 585-590.

Culpan, R. H., Davies, R. M., & Oppenheim, A. N. Incidence of psychiatric illness among hospital out-patients: An application of the Cornell Medical Index. *British Medical Journal*, 1960, 1, 855-857.

Davidian, H. Aspects of anxiety in Iran. *Australian and New Zealand Journal of Psychiatry*, 1969, 3, 254-258.

Eitinger, L. Studies in neuroses. *Acta Psychiatrica Neurologica Scandinavica, Suppl.*, 1955, 101, 1-47.

Essen-Möller, E. Individual traits and morbidity in a Swedish rural population. *Acta Psychiatrica Neurologica Scandinavica, Suppl.*, 1956, 100, 1-160.

Finlay, B., Gillison, K., Hart, D., Mason, R. W. T., Mond, N. C., Page, L., & O'Neill, D. Stress and distress in general practice. *Practitioner*, 1954, 172, 183-185.

Fraser, R. The incidence of neurosis among factory workers. Industrial Health Research Board of the Medical Research Council, Report No. 90. London: H.M.S.O., 1947.

Freud, S. The justification for detaching from neurasthenia a particular syndrome: The anxiety neurosis. *Collected Works*, Vol. 1. London: Hogarth Press & Institute of Psychoanalysis, 1894. (Paper reprinted in 1946.)

Garmany, G. Anxiety states. *British Medical Journal*, 1956, 1, 943-946.

Goldberg, D. P. *The detection of psychiatric illness by questionnaire.* Maudsley Monograph No. 21. London: Oxford University Press, 1972.

Hagnell, O. Neuroses and other nervous disturbances in a population, living in a rural area of Southern Sweden, investigated in 1947 and 1957. *Acta Psychiatrica Scandinavica, Suppl.*, 1959, 136, 214-219.

Hagnell, O. A Swedish epidemiological study: The Lundby Project. *Social Psychiatry*, 1968, 3, 75-77.

Hare, E. H. *The Bethlem Royal Hospital and the Maudsley Hospital 4th triennial statistical report, 1958-60.* Privately published, 1962.

Hare, E. H. *The Bethlem Royal Hospital and the Maudsley Hospital 6th triennial statistical report, 1964-66.* Privately published, 1968.

Kessel, W. I. N. Psychiatric morbidity in a London general practice. *British Journal of Preventive and Social Medicine*, 1960, 14, 16-22.

Lader, M. H., and Wing, L. *Physiological measures, sedative drugs, and morbid anxiety.* London: Oxford University Press, 1966.

Lader, M. H., & Marks, I. *Clinical anxiety.* London: Heinemann Medical, 1971.

Leighton, D. C., Harding, J. S., Macklin, D. R., Hughes, C. C., & Leighton, A. H. Psychiatric findings of the Stirling County study. *American Journal of Psychiatry*, 1963, 119, 1021-1026.

Lemkau, P., Tietze, C., & Cooper, M. Mental hygiene problems in an urban district. *I-V. Mental Hygiene (New York)*, 1941, 25, 624; 1942, 26, 100; 1942, 26, 275; 1943, 27, 279.

Logan, W. P. D. *General practitioners' records: An analysis of eight practices during the period April 1951 to March 1952.* Studies on Medical and Population Subjects, No. 7. London: H.M.S.O., 1953.

Mechanic, D. *Medical Sociology: A selective view.* New York: Free Press, 1968.

Pasamanick, B., Roberts, D. W., Lemkau, P. W., & Krueger, D. R. A survey of mental disease in an urban population: Prevalence by race and income. In B. Pasamanick (Ed.), *Epidemiology of mental disorder.* Publication No. 60 of the American Association for the Advancement of Science. Washington, D.C., 1959.

Registrar General. *Statistical review of England and Wales.* Mental Health Supplement. London: H.M.S.O., 1957-58.

Salkind, M. R. *The construction and validation of a self-rating anxiety inventory.* Unpublished doctoral dissertation, University of London, 1973.

Scadding, J. G. Diagnosis: The clinician and the computer. *Lancet*, 1967, 2, 882–887.

Shepherd, M., Cooper, B., Brown, A. C., & Kalton, G. W. *Psychiatric illness in general practice*. London: Oxford University Press, 1966.

Slater, E., & Shields, J. Genetical aspects of anxiety. In M. H. Lader (Ed.), *Aspects of anxiety*. London: Royal Medico-Psychological Association, 1969.

Srole, L., Langner, T. S., Michael, S. T., Opler, M. K., & Rennie, T. A. C. *Mental health in the metropolis: the Midtown Manhattan Study*. New York: McGraw-Hill, 1962.

Tan, E. S. The symptomatology of anxiety in West Malaysia. *Australian and New Zealand Journal of Psychiatry*, 1969, 3, 271–276.

Taylor, F. K. A logical analysis of the medico-psychological concept of disease. *Psychological Medicine*, 1971, 1, 356–364.

Taylor, S. J. L. & Chave, S. *Mental health and environment*. London: Longmans, 1964.

Trussell, R. E., & Elinson, J. *Chronic illness in the United States*. Vol. 3. *Chronic illness in a rural area—the Hunterdon Study*. Cambridge, Mass.: The Commission on Chronic Illness, 1959.

White, P. D., & Jones, T. D. Heart disease and disorders in New England. *American Heart Journal*, 1928, 3, 302–318.

Wood, P. Effort syndrome. *British Medical Journal*, 1941, 1, 767–772, 805–811, 845–851.

Yap, P. M. Anxiety reactions among Western expatriates in a plural society. *Australian and New Zealand Journal of Psychiatry*, 1969, 3, 339–342.

2

PSYCHOSOCIAL STRESS, INTERHUMAN COMMUNICATION, AND PSYCHOSOMATIC DISEASE

J. J. Groen and J. Bastiaans

Department of Psychiatry, University of Leiden
Jelgersmakliniek, Oegstgeest, The Netherlands

The professional commitments of medicine in our time are both widening and deepening. Although there is an increasing awareness of the need to extend medical efforts throughout the world, progress in modern medicine is not evenly distributed; diseases that have been conquered in the so-called Western countries are still wide spread in other areas. Growing realization that this inequality is due largely to poverty, backwardness, and authoritarian power systems in government and economy has made doctors more aware of the importance of social and political conditions as causes of disease. An increasing number of studies, therefore, are now being devoted to the mechanisms by which poverty, malnutrition, poor housing, and inadequate education produce disease. By eradicating these causes, we can improve health conditions in underdeveloped countries.

Acute infectious diseases, tuberculosis, rheumatic fever, and protein-caloric malnutrition have practically disappeared as mass phenomena from the Western world. Consequently, mortality has gone down impressively, especially in children, and the average life expectancy is now longer than ever before in history. We may even anticipate that neoplastic diseases will be conquered in the near future. Against this gratifying picture, however, there are other factors that may influence health conditions in the Western world which damp our optimism. A third world war, for example, could destroy in one stroke the lives of nearly everyone who has benefited from recent medical progress. "Minor" wars and violence from other causes such as traffic accidents are still important causes of death, and suicide is taking a heavy toll of life. So are arteriosclerotic heart, brain, and kidney diseases.

The situation looks even less positive if one devotes attention to morbidity. In this respect, the population of the Western countries are far from healthy. Apart from the large number of people who suffer from chronic, vascular, respiratory, and metabolic diseases, there is an appalling frequency of psychiatric, psychosomatic, and behavior disorders, including alcoholism, drug addiction, asocial behavior, and delinquency. Increased absenteeism from work because of functional and psychosomatic disease is another indication of the still unsatisfactory state of health in Western countries. There is ample reason therefore to devote equal attention to the health problems of our own society as to those of the underdeveloped countries.

It is naive to believe that poverty and underdevelopment are the only sociocultural factors that produce disease. There is always a relationship between society, the ways of human communication which go with it, and disease. Every society has the diseases it deserves. It is the purpose of this paper to inquire into the role of psychosocial factors that produce or promote disease in the Western countries. Our main attention will be focused on the so-called psychosomatic disorders. Before turning to this subject, it seems appropriate to introduce some basic definitions.

Society refers not only to the organized complexes of buildings, factories, engines, transportation systems, offices, farms, and agricultural equipment, but, more importantly, to the *people* who live in this environment. In the study of society, one must observe the ways people communicate, achieve gratifications or suffer frustrations, and strive to maintain or improve their status in the framework of their social value systems. The concept of society in the following discussion therefore refers not only to technical and economic conditions, but also to psychosocial and psychocultural factors.

We use the term *psychosocial* to accentuate our central interest in the ways society affects and influences people and vice versa. Society implies people and the ways they communicate, perceive, and interpret each other's behavior in the different social (cultural) subgroups to which they belong. Psychosocial stress refers to social situations that are frustrating (or threatening to frustrate) a group of individuals. The intensity and duration of psychosocial stress may seriously upset and alter the homeostasis of communications among people in a group, and disrupt their internal homeostasis, i.e., their health.

HUMAN COMMUNICATION: A SIMPLE PSYCHOSOCIAL MODEL

Figure 2-1 gives a diagrammatic expression of how the psychobiological interactions between two individuals determine both their outwardly directed behavior towards each other and the processes that take place within their internal organization. This diagram is an attempt to illustrate the main concepts on which this paper is based:

1. The behavior (output) of one individual is the information or stimulus (input) for another, and vice versa.
2. Information, after being scanned (cognitively evaluated) in the central nervous system, gives rise to externally directed behavior and to changes inside the organism ("internalized behavior").

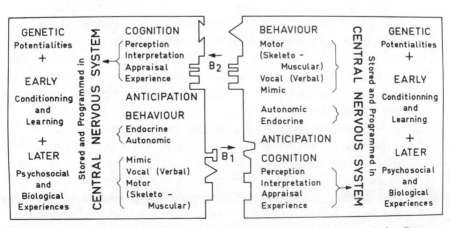

Fig. 2-1. The behaviour of Personality 2 is the stimulus (or stress) for Personality 1 and vice versa: $B_1 = S_2$ and $B_2 = S_1$.

3. The model depicted here seems to us better than the simple model of:

$$S(\text{stimulus}) + O(\text{organism}) \longrightarrow R(\text{response})$$

The most important stimulus for man by far is the behavior of his fellow man. The SOR model would hold only if man were a solitary animal. The present model conceptualizes man's behavior as primarily communicative exchanges with other persons, and assumes that the most common stress for man is the threatening actions or words of one or more of his fellow men. Thus, most human stresses are psychosocial.

4. The behavior of fellow human beings continually stimulates, inhibits, or modifies a person's *externally* directed behaviors and communications in his family, his work, and his society. The behavior of others also affects thinking, feeling, and autonomic and endocrine reactions. Man's behavior is directed towards preserving homeostasis, i.e., social harmony and biological health.

5. It follows that animal experimentation, e.g., on anxiety and behavior, to be applicable to man, should not be carried out on isolated animals, but with two or more animals and their communicative signals and behavior.

6. The behavior of man, in his communications with his fellow men, is determined by the biological structures and potentials he shares with other mammals. In addition, man has, in the course of his evolutionary history, especially developed the biosocial potentiality of vocalisation to verbalisation. In distinction to all other animals, man is able to learn to speak, understand, think, write, and read a word language. This vastly increases his psychological and communicative potentialities, and has enabled him to develop his orginally primitive social groups into cultures.

7. Society means people. Figure 2-1 oversimplifies the complicated and diversified human interactions and patterns of internalized behavior. Nor does it reflect the fact that the human individual communicates, as a rule, not with one but with many fellow human beings, in the different subgroups and subcultures to which he belongs.

8. The diagram is also incomplete because it does not depict the continuous dynamic development that takes place in the

behavior of individuals towards each other in the course of their childhood, adulthood, and senescence. Nor does it illustrate the continuous evolution and change in the subgroups in which people live and that influence and modify the ways of their communication.

PSYCHOSOCIAL STRESSES
IN WESTERN SOCIETY

Human communications take place in three environments: the family, the work situation, and in the large sociocultural subgroups of the society. We will try to describe how these three environments influence human behavior and health in modern Western society. It should be kept in mind, however, that this description is given by observers who are themselves members of Western society. Dr. Gregg, a former president of the medical division of the Rockefeller Foundation, had a favorite saying: "The last thing a deep-sea fish will ever discover is the existence of salt water." Similarly, the attention and curiosity of the scientific investigator is often caught more by what is strange and abnormal than by his own environment and his own nature. The following description of some of the ways that people of present day Western cultures communicate is, therefore, of necessity, colored by the environment in which the authors grew up, lived, and worked.

Sources of Stress in the Family

An important trend in Western family life has been the reduction in the number of children. Western families of all classes, nowadays, comprise no more than four or at most five individuals. Thus, the beneficial effects of *group support* are much less active now than in old-fashioned Western families, or than in most Eastern cultures. From the point of view of group dynamics, when there is rivalry and conflict between parents and children, there are fewer persons from whom the participants in the conflict can derive support. The so-called oedipal conflict, described by Freud, is more often present in small Western families than in the large Eastern families for the simple reason that the father and (often only) son have to compete for the (often only) female figure in the small group instead of sharing love and attention with several other female figures.

Another feature of the small family is the greater demands that children must make on their parents for their time and attention. When there are no brothers and sisters to play with, to speak and listen to, to ask for help when needed, children must appeal to the few figures available. Demanding children follow their biological urge for attention, and if it is not given by an older or younger sibling, they must seek attention from the parents. On the other hand, the tendency towards parental overprotection is stronger in small families than in larger families: when one or two children are the only "possessions" the mother has, she is more afraid that something may happen to them and, consequently, interferes too much with the child's trial and error exploratory behavior. In addition, common games that tend to encourage "team spirit" are played less often in smaller than in larger families. Playing games, singing together, and walking tours or excursions on bicycle are less conducive to the building of a family "esprit de corps" when the family is small. When the children grow older, the attraction of being home in the evening or returning home for celebrations is less when the group is small. All these features lead to relationships characterized by intrafamily ambivalence rather than by cohesion.

The diminution of cohesion and support in the Western family is accentuated by a decline in the religious practises of the family. The common ritualistic behavior of joint prayer, singing hymns, reading the scriptures, and going to church together all have a function which, beyond its religious significance, tightens the family bonds by the creation of mutual understanding. In many Western families this common behavior is disappearing; a vivid picture of the change is obtained if one compares the Sunday as it is now spent in many families with what it used to be a generation ago.

To obtain emotional support, Western children have come to depend more on other groups than on their own family. The kindergarten and the school, and later the hockey, football, or rowing club, the youth guild or church association may substitute for the communication children miss at home. A similar function is exerted by amateur jazz music bands and, on a different level, by political youth or student groups. But if a child is not sent to kindergarten, or if the teacher does not know how to encourage group cohesion in the class, or if a child is ill and stays in a hospital, or if the child or adolescent does not succeed in finding a place in such a group, needed compensation for the diminished group support of the family may be insufficient.

Transportation by automobiles is another factor that deprives modern children of communication with each other and their parents. Going to school or work together, or to church, or to pay a family visit, or to spend a day in the country in the olden days meant walking, cycling, or travelling in a railway compartment. Nowadays, father is driving and cannot be distracted by children climbing on his lap. He cannot stop to look at a tree, a bird, or something else for which the child wants his attention, and conversation is less centered on what interests the child. Anyone who has watched children being driven in a car for any length of time realizes the frustration imposed on them by the forced enclosement in a limited space with hardly any communication.

Another factor in the Western way of life that may have an unfavorable influence on the development of children is the growing tendency to diminish the burden of duties of women, both in the household and in the care of their children. Not long ago a baby, almost always born inside the home, would sleep with the mother in the same bed or certainly in the same room. When it cried during the night, the mother would take it to her and soothe it by pressing it against her, rocking it to and fro, trying to comfort it by her warmth, by soothing vocalizations, and by giving it her nipple to suck on. Now, most Western babies are born in hospitals where they are kept away from their mothers except at fixed feeding hours, prescribed by hospital routine. Many Western mothers are taught not to react to the baby when it cries during the night and not to take it too often in her arms because this would "spoil" the child. In the United States, breast feeding is regarded as old fashioned, as something almost indecent and a nuisance, or as something "not done" because it may spoil the shape of the breast and thereby the mother's feminine figure. This practice is an impressive example of how far human culture sometimes interferes with biological nature.

Both the mother and the father in Western culture tend to restrict the time their children spend with them. Many parents have substitutes replace them when they go on vacation, or send the children away when they entertain guests. A modern child often comes home and finds the mother not in. Going to watch a football game or to see friends, receiving guests or looking at television are among the reasons that many present-day Western parents refuse their children the attention they need. This holds especially for many fathers when they come home in the evening. Instead of playing with their children, the fathers direct them to gramophone records or to watch the television by themselves. These passive activities are insufficient substitutes for educative play behavior. No wonder that many children develop differently from their father's expectations—they hardly undergo their father's influence. The same is true when the husband spends his evenings away from home (e.g., to go to scientific meetings!).

There is also a tendency in Western culture to wean babies at an earlier age from bottle feeding. If given properly prepared artificial diets, this is apparently without harm to the bodily growth of the baby; indeed, it may enhance the rate of gain in height and weight. On the other hand, early weaning diminishes the time during which the child is coddled and hugged on mother's lap. At an early age, the Western baby is put into a playpen, separated from the mother by bars, and this again diminishes the bodily contact between the child and the mother. Similarly, many Western mothers refuse to coddle a child when he asks for it, because "he is too big for this now." As a result, some Western children are conditioned, already at an early age, to deprivation of bodily contact. This is characteristic of the manner in which adults communicate in Western society; more and more, Western people only talk and look at each other, but hardly touch one another. Caressing by gentle stroking, kissing, petting, embracing, and hugging are restricted to the short foreplay of intercourse but are rarely practiced in other situations.

Dancing as a form of intense group communication by means of rhythmic bodily contact, which plays such a large role in African culture, is hardly practised in the West. There is a general fear of being regarded as "sentimental," "oversexed," or "emotional" in Western countries, especially in Northern Europe, where people take special care to restrict their bodily contact to a shake of hands or a symbolic touching of each other's cheeks during a kiss-resembling ceremonial greeting. This taboo against tactile contact is sometimes rationalized by psychoanalytical concepts. Fathers refrain from letting their daughters ride horseback on their knees or shoulders and mothers do not participate in bodily hugging with their sons for fear of inducing incestuous fixations!

Children need to feel their parents' love by gentle touches, but they are increasingly taught that this is only for small babies. A "big" boy or girl is no longer hugged or kissed. Even tucking in a child before he goes to sleep is accomplished by many modern parents routinely and almost apologetically. The work of Harlow and other researchers with regard to the effect of handling on the health and behavior of animals may explain what happens to many human infants and children. Harlow's experiments support the everyday common-sense observations that the Western tendency to restrict human bodily contact is a deprivation which, when practised too early and too rigidly, disturbs the later development and communicative behavior of the child. Tactile deprivation may lead to social isolation and autostimulation.

Clinical observations suggest that children who have been deprived from touch contact may try to find compensatory gratification, e.g., by masturbation or other forms of autoerotic behavior. They may also substitute for the pleasant sensations of touch those induced by smoking or by drugs. Such children, when they become adults, are often incapable of expressing love by gentle touches to their marriage partners or children.

It is widely believed that children are better off in modern society than in previous times or in other cultures today. Certainly in most Western countries children are no longer forced to work in industry or agriculture. Their physical development is much better and they have better clothes and food, more toys and gadgets, more "fun," and they get more sweets and money. They need also be less afraid of their parents because beating children is now forbidden both by written and unwritten laws. In general, children in our society have more rights and less duties; they are "emancipated." On the other hand, as we have pointed out, the price they pay for their emancipation is a less warm, less supporting family situation. Furthermore, as far as the decrease in beating as a form of punishment is concerned, we are not so sure this is really an advantage. A moderately painful slap is a short, clear form of punishment, which, when over, has served its purpose. Without beating, some modern parents remain angry with their children and, from the life histories of our patients, this seems much more difficult to bear than mild physical punishment. Patients whose fathers did not beat but who showed a threatening face or did not speak to the child for days on end, had more "basic insecurity" and tendency to "anxiety trait" than those who (sometimes even proudly) told about being spanked.

The deprivation of mutual bodily touching as a form of human communication seems to be a part of a growing tendency in Western cultures to suppress emotional expression. This tendency started and is still more manifest in well-educated classes whose members communicate primarily by the spoken or written word, and tend to suppress other forms of vocalization behavior like weeping, sobbing, shrieking, shouting, and cursing. They also refrain from vivid gesticulations, such as beating the table with the fist, stamping feet, slamming the door, throwing things, slapping or tearing one's hair or clothes, which were not uncommon in the past and still occur in "lower" more "primitive" classes or societies. Aggressive behavior is also punished at a too early age by Western parents and educators.

Western children and adolescents are taught and conditioned from an early age to control and inhibit all forms of communications other than by speaking, writing, and reading and some ritualized motor responses like nodding, smiling, shaking of hands, standing at silent attention, etc., which are considered civilized ("higher") forms of communications. More and more, Western people learn to speak and act in a "detached" way. In situations they formerly reacted to by intense motor, mimic, and vocal discharges to express their feelings, they now behave as if they were not experiencing any emotion.

Detached behavior has certain advantages. We all use it as scientists when we suppress our feelings in the study of such terrible situations as cancer, accidents, delinquency, suicide, and war. But too much detachment is potentially harmful because speech alone is an insufficient vehicle for the transfer of all the feelings that human beings need to convey to each other. Only an adequate abreaction of the emotions brings understanding and sympathy from others and thus gives the support that is needed in situations of frustration. The effects of growing up in too-small family groups, and being conditioned to behave like well-controlled boys and girls at an early age, deprive many people in the Western world of the ability to tell others in words what they feel. They are "ashamed" to ask for attention, understanding, and support; and they are unable to express normal aggression or frustration even by words when this would be appropriate. This exaggerated "bottled up" behavior is not only a characteristic of communication with strangers, but also between parents and children, marriage partners, friends, colleagues, and supporting figures like doctors. Showing feelings and speaking about emotions exposes one to the risk of being considered socially inferior, weak, "nervous," dependent, and immature.

Source of Stress in the Work Situation

After World War II, the 8-hour working day was introduced by law in most Western countries, but this did not mean that all men automatically devoted their free time to communicate with their wives and children. A large number of men in all classes do extra jobs in their leisure time; others, especially intellectuals or business executives, are home but read their reports, or study in the evenings, or go to meetings (where they discuss how to improve our society!). Thus, many men in Western cultures have not more but less time to communicate with their wives and children.

Modern transportation enables more people to be away from home, even during the long winter evenings which used to keep them indoors in the past. This lack of contact can be potentiated if the wife is also working and no suitable substitute is available. When everyone in the family follows a detached pattern of nonemotional, businesslike behavior, we find a family in which people live together but hardly communicate.

The conglomeration of people in big cities has not promoted their cohesion. On the contrary, city life has diminished possibilities of communication. This is obvious when one simply looks at the crowd going to or from work everyday. People used to greet each other and chat while walking to work. They are now driven in buses or underground railways where the noise makes conversation impossible; this further diminishes communication. In many Western cities people in buses and trains not only are careful not to touch each other, but they avoid looking, nodding, or smiling at each other. The greetings that occur in the villages do not occur in the cities. The car also isolates people. Hurrying to and from work in cars, people are physically prevented from communication with their fellow human beings other than by an occasional hooting. Thus, in the typical Western culture, there is *alienation* or "loneliness in the midst of the crowd."

Nowadays, one finds much interest in interaction with larger, loosely knit groups, often in other countries and cultures. In the olden days (as is still the case in most Eastern cultures), strong in-group cohesion and support existed inside the family, tribe, clan, or social class; but hardly any communication was extended to fellow human beings outside these groups. Outsiders were regarded as strange and hostile. Nowadays, many Western people belong to large trade unions and to political and idealistic groups. Fraternal feelings for oppressed people in distant countries are expressed; but not for brothers and sisters, neighbors in the same apartment building, or fellow citizens of their own city or country. In the Western culture, built on such feelings of cohesion with "humanity" in the widest sense, there is a hope for a future international community of nations and for the eradication of war.

If realized, these ideals would undoubtedly mean great progress for human civilization. Unfortunately, adhesion with far-away people cannot replace direct support from fellow members of groups who are physically nearby when one needs them. This is especially obvious in situations of bereavement, conflict, or frustration, when loneliness and emotional isolation become acutely stressful. Children, especially, need to experience support from the key figures in the family and in the immediate environment whom they can see, hear, and feel. For children the widening of human ties to encompass all of "humanity" only partially compensates for loosening ties within the family. The same is true for housewives who do not participate in the wider social activities and miss their husbands' presence.

Rewards and punishment in the work situation are often inhuman to a degree that they resemble the experimental conditions of the animal behavior laboratory. Every Western man learns at an early age to go to school, and, later, to work at fixed hours. The average worker cannot choose between alternative possibilities like those offered by nice weather, a job to do at home, or an interesting book. In short, he cannot do what he would like to do because he *must* participate in school or work situations, just as experimental dogs or monkeys must enter into the harness or experimental cage. There is no escape, for either experimental animals or Western man, from the work situation. Almost all Westerners learn this work behavior so well that, when the work is not satisfying, they at most consider "fleeing" to another job, not escaping work as such.

In the small workshop of the past, each worker knew the boss personally, or he was an independent craftsman who could decide for himself when and how to work. In modern industry, workers are brought together in large factories or offices. The work is often monotonous, and the machine or production line requires constant attention so that there is no time for the workers to exchange more than a few words or signals. Noise further impedes their communication.

Office workers are often separated by glass walls to prevent communication during work. Among white-collar workers, the drive for material prosperity, which serves as the main reward, makes coworkers competitors. As in the family, this situation increases ambivalence and conflict rather than mutual support. Further distrust between workers and bosses is sown by management and trade union propaganda. The enormous increase in size of our industrial enterprises has destroyed "fatherly" relations that formerly existed in smaller firms.

Not only the work but the whole social life in Western cultures is conditioned to time signals. Practically everyone carries a watch and an appointment book that codes the timed tasks expected from him. Most Westerners have been so intensely conditioned to fulfill time-expected behavior that they regard this as normal; one has to live in another culture to realize that this is not so. It is interesting to observe the development of "experimental neurosis" in people whose colonial country becomes independent and they are expected to respond to tasks according to watch and notebook signals. It is equally interesting to observe Westerners whose time schedule (read: time conditioning) is upset, i.e., made unpredictable.

The reward for work in Western culture is a conditioned reinforcer, money, which may be used to purchase pleasant stimuli, e.g., food, a home, clothing, cigarettes, music, etc. Money is also the means to obtain the love (both bodily and socially) of a marriage partner and the gratifications that go with culturally sanctioned forms of copulation and procreation. But money is an indirect reward and only incompletely substitutes for the direct interpersonal gratification that comes from a boss or customer for whom people used to work. Most people work now for impersonal companies or government. This is what sociologists have described as the alienation of workers from their product.

Punishments handed out frequently at work require effort and coping to avoid. These include unjust demotions, threats of dismissal, and humiliating remarks when work performance is too low or a mistake is made. Since flight from the industrial cage is impossible, small wonder that absenteeism is increasing, especially after a minor illness or accident. A large part of the so-called "secondary gain" from illness is understandable as an attempt to escape, at least for a few days, from a frustrating work situation.

The money rewards of our society often become ultimately a punishment. The increased income of Western workers leads to increased expenditures, under the influence of the seductive advertising of a consumer-oriented society. Consequently, they sometimes have more worries over how to balance their finances than did their parents, who were really poor. Others become "men of small property" and must now worry about the threatening signals of the stock exchange, about which their parents knew nothing.

In Western cultures, the period of education is made extra difficult by the complicated, often contradictory rules and customs that prevail and by the rapid changes that occur. The majority of parents and teachers try to educate their children according to the norms of behavior to which they were conditioned by their own parents. Very often these forms of behavior are no longer appropriate when the children become adults, or when they enter into different social environments and have to communicate with new or strange cultural subgroups.

Special risks confront the adolescent human in learning to adapt to the manifold influences of his culture. During the long period of his immaturity (longer than most animals known to us), he must live in an inescapable intercommunication with his elders and peers because he is dependent on them for his nutrition, housing, and protection. This is the more frustrating because biologically man matures at age 12–14 years; at this age, young men and women are able to mate, produce sperm, ova, and offspring. But to take adequate care of their offspring in the framework of their culture, they must be socially mature. Social maturation requires the learning of occupational skills, which takes longer than biological maturation. For this reason, sexual activities and marriage are forbidden in Western cultures at an age when these would be biologically normal. This may lead to conflict and to the separation of love, sexual activity, and marriage.

In Western society, the adult male is educated to behave as both a competing and dutiful member of his community. He must strive for social responsibility and success while providing care for his wife and children. He must strive to be vigorous, energetic, fearless, enterprising, hardworking, self-relying, and self-controlled if he, as a male, wants to maintain the appreciation of his fellow men and the admiration of his wife, as well as his own self-esteem. This prescribed, controlled-aggressive, dominating behavior that enabled males to fit in the family and cultural setting as a respected, partly beloved, partly feared authority figure of 19th-century Western society is now producing conflict.

The development of our 20th-century Western culture has brought emancipation, within the family, for the wife and children; the previously normal, dominant behavior of the husband and father has become socially less acceptable. No longer inhibited by tradition and upbringing from disobeying or contradicting their husbands, many wives in modern Western culture criticize their husbands and independently pursue their own career goals. Formerly, a Western husband would have told his wife off or even beaten her if she irritated him, but these aggressive outlets are now forbidden, by both social laws and the husband's upbringing, which requires him to inhibit such emotional outbursts. Our interviews with Western wives suggest that they were often unaware of how irritating and even frustrating to their husbands is their refusal of submissive behavior. The same holds for the behavior patterns of Western adolescents, who no longer submit to paternal authority, but go their own way, leaving the parental home as they please and often marrying without asking parental advice or consent. These young people do not make life easy for a dominant and aggressive middle-aged man who feels that, because he works hard to support his wife and children, he is entitled to their respect, love, and submission as a reward.

The position of the husband and father in 20th-century Western culture has thus changed considerably. To provide an acceptable standard of living for his family, often in hard competition with other males and with few rewards in his work environment, he has to work very hard. When he fails, he loses his authority in the family; even when he provides well, he is often poorly rewarded in affection by the family. Consequently, many Western fathers feel lonely in their own family, deprived of love and affection, and often left out in matters of importance.

If we compare Western man with the position of the husband and father in "primitive" Eastern cultures, such as the Bedouin in the Negev and Yemenite Jewish immigrants in Israel, we find marked differences.

First, there is a striking difference in attitudes towards work. Most middle-class Eastern males avoid working when they can. A respectable man lets others do the work for him: the poor, the illiterate, and the women. The traditional Arab society man is as much respected for not working as is the Western citizen for working hard.

Second, marked differences exist in the attitudes of men towards women and vice versa. An essential feature of traditional Eastern cultures is based on the concept of the inferiority of women. Girls do not go to school, and practically no woman can read or write. From childhood, a girl is taught that her greatest fortune must come from a man, for whom she has to do the work and bear sons (not daughters). Family situations such as the ones we have described, are nonexistent in traditional Eastern families. In contrast to the Western male, the Eastern husband is sure to find at home at least one wife (sometimes more) who always looks upon him with admiration and affection and who is always ready to be his submissive servant.

Third, there is a great difference between technologically advanced, urbanized Western society and primitive rural or small society of the Middle East. In the latter, there is no industry, and there are no problems of rigidly required behavior as in Western employment. One is a farmer or a herdsman, a shopkeeper, or a simple artisan who makes shoes or garments to order and at his leisure, since the customer is also unhurried. The hours of work are set by the sun or by one's own mood, or by "tradition," but certainly not by the watch, the world market, or by the order book. There is no stock exchange, no installment system, no need to climb the social ladder. Financial worries are much less and are not a source of stress with which one must cope. Poverty and belonging to a lower social structure are accepted as fate, like disease and death, but not as signs of failure. In short, the social system is much less competitive; therefore, behavior is less determined by the rewards and punishments given by a system from which one cannot escape.

To describe the psychosocial stresses for the female in Western society would almost require a review of all social changes of the past century. Western woman, until about a hundred years ago, had as her main tasks to care for the cleanliness and other work in the home; to produce and take care of numerous offspring; and to be her husbands' obedient servant, both in his sexual activities and in those parts of his social task (work) which he cared to order her to do. She had to find gratification in serving husband and children and received, at most, protection and the signs of her husband's love and esteem. Her social behavior, unlike that of the males, did not take place in the three social subgroups of family, work, and society at large, but only in the family.

All this has changed for many women, but not for all to the same degree. One of the most important psychosocial stresses for modern Western women is the double aspect of her position. On one hand, she can still behave as the submissive love partner and mother who seeks her main gratification in her function in the family. Even while accepting the political and other rights that emancipation has given her, many women still behave, think, and feel very much as in previous times. Many women are satisfied if the male partner responds to this behavior by giving her the time, attention, love signals, and protection she expects for it. When he is too busy, or puts his work before her, or expects her to serve him but does not respond as she expects from him, she may become frustrated.

Other women go to work. A relatively small group manages to compete successfully in the work situation and to share with men the frustration and psychosocial stress associated with work in Western societies. Especially difficult is the psychosocial situation for Western females who try to function both as the key figure in the family as of old and as a modern, equal-to-the-male member of society. The successful combination of these two roles, in the authors' experience, is still relatively rare. Such women are generally less submissive and often even dominant in their sexual behavior and other interfamilial communications.

In this description, we have pointed out that the position of the male in Western society has become more difficult during the last hundred years; for women this is only partly true insofar as they share with males the same stresses at work and in larger societal subgroups. But the position of women in the family has certainly improved. The same technical developments that have dehumanized work in modern industrialized settings, have made life easier and less stressful for the housewife. The diminution in the number of children has enabled the modern mother to devote more time to her own interests whereas many males have used the reduction in their working hours to make additional money. Many more women than formerly read books, attend concerts, or enroll in university extension courses. In contrast, it seems as if the majority of modern Western males seek their main distraction in watching football games, or television, or in alcohol. Even if the number of women in top positions in government, in industry, and in the universities is still small, the progress in social position of the majority of women is so widespread that one does not need statistics to prove it.

There is one more psychosocial stress that operates less in women than men, viz., they are not so strictly conditioned to inhibit the expression of their emotions. Crying, complaining and asking for help, and aggressive verbalizations against husband and children are not socially condemned in women as they are in men. It is only recently (and in relatively small proportion) that women are beginning to show "detached" behavior, to appear "cold," matter of fact, or businesslike, like the majority of the Western males. In contrast, the Western male who behaves aggressively towards women in words and action (e.g., by beating his wife), as was his undisputed right in the past, would now be severely censured by other males and by his own internalized (conditioned) norms of morally justified behavior.

Finally, social change produces psychosocial stress that seems to make life increasingly difficult for people in Western society. Moving to another place to live, the displacement of people from rural to urban environments, has created different circumstances for millions of people. The change from an agricultural to an industrial worksetting or to another social class (both upward and downward) requires coping and adjustment. Social change is also inherent in events such as war or revolution, or the evolution of Western society which has brought more power to the organized working classes, previously colonial countries, and oppressed races. When war or revolution takes place in neighboring countries, they produce social stresses because of this threat effect. The same is true for the threat to our survival of air and water pollution.

The so-called generation conflict makes many adult and elderly people insecure about the future of society, themselves, and their possessions. The same is true for economic changes such as devaluation of money, or the decline of the security derived from the stability of institutions like the church or the universities. Social threats are sometimes more stressful than the actual changes because they are unpredictable. The threats are often signified by modern techniques of mass communication: movies, newspapers, and television bring people stressful news from all over the whole world, whereas, in the olden days, many stresses did not reach them because of sheer distance. Any crime, especially when associated with sex or drugs, any fatal accident or brawl between police and rioters, anywhere in the world, has news value and is accentuated by the mass media, whereas reassuring information about social or political stability is rejected. Thus modern telecommunication has the reverse function of the "normal" defense mechanisms. While this has advantages, there are also harmful effects.

PSYCHOSOCIAL STRESSES AND DISEASE

The role of social stresses in modern Western life, outlined in the previous discussion, can be summarized briefly as follows:

1. Psychosocial stresses influence the early conditioning (learning) period of development and the adult life of practically all members of Western society, but affect individuals to a widely variable degree.
2. Some psychosocial stresses are clearly analogous to the factors that produce "neuroses" in experimental animals in which associations between stimuli, reward, and punishment, after having been established by classical conditioning, are randomized and thereby become unpredictable. This seems to lead to severe neurotic behavior when the randomization is done by parent, other family member, teachers, boss, marriage partner, or members of a subgroup to which one belongs, i.e., people from whom one expects understanding and predictable support and cooperative behavior. Experimental neurosis is, as Pavlov suggested, quite analoguous to human neurotic behavior.
3. Inappropriate conditioning by key figures, during early and/or later periods of life, is found in the histories of patients with psychosomatic diseases, e.g., bronchial asthma, peptic ulcer, ulcerative colitis, and essential hypertension—and even in patients with coronary heart disease, rheumatoid arthritis, diabetes, and multiple sclerosis.
4. Clinical observations derived from the biographical anamneses of psychosomatic patients, compared with those of healthy controls, reveals that such patients have been exposed to a larger number of psychosocial stresses. Observations during war, of slum dwellers and in-migrants, confirm that massive psychosocial stress is an important factor in the production of

asocial and delinquent behavior, as well as of neurotic and psychosomatic illness.

5. The common feature in the multiple psychosocial stiuations leading to different forms of abnormal behavior seems to be *unpredictability of the future.* The individual or group (whether real or imagined) is not able to anticipate future events in the external environment nor the effects of their own coping behavior on such events. In this connection, it should be emphasized that the most important factor in the human sociocultural environment is predictability of the behavior of key figures (parents, marriage partners, children, coworkers, and leaders of industry or government). The psychosocial stresses that we have noted as stress-producing factors in modern life, all seem to decrease predictability and confidence, especially when they occur in combination. It is the complicated, randomized combination of multiple, contradictory psychosocial factors that makes human communication in our modern society so stressful.

6. In individuals exposed to many and even severe psychosocial stresses, the development of disordered behavior and disease differs widely. There is a wide variation between people in the amount of psychosocial stress to which they are exposed and in their "stress tolerance", i.e., the amount of stress with which they can successfully cope and maintain psychological, biological, and social homeostasis. "Stress" is determined not only by the "objective" psychosocial factors described here, but also by the "sensitivity" or "resistance" of the individual or group.

7. Stress tolerance may be partly a hereditary potentiality, but we have found considerable evidence in the life histories of our patients that early life experience (i.e., early conditioning) of the individual in his communications with the key figures in his primary groups is an important determinant of his later resistance to psychosocial stress. Growing up in a warm, consistently communicating family that provides adequate support seems not only to protect the child from developing "neurotic" behavior, but also appears to endow such individuals with what psychiatrists have called "basic security." In psychobiological terms, this means that such individuals can,

as adults, endure more psychosocial stress than others without developing disease or disordered ("asocial") behavior.

8. In contrast to people who decompensate under stress by developing neurotic or socially disturbed behavior, those who develop psychosomatic disease tend to inhibit the acting out of their emotions.

A major hypothesis of psychosomatic medicine is that inhibited communication is an important factor in the causative constellation of psychosomatic disorders. According to psychosomatic theory, input into the organism must be followed by an adequate output. When verbal or motor components of emotional states are partly or completely inhibited, the organism tends to *substitute* other forms of behavior along other output channels. Psychosomatic diseases are substitute forms of behavior, becoming manifest when the expression in speech or musculoskeletal action that would be appropriate in a response to psychosocial stress, is inhibited. This inhibited energy may ultimately find an outlet in increased autonomic, visceral, or endocrine activity (see Figure 2-1).

Psychosomatic theory makes use of the ethological concept of *displacement;* psychosomatic disorders are displaced or substituted reactions to frustrations. The ethologists have shown that, in general, displacement behavior, insofar as it is appropriate, may fulfill a useful function in maintaining the homeostasis of the organism. But when the frustration is intense or long lasting, and inhibition of adequate behavior persists, the substituted discharges are exaggerated in intensity and duration and may become harmful either socially or bodily. The cultural tendency towards greater self-control in the Western world is, according to psychosomatic theory, one of the main reasons for the increasing frequency of certain psychosomatic disorders in Western culture.

Apart from attempting to relieve the psychosocial stresses to which people are exposed in modern Western society, there are at least two other avenues for preventing emotional disorders: viz., by improving communication in the family to facilitate future stress tolerance (basic security), and by encouraging people not to overly inhibit their emotional behavior. In other words, let them learn how to act out "harmoniously" along all available channels.

PSYCHOSOCIAL STRESS AND
PSYCHOBIOLOGICAL BEHAVIOR

The human organism, as it has emerged from evolution, possesses a number of mechanisms to perceive, appraise, and cope with its environment and with the stresses inherent in communication with its conspecifics. All these mechanisms function as cybernetic feedback processes that have their scanning mechanisms in the central nervous system. The human central nervous system is partly the same as that of the other mammals; there is a *triune brain*, as MacLean has described it, consisting of the "reptilian" brainstem, midbrain and forebrain, the palleo-cortex (belonging to the limbic system), and the neocortex (regulating the sensory-motor functions). In addition, the human has a "word-language brain" in the frontal-temporal area, which serves the feedback mechanism of speech and thinking.

During the last decades, great strides have been made in the elucidation of the central nervous system substrates of human behavior. Especially important has been the discovery of the Ascending Reticular Arousal System and its function in anxiety and aggressivity; the reward and punishment system in the septal area of the limbic brain and its role in the processes of conditioning and learning; the ventromedial hypothalamic system and its role in avoidance behavior; the elucidation of the transmitter substances norepinephrine, dopamine, and serotonin and their specific function in the different central and peripheral nervous feedback machanisms; the elucidation of the mechanisms of sleep and dreams; and the hypothalamic-adrenalcortex axis and the feedback mechanisms of sexual behavior in the hypothalamus and its release hormones. These new additions to our knowledge, together with the results of psychophysiological and ethological behavior studies in animals (and in men) allow us now to formulate comprehensive hypotheses about (a) the psychosocial stresses of modern life and their effects on people's communications and (b) the psychobiological mechanisms that mediate the effects of psychosocial stresses on behavior.

It is beyond the scope of this paper to describe these new psychosocial-biological concepts in detail. It should be clear, however, that they are of utmost importance for modern psychiatry and psychosomatic medicine, which must deal with both normal and disturbed psychosocial and psychobiological behavior. Knowledge of the three "dimensions" of human behavior (psychic, social, and biological) will multiply, by a factor of three, our possibilities of manipulating disturbed human behavior for the sake of human wellbeing.

SUMMARY

Man is a social animal living in a human culture. In this culture, he has to maintain his social and internal homeostasis (i.e., his health) in continuous communication with his fellow men and, especially, with the key figures in the social subgroups to which he belongs. Every society and every social subgroup has its own psychosocial stressors that consist of the behavior patterns of its members, which require more than the usual cognitive, appraisal, anticipation, and adaptative behavior. Successful coping with these stressors leads to gratification; failure to cope leads to frustration.

In this report, the authors have described a number of cultural factors which, according to their clinical experience, operate as psychosocial stressors in Western society. The common denominator in these factors is that they make it difficult or impossible for particular individuals or groups to anticipate future events in their social environment and in the efficacy of their own coping behavior to such events. Compared with earlier or more simple cultures, Western society is characterized by complicated, randomized complications of multiple (often contradictory) psychosocial signals, rewards, and punishments. Insufficient capacity to cope with this complicated human environment is an important factor in the causation of behavior disorders and psychosomatic disease.

The tolerance to cope with psychosocial stress varies widely among different persons. Next to genetic factors, the stress tolerance of adults seems to be determined mainly by the basic security that individuals acquire from consistent conditioning during their early development. While the neurophysiological bases of the complex mechanisms that play a central role in the process of psychosocial communication are still incompletely elucidated, existing knowledge opens possibilities for interdisciplinary prevention of disordered social behavior and psychosomatic disease.

3

ANXIETY AND THE NATURAL HISTORY OF NEUROSIS

H. J. Eysenck

Institute of Psychiatry
University of London
London, England

Of all the terms used by psychologists, "neurosis" is probably rivalled only by "intelligence" in the way that it has been taken up in popular language and in the degree to which it is being used by all and sundry. It certainly excels all other psychological terms in the extent to which it is left undefined; a search through many psychiatric and psychological textbooks failed to unearth anything like an agreed-upon definition.

The term "neurosis" seems to have been coined by William Cullen (1712-1790), one of the originators of the science of "neural pathology." An indication of the way the term was understood prior to Freud's systematic efforts to create a causal theory is given by the very influential medical dictionary of Littre and Robin. In the 10th edition (1855) the definition runs as follows: "Nom générique des maladies qu'on suppose avoir leur siège dans le système nerveux, et qui consistent en un trouble fonctionnel sans lésion sensible dans la

I am indebted to the Colonial Research Fund for the support of experimental studies that have been instrumental in constructing this model of neurotic behaviour.

structure des parties ni agent matérial apte à le produire." (General term referring to diseases believed to have their site in the nervous system, and which consist of functional troubles without visible lesion in the structure of its parts, nor material agent capable of producing it.) In the 15th edition (1884) the phrase "sans lésion sensible" was changed to "sans lésion actuellement appréciable." Thus, we have a *disease* (a concept left severely undefined) with an unspecified locus in the nervous system which is characterized exclusively in a negative fashion, i.e. by the denial of any lesions in that system.

Modern authors do not do much better. Thus, Henderson and Gillespie (1969) say that the term "neurosis" has two connotations. The first is purely descriptive: "it is a term referring to conditions characterised by certain mental and physical symptoms and signs, occurring in various combinations." The second is aetiological: "the existence of neurotic reactions is an indiciation of mental conflict. . . . The pathology of neurotic reactions, in other words, is essentially a pathology of personal relationships." This second connotation seems somewhat circular; as Greenson (1967) puts it:

> Psychoanalysis maintains that psychoneuroses are based on the neurotic conflict. The conflict leads to an obstruction in the discharge of instinctual drives eventuating in a state of being dammed up. The ego becomes progressively less able to cope with the mounting tensions and is ultimately overwhelmed. The involuntary discharges manifest themselves clinically as the chief symptoms of psychoneurosis.

Thus, *neurotic* conflict causes *neurosis;* this definition is not very informative in the absence of independent definitions of "neurotic conflict."

FREUD'S CONCEPTION OF NEUROSIS

These authors take for granted one particular paradigm (to use Kuhn's term), namely that of Freud; they do not attempt to look at this paradigm in any critical way. What precisely is Freud's paradigm, and to what extent do the known facts support it at the present time?

We can do no better than to quote Freud himself: "Starting from the mechanics of cure, it now becomes possible to construct quite definite ideas of the origin of the illness. It is only experience in childhood that can explain susceptibility to later traumas" since ". . . it is only by uncovering these almost invariably forgotten memory traces and making them conscious that we acquire the power to get rid of these symptoms [Freud, 1962]." Thus, we are told quite categorically that (a) the curative treatment is primary, leading to the elaboration of the causal theory; (b) uncovering childhood experiences enables us to effect cures, which are here defined as the removal of symptoms; (c) it is *only* by this uncovering that such cures are to be achieved, and, finally, (d) any causal theory must concentrate on childhood experiences—these and only these can explain the development of neurotic illness.

I shall argue that the evidence now available is sufficient to warrant dismissal of Freud's theory of neurosis as failing to account for important, well-documented facts that are crucial to any proper evaluation of it. Furthermore, I shall argue that an alternative theory is available which is more in conformity with these data. Using Kuhn's phraseology, I shall argue that the existing paradigm has broken down irretrievably and that another paradigm has taken over. The main point of this paper is to discuss this new paradigm in some detail.

The main points against Freud's theory can be put very briefly.

1. There is strong evidence that indicates that "uncovering childhood experiences" does not in fact, get rid of the symptoms of which Freud speaks.
2. Such uncovering is not required for the purpose of getting rid of the symptoms—spontaneous remission does so as quickly and efficiently as does psychoanalysis while behaviour therapy does so much more quickly and efficiently.
3. Furthermore, neither spontaneous remission nor behaviour therapy is followed by relapse or symptom substitution, as they should be if Freud's theory were right.

Thus, taking our cue from Freud and "starting from the mechanics of cure," we come to conclusions exactly contrary to those suggested by Freud. The evidence has recently been reviewed in considerable detail by Rachman (1971), and it leaves very little doubt about the failure of the Freudian theory in these vital respects. It would be a task of supererogation to continue the task of disproving other details of Freud's system; what has been said is sufficient to show that it cannot begin to serve as a useful model of neurotic behavior.

A BEHAVIOURAL CONCEPTION OF NEUROSIS

The alternative paradigm to Freud is based on Pavlov's contribution in the field of conditioning. This paradigm postulates, essentially, that so-called neurotic "symptoms" are not to be understood as the outcome of intrapsychic conflict, reaching back into childhood experiences, but are to be regarded as conditioned responses, particularly autonomic or "emotional" responses, which have become nonadaptive. This general view goes back at least as far as Watson and Rayner's (1920) description of the case of little Albert, and the work of Mary Cover Jones (1924 a, b) on the elimination of the children's fears. In its simplest form this theory says that all neurotic behaviour and the symptoms associated with it are due to classical conditioning, and that recovery from "neurotic symptoms" and changes in this behaviour are due to extinction.

As I have pointed out elsewhere (Eysenck, H. J., 1960), the Pavlovian theory presents a profoundly different account from the Freudian. For psychoanalysts, "symptoms" are merely the outward expression of internal conflicts and complexes (which constitute the real "disease"), while for learning theorists the symptoms are simply conditioned responses, without any underlying "disease." "The symptoms are the neurosis," as I put it then, and one ought perhaps to abandon the term "symptom" altogether in this connection, because according to this theory they are not "symptomatic" of anything. This fundamental difference is responsible for many subsidiary ones; thus the Freudian rejects what he calls purely symptomatic treatment and predicts relapse and symptom substitution to follow any such treatment, whereas learning theorists consider symptomatic treatment the only possible and relevant kind of treatment, and do not expect relapse and symptom substitution. The Watsonian theory never caught on, and it is easy to see why it failed to do so; it is much too simple to accommodate all the known facts of neurotic breakdown and recovery. As we shall see, the facts are very much more complex than this simple account suggests, and a properly behavioural theory of neurosis, based on learning theory, must accordingly also be much more complex.

Curiously enough, no attempt seems to have been made by learning theorists to elaborate such a theory. H. J. Eysenck and Rachman (1965) gave an outline which, while taking into account many of the facts that require explanation, must still be judged inadequate. Gray (1971) pointed out several important relationships between neurotic behaviour and experimental studies of rats and other animals; however, current conceptions have centered almost exclusively on methods of behaviour therapy, rather than on methods of neurosis acquisition. Before turning to an attempt at remedying this omission, let us consider for a moment the descriptive account of the term "neurosis." It is important not to reify scientific concepts; there is not something *out there* which constitutes the Platonic idea of neurosis, and with which we can compare our inadequate notions. We create concepts to serve our purposes, and the only criterion by which we judge these creations is the degree to which they are useful in our scientific enterprise. With this criterion in mind let us consider the characteristics of neurotic behaviour. The first of these, already implicit in the older definitions quoted earlier, is that these types of behaviour are *learned;* they are not due to injury, lesions, or other externally imposed permanent modifications of the cortex, CNS, or autonomic system. The second is that these behaviours are *maladaptive;* they do not serve our purposes as these are recognized by ourselves. The third is that they involve strong emotions, particularly *anxiety;* indeed it is this third criterion that brings neuroses and their natural history into the framework of this book.

It is important to realize that what are commonly recognized as the prototypical neuroses (hysteria, anxiety state, reactive depression, obsessional and compulsive disorders, etc.) are not the only types of disorders classed as neurotic; antisocial conduct, as shown by professional criminals, also comes into this category. Their conduct, too, is learned; it is maladaptive; and criminals often show a high degree of anxiety. It could be said that while the conduct of the classical neurotic harms no one but himself, that of the criminal harms society (i.e., other people); but this is only partially true. The neurotic often harms other people (particularly members of his family) by his conduct, and society in general by making himself a financial burden; the criminal often harms himself, in the sense that a life behind bars is not what he is really aspiring to.

Different Types of Neurosis

H. J. Eysenck and Rachman (1965) have made the distinction between disorders of the first kind (consisting of the traditional neurotic disorders), which are acquired through a process of conditioning, and disorders of the second kind (consisting of criminal behaviour and other antisocial sorts of conduct), which are mediated through a failure of conditioning that creates, in socialized human beings, a conscience that causes them to refrain from antisocial activities (Eysenck, H. J. 1970a). Thus, conditioning is a vital feature in both forms of neurosis, but in the one case (disorders of the first kind) the neurotic conduct is mediated through such conditioning, while in the other case (disorders of the second kind) the neurotic conduct is mediated though the failure of proper conditioning to occur.

Conditioning as a neural process is of course neutral, in the sense that what is being conditioned may be useful, useless, or actively harmful; it is equally bad to condition senseless fears which may lead to maladaptive behaviour as not to condition useful fears which prevent us from doing things to our disadvantage. Some psychiatrists (particularly those whose profession brings them into contact with prisoners) would agree with the proposal to include people of this kind in the general rubric of "neurotics," others would probably disagree. We shall adduce some further evidence to demonstrate the usefulness of this classification later on. It is important to recognize in this connection that many sexual disorders, which are widely recognized as neurotic (homosexuality, fetishism, transvestism), probably also belong in this second category; so may drug addiction, alcoholism, and other forms of addiction, at least in certain cases.

Neurosis and Personality

One way to look at the "two kinds of neurosis" is by way of individual differences, i.e., by asking whether perhaps different people are likely to fall prey to either of these two kinds of maladaptive behaviour. My own answer has been in terms of the two major dimensions of personality, neuroticism (or emotionality) as opposed to stability, and extraversion as opposed to introversion (Eysenck, H. J., & Eysenck, S. B. G., 1969). Both neurotics and criminals are characterized by high degrees of emotionality (N); indeed, there is little difference between the groups with respect to this variable. However, there is a marked difference between the groups with respect to extraversion (E); criminals are high on extraversion, neurotics of the traditional kind are high on introversion. These differences are not due to the influence of situational factors on personality; it is not incarceration that makes criminals emotional and extraverted, or hospitalization which makes neurotics emotional and introverted.

Burt (1965) followed up 763 children who had been rated for these personality variables by their teachers in school. Of these, 15% and 18%, respectively, later became habitual offenders or neurotics. Of the offenders, 63% had been rated as high on N and 54% as high on E; only 3% had been rated as high on introversion. Of the neurotics, 59% had been rated as high on N and 44% as high on introversion; only 1% had been rated as high on E. Other follow-up studies are available to show the same thing—child personality predicts with some degree of accuracy future conduct, whether neurotic or criminal (Eysenck, H. J., 1970a).

These facts can to some degree be brought in line with the causal theory of personality (Eysenck, H. J., 1967), according to which the underlying biological basis of the N factor is the autonomic system and, in particular, the visceral brain. In high N subjects there is a lability of this system that leads to quick overarousal and slow return to normal of this system when emotional unconditioned stimuli (UCS) and conditioned stimuli (CS) are presented to the person concerned. The biological basis of the E factor is the degree of cortical arousal, as mediated by the ascending reticular activating system; in high E subjects this system mediates a low degree of arousal, leading to poor learning and conditioning. Thus, criminals and neurotics both share the high emotionality produced by a labile autonomic system; however, criminals condition poorly and, hence, fail to acquire the conditioned socializing responses we call "conscience," whereas neurotics condition all too well and hence acquire all sorts of fears and irrational anxieties.

In addition to conditioning proper, neurotics, criminals, and normals also differ in many other ways connected with our theory. For example, neurotics have been found in several studies to show greater stimulus generalization; whether this is connected with E or N or both is not known (Mednick & Freedman, 1960). N and E are also probably involved with such phenomena as peak shift (Nicholson, 1972; Nicholson & Gray, 1971).

Gray (1971) suggested the involvement of the pain and pleasure centres with personality differences. He suggested that extraverts are more sensitive to stimulation of the pleasure centres, introverts to the stimulation of the pain centre. While N increases sensitivity generally, the direction depends upon the person's position on the E dimension. It is not our purpose to trace these connections between personality and various psychophysiological mechanisms, but it seemed worth while to mention a few of the possibilities that have cropped up in the recent literature. A review of the relation between anxiety and learning (as opposed to conditioning) is given by H. J. Eysenck (1973b).

This account is of course partial, in that it omits all mention of the environmental conditions that mediate the conditioning process; these are too well known to merit detailed discussion here. What is being asserted is not that personality variables such as N and E are sufficient to determine whether a person will become a neurotic or a criminal or neither, but merely that they play a part in the genotype-environment interaction that ultimately leads to one outcome or the other.

Genetic Determinants of Neuroses

The hypothesis that genetic factors play an important part in predisposing a person to criminal or neurotic conduct has been disregarded for a long time by psychologists, but the evidence in its favour is strong; I have reviewed it elsewhere (Eysenck, H. J., 1975) and will not go into detail here. However, a few words may not be amiss with respect to the hereditary determination of N and E.

Jinks and Fulker (1970) reported a biometric genetical analysis of the data collected by Shields (1962) on monozygotic (MZ) twins brought up in isolation; they also made estimates based on his data comparing MZ and dizygotic (DZ) twins brought up together. For N, using the MZ data only, they estimated heritability as 60% ± 11%. Using MZ and DZ values, they arrived at an estimate of 54% ± 9%. [The standard errors for the heritability ratios were calculated using Kempthorne's (1957) formula.]

Jinks and Fulker found some (not significant) suggestion of assortative mating, independently verified elsewhere (Eysenck, H. J., 1975) and an absence of dominant gene action. Their findings strongly suggest that an intermediate level of neuroticism has been favoured by natural selection and constitutes the population optimum for this particular trait. The narrow heritability was found to equal the broad heritability; thus, all genetic variation is available for natural or artificial selection to act upon.

Cattell's (1963) nurture : nature ratios indicate that the differences in N observed between families is entirely genotypic in origin—evidently cultural and class differences have no effect on this personality variable. S. B. G. Eysenck and H. J. Eysenck (1969) found slight but significant differences in N due to social class, with high N scores being somewhat more frequent in lower social class groups. It is possible that the causal link might be in the direction of high N causing affected individuals to have negative social mobility, i.e., to move downwards. The data fit the model perfectly, thus leaving little doubt that the heritability ratios given are a conservative estimate of true values. (The formulae used make test unreliability part of the environment variance, hence any reasonable correction would increase the heritability variance ratio.)

For E, the heritability ratio was found to be 67% ± 8%. For this personality variable the simple model was not found fully adequate, probably because of intrauterine "competition" between DZ twins, a phenomena well documented in plant and animal work. The test for the genotype-environment interaction yielded a correlation of —.37 for the MZ twins; this is interpreted by Jinks and Fulker in the following manner: "This negative correlation indicates that introvert genotypes are more susceptible to environmental influences than extravert genotypes, the latter being relatively impervious [p. 332]." This is, of course, in good agreement with our theory, which posits better conditioning and learning in introverts (Eysenck, H. J., 1967), although the genetic investigation does not have anything to say directly about the manner of the environmental influence. It may seem at first somewhat paradoxical that introverts are *innately* predetermined to be more easily modifiable by *environmental* influences, but the statement makes perfectly good sense genetically and psychologically.

Another study along similar lines has been carried out by H. J. Eysenck and L. Eaves (The inheritance of personality. Unpublished manuscript. London, 1974) on a very large sample of approximately 800 MZ and DZ twins; the results of this study have not yet been published, but may be quoted briefly. The large number of subjects makes the study unique; in view of the large standard errors of variance ratios it must be said that the majority of the published twin studies are not of very great value, the heritabilities found being compatible with a very wide range of true values. In addition, nearly all the published studies make simplifying assumptions, the appropriateness of which must remain in doubt in the absence of proper biometrical calculations and model fitting. When the proper methods of analysis were used on our sample, it was found, for both E and N, that heritability values (uncorrected) were around the 50% mark, and that the kind of genetic model postulated by Jinks and Fulker gave a very good fit. We may therefore conclude that genetic factors play a very important part in the determination of personality factors that have been found to enter into the genesis of neurotic and criminal conduct.

Concordance Studies

Concordance studies of neurotic and criminal twins are very relevant here. H. J. Eysenck (1970a) summarized such studies for criminals and concluded that MZ twins are markedly more concordant than are DZ twins for criminality. Table 3-1 gives detailed figures. Out of 231 MZ twins, 55% are concordant; of 535 DZ twins, only 13% are concordant. Thus concordance is over four times as common in MZ twins as in DZ twins.

Table 3-1.

Concordance Rates for Criminality in 9 Twin Studies

Investigator	Date	MZ twins[a]	DZ twins[b]
Lange	1929	10/3 = 77%	2/15 = 12%
Legras[c]	1932	4/0 = 100%	0/5 = 0%
Rosanoff et al.	1941	25/12 = 68%	6/54 = 10%
Krantz[c]	1936	20/11 = 65%	23/20 = 53%
Stumpfl	1936	11/7 = 61%	7/12 = 37%
Borgström	1939	3/1 = 75%	2/3 = 40%
Yoshimasu	1965	17/11 = 61%	2/16 = 11%
Hayashi	1967	11/4 = 73%	3/2 = 60%
Christiansen[d]	1968	27/54 = 33%	23/340 = 6%
Total		128/103 = 55%	68/467 = 13%

[a] Monozygotic twins.
[b] Dizygotic twins.
[c] Quoted by C. Stern (1960).
[d] This is an unbiased and practically complete sample.

Rosanoff, Handy, and Plesset (1941) and Yoshimasu (1965) introduced a distinction similar to that made by H. J. Eysenck (1967) between *neuroticism* and *neurosis* (see the next section). Rosanoff et al. wrote about criminalism and criminality, applying the former term to a persistent constitutional tendency while considering the latter to be more incidental in character and less dependent on heredity. It is noteworthy in this connection that Stumpfl (1936) examined concordance at five different levels: both twins punished for crime, the same degree of recidivism, the same kind of crime, the same kind of antisocial acts, and the same kind of psychopathic features. The difference between MZ and DZ twins with respect to concordance increased from level 1 to level 5, where all MZ pairs were concordant and all DZ pairs discordant. Level 5 seems most closely related to personality, with earlier levels strongly influenced by social definitions of "crime" and accidental factors of discovery and punishment.

B. Hutchings (Environmental and genetic factors in psychopathology and criminality. Unpublished manuscript. London, 1972) and Schulsinger (1972) used detailed studies of foster children who did or did not behave criminally to demonstrate that genetic factors play an important role in criminality; the criminality of the biological father was found to be more important in determining the child's future conduct than was the criminality of the foster father. A general survey of the literature was given by Hutchings.

A similar result emerges from studies of neurotics. Thus Shields (1954) found much higher concordance rates among MZ twins aged between 12 and 15 years than among DZ twins. He also made a check on the degree of closeness of social relationships, finding, as expected, that MZ twins were closer to each other than were DZ twins. This degree of closeness, however, was not related to degree of concordance, thus disproving the hypothesis frequently voiced to discount the value of twin studies, viz., that MZ twins, being closer to each other, are growing up in an environment which is in fact more alike than that provided for DZ twins, who are less close. Shields also found some evidence of specificity; i.e., MZ twins resembled each other with respect to the specific symptomatology of their neurotic disorder. In this regard, they were rather like some of the criminal MZ twins where a certain degree of specificity was also observed, twins being concordant not only for criminality, but also for specific types of crime.

The later work of Shields and Slater (1966) and Slater and Shields (1969) with adult twins confirms these impressions. Of adult neurotics, MZ twins showed higher concordance rates than DZ twins, particularly for anxiety state and personality disorder; for reactive depression there seems to be little difference. For anxiety state the concordance figures are 41% and 4%; for personality disorder, they are 33% and 6%, respectively. These two types of disorder would be typically introverted and extraverted neuroses, thus presumably combining the heritabilities of E and N in some measure. Shields (1968) gives a table (p. 176) where the ratios of MZ concordance to DZ concordance are given for different specificity of diagnosis; these go from 1.7 for the most general form of diagnosis to 9.3 for the most specific. There are 5 degrees of specificity, and with each increase in specificity there is a monotonic increase in the ratio. (The least specific diagnosis is "any coded psychiatric abnormality in co-twin"; the most specific diagnosis is "both twins same diagnostic code, smallest subdivision used.") Thus, concordance figures are in good agreement with those derived from personality inventory studies in stressing the importance of genetic factors, right down to the most specific details of neurotic disorder, i.e., whether extraverted or introverted in type.

Neuroticism and Neurosis

Having set the genotypic scene for the appearance of the phenotypic "neurosis," we must try to differentiate "neurosis" from "neuroticism." In theory, the latter is the genotypic predisposition of the autonomic system and the visceral brain to overreact to emotion-producing stimuli; this is measured very imperfectly by such questionnaires as the Eysenck Personality Inventory (Eysenck, H. J., & Eysenck, S. B. G., 1965). Alternatively, we might use autonomic measures to estimate a person's degree of neuroticism; such measures form a factor, and this factor can be shown to have a significant degree of heritability (Eysenck, H. J., 1956). (The Holzinger h^2 for the autonomic factor was .75, calculated on 26 pairs of MZ and 26 pairs of DZ twins.)

By contrast, a neurosis (if the term has any meaning at all) must denote a substantial and, if possible, qualitative departure of an individual's behaviour either from that of the great majority of nonneurotic individuals, or from the mean of his own habitual behaviour patterns. In extreme cases such a departure (along either path) can be documented without any difficulty; these cases constitute the "descriptive conditions" mentioned in the Henderson and Gillespie (1969) definition quoted previously. Such a "breakdown" should be envisaged as a combination of genotypic predisposition and environmental stress; it may be sudden and apparently unexpected, or it may be slow and long continued in its origin. It would be useful if "neurosis" were separtely measurable from "neuroticism"; unfortunately (and inevitably), a person's neuroticism scores are raised during a neurotic breakdown, and return to his normal level after recovery (Eysenck, H. J., & Eysenck, S. B. G., 1969). Much the same is probably true of scores of tests of autonomic lability; "breakdown" signifies an exacerbation of the endogenous traits that normally characterize an individual.

Different neuroses differ widely in the degree to which they generalize; a person with a monosymptomatic phobia for snakes may appear perfectly normal at all times in a country like Ireland where there are (proverbially) no snakes, while a person with a phobia for cats may have his life ruined for fear of going out and meeting a feline (Freeman & Kendrick, 1960). Usually N scores are *more* elevated in cases of *more* widespread, generalized disorder; but even simple monosymptomatic phobics are usually found in the high-N/ low-E quadrant.

CAUSES OF NEUROSIS

Innate Fears

Given the presence of a "neurosis" so defined, how can we account for its presence? There appear three main causes which might be adduced in this connection. The first is entirely genetic; there is much evidence in the ethological literature of innate fears of a fairly specific character, and there is every reason to believe that, in man, too such fears exist in varying strength. Watson (1924) limited the innate causes of fear to three: loud noise, sudden loss of support, and pain. Typically he generalized this theory to all species. The work of Tinbergen (1951), Lorenz (1957), Hinde (1966), and many others has conclusively shown that this view is vastly oversimplified; many different species show quite specific fears even though all means of learning or conditioning have been eliminated through careful controls. Animals apparently have an innate mechanism that enables them to detect the complex set of stimuli characteristic of a predator and to experience fear (autonomic reaction) on perceiving such stimuli. Such fears (e.g., of snakes) are also found in humans, and appear subject to maturation.

Gray (1971) reviewed the evidence and substituted a four-fold classification of innately fear-producing stimuli: intensity, novelty, "special evolutionary dangers," and stimuli arising from social interaction. The phrase "special evolutionary dangers" suggests specific fears of animals which, during the evolution of the species, have been dangerous predators, and where consequently innate fears of such stimuli as are associated with these animals would confer evolutionary benefits.

According to Gray (1971):

The fourth class of fear stimuli—those arising from *social interaction with conspecifics*—is the result of more complex evolution, involving the development of mutually interacting forms of behaviour (such as those characteristic of dominance and submission), of the sign-stimuli produced during these forms of behaviour, and of the mechanisms for recognition of these sign-stimuli.

Evidence shows that the first two principles (intensity, novelty) all diminish fairly rapidly with age, a diminution in effectiveness which may be due to adaptation and habituation. In contrast, the other two principles seem subject to maturation; they tend to become stronger over time. This makes good sense in evolutionary terms; very young animals can do nothing about the appearance of predators, nor can they indulge in proper intercourse with conspecifics, and hence fear reactions to such stimuli would be useless and out of place.

Observational Learning

Even where innate fears are not strong enough to become very apparent, they may nevertheless interact with the remaining two principles of fear acquisition, viz., imitation or modeling, and conditioning. It is probably much easier to acquire a fear of snakes than of sheep through either of these two modes! "Observational learning," which is the generic term covering both imitation and modeling, was given proper scientific status by Miller and Dollard (1941); in recent years, the work of Bandura and Walters (1963) and Bandura (1969, 1971), in particular, has attracted a good deal of attention to this particular approach to the study of the growth and extinction of anxiety.

Rachman (1972) has drawn attention to the "long pedigree and wide implications of observational learning." He points out, "in addition to its potential therapeutic value, observational learning is of importance in theorising about the etiology and course of certain types of behavioural abnormality." For example, it has been found necessary to revise and extend the traumatic theory of phobias to encompass the research produced by observational learning (Rachman, 1968). Observational-learning theories can cope with awkward findings such as the occurrence of fears in large numbers of people who have no recollection of any direct contact with the feared object.

In the light of findings on observational learning, it is extremely likely that many fears are acquired by vicarious experience.

Such research also helps explain the unduly common fears, such as snake phobias, and the fact that there are some objects which seemingly never become items of fear-producing quality (e.g., lambs). The possible role of observational learning in the prevention of behavioural abnormalities, while recognized, has not yet been the subject of intensive study [Rachman, 1972, p. 380].

Conditioning

Fears and anxiety can be regarded as either innate or acquired by observational learning. A third major method of acquisition of fears is, of course, conditioning along classical Pavlovian lines. Such conditioning can either be traumatic single-trial conditioning, or it can be repeated pairing of subtraumatic UCS with appropriate CS. In any social situation the term "CS" will generally stand for a multiplicity of stimuli; it is rare to encounter a situation in which single stimuli, of the kind encountered in the laboratory, can be dissected out of the complex set of changing background and foreground factors involved in the total situation. Occasionally there is a clear-cut single CS of this kind, particularly in traumatic single-trial learning, but this is the exception rather than the rule. Many critics have felt that this fact makes the application of conditioning theory to the genesis of neurotic disorders impossible, but it is difficult to see why this should be so. Clearly the problem becomes more complex and difficult when there is a multiplicity of CS, but in principle the general laws of conditioning should apply as readily to this as to the simpler situation. There is much experimental work, largely with animals, in which multiple CS have been used; the results of such studies can guide our expectations in the human field also.

Conditioning theories, such as Watson's, tend to recognize only fear and pain as the unconditioned response (UCR) which enter the conditioning situation; it would seem that this produces too restrictive a basis. Gray (1971) argued that "frustrative nonreward" has effects very similar to punishment, and that frustration is functionally and physiologically very similar to—and perhaps identical with—the state of fear. There are a number of characteristics of fear-producing situations; and, in order to demonstrate that frustrative non-reward has similar properties to pain/fear, it is necessary to demonstrate that similar characteristics can be found in the case of frustration. Research on the whole has shown that these similarities tend to be present whenever they are looked for:

1. The defining characteristic of a punishment (pain) is that it is aversive; i.e., the animal will work to terminate or avoid it. Several investigators have shown that animals will work to terminate or avoid frustrative nonreward (Adelman & Maatsch, 1956; Wagner, 1959).
2. Punishment can increase the vigour of ongoing or immediately subsequent behaviour; it interacts with other drives present according to Hull's "drive summation" hypothesis. Amsel and Roussel (1952) provided evidence for this property of frustrative nonreward.
3. Extinction is slower following partial reinforcement; this is theoretically explained in terms of conditioned frustration acquired during the organism's performance of the instrumental response. It has been found possible to substitute punishment for frustrative nonreward in such experiments (and vice versa) and obtain similar results (Brown & Wagner, 1964).
4. It is known that in approach-avoidance conflict, the strength of the avoidance tendency falls off more rapidly with stimulus change than does that of the approach tendency. Wagner

(1966) has shown that what is true of fear responses in the classical Miller situation is also true when frustration is substituted for fear.

5. It is possible to show that punishing animals on a proportion of rewarded trials (a "partial punishment" schedule) affects subsequent resistance to continuous punishment in much the same way that a partial reinforcement schedule affects resistance to extinction.

6. The effects of fear-reducing drugs, such as amytal and alcohol, have similar effects on frustrative nonreward; i.e., they reduce the observed effects of frustration (Dollard & Miller, 1950; Gray, 1971).

7. Rats, which are specially susceptible to fear, are also especially susceptible to frustrative nonreward (Savage & Eysenck, 1964).

There are other points of similarity, as Gray's review shows, but these will suffice to indicate that it is not unreasonable to regard these two concepts as being differentiated mainly on a quantitative basis—pain/fear responses tend to be stronger than responses to frustrative nonreward.

The consequences of this extension of the original oversimplified Watson model are quite important; actual physical pain is not a frequent UCR in typical neurosis-producing situations, but frustration probably plays a much larger part. It is sometimes possible to discover actual physical pain and trauma as a causative factor in neurotic disorders, particularly those arising in war, but it is far more usual to find certain forms of frustration which can take the part of the UCR in our paradigm. Thus, the extension of the paradigm from animals to humans coincides in part, with the extension of the UCR from simple physical pain to frustrative nonreward. Furthermore, such an analysis enables us to understand the role of alcohol and barbiturate drugs in the lives of many addicts and alcoholics; the difficulties with which such people are faced seldom involve actual pain, but they do very often involve frustrations of one kind or another, disappointed expectations or frustrated hopes, as the case might be. On the fear-frustration hypothesis, "these are no less able to establish the avoidance component of an approach-avoidance conflict than is a painful blow; and according to the experimental evidence, alcohol and the barbiturates are able to alleviate the distress of conflict just as well when this arises from frustrative non-reward as when it arises from punishment [Gray, 1971, p. 160]."

THE NATURAL HISTORY
OF NEUROSIS

The Role of Conflict

We have now discussed at some length the origins of anxiety through genetic factors, through imitation/modeling, and through classical conditioning, or through some combinations of these; we must now turn to the conditions under which these acquired fears and anxieties may turn into neurotic disorders. It would be quite inadmissable to argue that because a person had acquired unreasonable fears and anxieties in one or other of the ways described, therefore his conduct could be termed "neurotic." A person may have a strong fear of snakes that might even border on the pathological when we consider the contrast between the strength of the feeling as opposed to the harmless nature of the CS; nevertheless, in a country where there are no snakes, such a person would not be exposed to the CS and hence the very existence of his disorder would remain unknown, possibly even to him.

Neurotic behaviour is the consequence of fears and anxieties, such as snake phobias, coming to the fore in certain types of social situations that give rise to what we commonly term "passive avoidance" in the laboratory. In such situations the animal is positively motivated to carry out activity a, or seek goal x; however, to do so brings the animal into contact with the CS which produces fear/anxiety. A thirsty animal who in the past has been shocked when approaching the bottle is in such a situation; he wishes to drink, but the sight of the bottle acts as a CS which produces fear/anxiety.

Note that passive avoidance can also be a response to the UCS; there is an unavoidable ambiguity in the situation in the sense that the animal cannot know whether the shock device has been connected with the bottle. If it has, his avoidance conduct would be "reasonable"; if not, it is "maladaptive" and hence might be considered "neurotic." With humans there is the possibility of verbally informing them of the harmless nature of the CS; "neurotic" conduct is diagnosed only when it is evident that the patient understands that the CS is no longer connected with the UCS. (It is not considered neurotic to be afraid of poisonous snakes!)

In passive avoidance, therefore, we have an element of conflict; in this particular the situation is different from that obtaining in active avoidance, where the animal is punished for any response except the one which the experimenter has specified—moving from one compartment to the other in a shuttlebox, for instance. Here too there could be conflict (i.e., if the response the experimenter wishes to induce is in some way undesirable to the animal); but this is not an inevitable feature of the total situation, as it is in passive avoidance. When there is a conflict in active avoidance learning, it is an avoidance-avoidance conflict; in passive avoidance learning, it is an approach-avoidance conflict, and it is this type of conflict that is typical of the neurosis-producing situation.

In postulating that conflict plays an important part in neurosis, we seem to be returning to our starting point in psychoanalytic theory. However, this is not so in any meaningful sense. The type of conflict referred to here is quite different from that postulated by psychoanalytic writers; the origins of the anxiety involved are quite different in the two cases; and the solutions to the problems posed by the existence of the conflict in question are entirely different. We have already looked at the origin of the anxiety generated in these approach-avoidance situations; it is in no way similar to the anxiety postulated by Freudian writers who deduce it from infantile traumas and sexual rivalries repressed and giving rise to "complexes" of one kind or another. The type of conflict posited by the Freudians is between ego and id (or sometimes between superego and id); it bears no relation to the conflict posited in our theory.

We are fortunate in having a detailed, experimental analysis of the approach-avoidance type of conflict (Miller, 1959); this can be transferred with a minimum of modification to human conflict behaviour. Miller's equilibrium model postulates that an animal, in approaching a stimulus situation containing CS for both approach and for avoidance, will come to rest at that point of his environment at which the forces impelling him towards and away from the stimulus situation are equal in strength. A second postulate concerns the slopes of the respective drive strengths of the two types of reaction; the strength of avoidance increases more rapidly with nearness to the goal than does that of approach. A third postulate tells us that stimulus similarity affects approach and avoidance in the same way as distance from the goal; changing the properties of the CS in the experiment will decrease the strength of the avoidance response more than the strength of the approach response. These general laws, which have received considerable experimental support, are of enormous help in understanding many features of "neurotic" conduct and behavior.

Approach–Avoidance Conflict

Consider for example some consequences of the third and last law mentioned. Gray (1971) gives the following account:

> These effects of stimulus similarity are very important. They are probably involved in the causation of patterns of behaviour in which a response is directed towards an apparently inappropriate stimulus. Consider a man who is, for whatever reason, frightened of women, but sexually attracted to them. Such a man might not be able to direct sexual behaviour towards women but be able to do so with individuals of a moderate degree of similarity to women. The outcome might well be that he was able to behave sexually only with men, or young girls, or young boys. Alternatively he might still direct his sexual behaviour towards mature females, but find that there was a point at which the avoidance tendency overcame the approach tendency. The outcome now might be a "peeping Tom" syndrome, or a fetishism directed towards articles of female clothing.

It is not claimed that, at the moment, there is much direct evidence in favour of these particular deductions from Miller's principles; they are not presented as established facts, but rather as hypotheses to be investigated empirically.

An interesting example of the approach-avoidance conflict situation relates to the clinically well-known sexual proclivities of hysterics; these were described by Lewis (1956) as "coquettish and frigid," whereas Chodoff and Lyons (1958) mentioned both the lasciviousness and sexualization of all nonsexual relations, the coquetry and the provocativeness of the hysteric, sexual frigidity, intense fear of sexuality, and failure of the sex impulse to develop towards its goal. O'Neill and Kempler (1969) and Jordan and Kempler (1970) published experimental studies that made use of the concept of approach-avoidance conflict in this connection, and H. J. Eysenck (1971) showed that this conflict may in part be due to the personality combination of high N and high E that characterizes the hysteric; E predisposes towards overt sexual behaviour, while N predisposes towards fear and avoidance responses. Thus, the personality makeup of the hysteric makes sexual conflict along these lines almost inevitable.

The points that we are trying to make are that certain principles originating in the animal laboratory are capable of producing explanations of complex human conduct; these explanations are quite different from those hitherto used in similar contexts; and these deductions are testable, in a sense that Freudian hypotheses never have been (Eysenck, H. J., & Wilson, 1973). Furthermore, they give rise to certain types of treatment (desensitization, aversion therapy) that also are quite different from the types of treatment deriving from Freudian theories; the relative success of these different types of therapy should throw much light on the relative adequacy of the causal theories involved.

It would be wrong to give the impression that approach-avoidance conflict is the only type of conflict that can generate neurotic behaviour; it seems quite likely that approach-approach and avoidance-avoidance problems, too, can generate neurotic behaviour. Unfortunately, there has been much less work done in these areas, so that we lack the carefully worked-out principles that alone could enable us to tackle the application of these principles to the human field. These types of conflict (particularly approach-approach) are probably much more difficult to induce in rats than are conflicts of the approach-avoidance type. Human beings seem uniquely gifted to react with delay, worry, and, possibly ultimately, anxiety to approach-approach conflicts; even in humans, however, the strength of the conflicts produced is usually much less than those produced by approach-avoidance conflicts.

Work on cognitive dissonance (Festinger, 1957; Lawrence & Festinger, 1962) is possibly relevant here, but this has never received the amount of corroboration from independent studies so characteristic of Miller's work on approach-avoidance conflict. Therefore, at the moment, it is impossible to derive any general principles from dissonance research which would be relevant to our problem. It may be said in passing that possibly one of the reasons for the comparative difficulty of replicating Festinger's work, which many investigators have experienced, may lie in the failure of taking personality into account; it would probably be a safe prediction that cognitive dissonance is more easily resolved by choice behaviour in extraverts than in introverts. Indeed, it seems possible that, for introverts, choice may have the opposite effect, leading to exacerbation of dissonance. Such a view seems supported by causal observation; introverted neurotics seem to find considerable difficulties in choice behaviour even when both choices involved are positively reinforced, and they often seek to annul choices already made; psychopaths and criminals, however, seem to follow the principles laid down by Festinger. Obviously casual observation furnishes no proof, and proper experimental study of this point would seem urgently desirable.

The Mowrer–Miller Theory

We have now arrived at the stage in the development of the neurotic disorder where predisposition, conditioning, and external situation have between them succeeded in producing a genuine functional (behavioural) disorder, characterized by anxiety and by conduct primarily designed to relieve this anxiety. Such conduct follows from the Mowrer-Miller two-process theory of passive avoidance learning (Mowrer, 1947; Solomon & Wynne, 1954; Turner & Solomon, 1962; see also Herrnstein, 1969). The first process is the establishment of a conditioned emotional response, which takes place as a result of the contiguous presentation of the CS and UCS; this is the classical conditioning stage. The second process is the reinforcement of the instrumental escape response, which takes place by means of drive reduction, i.e., elimination of shock; this is the instrumental conditioning stage.

As Gray (1971, p. 164) points out, the essential features of the Mowrer-Miller theory are as follows:

(1) That initially neutral stimuli which are followed by punishment acquire secondarily aversive properties, in the sense that the individual exposed to them will take action to terminate this exposure; (2) That termination of these conditioned fear stimuli ("CS-termination") is the critical reinforcing event for active avoidance learning; and (3) That avoidance of the punishment ("UCS-avoidance") does *not* have any reinforcing effect. Using the language of the emotions, this theory is often stated by saying that:

(1) The stimuli followed by punishment come to evoke conditioned fear; and (2) That it is reduction in this fear which reinforces avoidance behaviour.

There are two entirely different ways along which this second stage can proceed, and it is important to bear the distinction in mind. A patient may suffer from strong anxieties on coming into contact with a class of stimuli (e.g., dirt), and he may then discover that on washing himself carefully, this anxiety is reduced. Repetition of this sequence may give rise to a typical compulsive washing syndrome in which the motor activity, instigated by the conditioned anxiety, constitutes a major symptom of the neurotic disorder, (Hodgson & Rachman, 1972). Note that in this example we have neither "escape" nor "avoidance" of the CS, as in the typical animal experiments; this type of reaction seems particularly appropriate to human subjects.

An example of the second major way of reacting to a conditioned fear CS would be that of the woman in the Freeman and Kendrick (1960) experiment, already mentioned, who first developed a conditioned fear response to cats, and then proceeded to stay at home for fear of encountering cats in the street, or in the garden. In her case the second (instrumental) stage of conditioning protected her from coming into contact with the fear-producing object altogether, thus producing "avoidance" behaviour. This second type of instrumental conditioned behaviour is what psychiatrists refer to as "making reality-testing impossible," and clearly it plays an important part in "protecting" the neurotic (classically conditioned) CR from extinction. It is possible that, on occasion, the symptom-producing, instrumentally conditioned response exemplified in our obsessional-compulsive patient, may also have this effect; we have encountered patients in whom prevention of the washing response did not in fact produce any strong anxiety. However, this is quite unusual; presumably in these cases habit has taken over completely (Allport's "functional autonomy").

What would we expect to be the next stage in our natural history of neurosis? According to learning theory, we now have a CS which is followed no longer by a UCS (if the UCS were still present, the patient's reaction would be quite sensible, and we would hardly accuse him of neurotic disorder of any kind!). Given that this CS is presented frequently to the patient (a condition which is undoubtedly nearly always fulfilled, as otherwise he would have no cause to complain of his strong anxiety reactions to a CS which was never presented!), under conditions of no reinforcement, we would undoubtedly expect extinction to take place. As I have pointed out (Eysenck, H. J., 1963), the facts of spontaneous remission are in good accord with this prediction; the evidence indicates that without any form of psychiatric treatment something like two out of three neurotics recover within a period of about 2 years (Rachman, 1971). I have argued that this effect is in fact due to certain events taking place in the life of the patient—time by itself can of course have no effect; it must be events within time which produce the remission— and that these events are similar in kind to those which take place during behaviour therapy, but are of course less concentrated, less well timed, and hence much less effective.

I have also argued that, in so far as psychotherapy is effective, it is precisely because it resembles in nature the events that take place during spontaneous remission (Eysenck, H. J., 1963; Eysenck, H. J., & Rachman, 1965). The nature of these events will be better understood once we have discussed the major principles of behaviour therapy; here let us merely note that extinction is expected on theoretical grounds (and very much counter to Freudian predictions), and extinction is indeed found in many empirical studies. Indeed, it might be said that few neurotic phenomena are better documented than the facts of spontaneous remission. Thus, we would seem to have strong support for our theory. Unfortunately, there are some difficulties which make such an interpretation less acceptable than one might wish.

The main difficulty is the fact that while a majority of patients recover, many do not. Our prediction, therefore, would not cover quite a sizeable proportion of neurotics, including the majority of those who are most difficult and troublesome; a theory can hardly claim to be effective when it cannot deal with such an important group. It might of course be said that perhaps these are the people who fail to "reality test," in the manner explained previously; using the Mowrer-Miller two-process theory, we may claim that these patients have used the instrumental conditioning paradigm to insulate themselves from the presentation of the CS, and have thus opted out of the extinction paradigm. This theory was advanced by H. J. Eysenck and Rachman (1965); but although it undoubtedly accounts for some portion of the group of nonremitters, it does not account for the majority. Either there is something seriously wrong with our theory, or else the law of extinction is in need of a major revision. I have argued that the evidence strongly suggests that the latter alternative is preferable (Eysenck, H. J., 1968) and have suggested a revised law of extinction that takes into account the important facts of incubation of anxiety.

Incubation of Anxiety

This revised law states, in essence, that administration of the unreinforced CS (symbolized as $\overline{CS}$), which has in the past been associated with a pain/fear/anxiety-producing UCR, has two separate and contradictory effects: (a) As traditionally suggested, $\overline{CS}$ produces extinction of the CR and (b) $\overline{CS}$ produces incubation or enhancement of the CR. (The so-called Kamin effect has also been called an "incubation" effect, e.g., McAllister & McAllister, 1967. This refers to a growth of fear over a time interval that follows some aversive stimulus and is probably to be understood in terms of reminiscence, i.e., the consolidation of the memory trace; it does not seem desirable to use a special term to designate this effect. If a special term is needed, then the more widely used term "Kamin effect" is probably preferable.)

Experimental conditions favourable to the production of extinction are the reverse of those favourable to the incubation of the CR; relevant here are the strength of the UCR, the duration of the $\overline{CS}$, the emotionality of the subject, etc. The outcome of the experiment depends on the interplay of these conditions, which jointly determine the strength of these two tendencies. The experimental evidence regarding the revised law has been reviewed by H. J. Eysenck (1968), who concluded that many well-designed experiments report the incubation effect, both with humans and with animals, and that there can be little doubt about its reality. A typical example is the work of Napalkov (1963); working with dogs, he found that various novice stimuli produced increases in blood pressure of less than 50 mm., complete adaptation (habituation) occurring after some 25 applications of the UCS. A single conditioning trial, however, followed by repeated administrations of the $\overline{CS}$ (never the UCS) brought about increases in blood pressure of 30–40 mm. at first, rising to 190–230 mm.; the hypertension state that was produced lasted over a year in some cases (see Fig. 3-1). Campbell, Sanderson, and Laverty (1964) produced similar effects in humans.

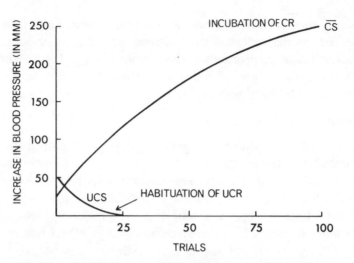

Fig. 3-1. Habituation to UCS, contrasted with incubation (enhancement of $\overline{CS}$ (unreinforced CS). Diagrammatic representation of results reported by Napalkov (1963).

While the facts will probably not be disputed, the question of an explanation is, of course, quite a different one. H. J. Eysenck (1968) has put forward a theory to account for the facts which is ultimately based on certain peculiarities of the anxiety CR which distinguish it from any other type of CR (with the possible exception of the sexual CR). These special features have been reviewed elsewhere (Eysenck, H. J., 1968). To put it briefly, anxiety is a term denotative of a secondary drive, and also a source of secondary reinforcement. The primary drive involved in this case is pain or frustrative nonreward, probably acting through stimulation of the pain centres. Neutral stimuli associated with pain give rise to anxiety/fear responses, which are very similar to responses to pain, and the proprioceptive consequences of these learned responses produce the drive stimuli (S_D) that serve the secondary drive. Anxiety may be unique in having both these functions: few other examples come to mind of secondary *drives*, although there are many studies using secondary reinforcers. Tokens that may be exchanged for food will act as secondary *reinforcers* for hungry chimps, but they will only cause him to work when hungry (primary drive); they will not produce a secondary hunger drive.

Miller, in his classical studies, showed that anxiety, i.e., conditioned pain reactions, acted as a drive as well as providing reinforcement. In these studies he demonstrated, first, that neutral stimuli become fear arousing after association with noxious stimuli and can serve as the basis for motivating an animal in a learning situation so that it strives to escape from them. Second, he showed that reduction of the fear through cessation of the conditioned fear stimulus constitutes a reinforcing event in that it leads to the learning of those responses which it follows. To put these points very briefly, it seems that the conditioned pain reaction shares with the unconditioned pain reaction all the drive-producing and reinforcing properties which are characteristic of primary drives. Therefore, for all practical purposes, conditioned pain reactions may be regarded as equivalent to a primary drive.

Aversive Conditioning

Consider now the usual account of aversive conditioning. A CS is followed by a UCS, say shock, which produces a great variety of UCR's; some of these, or even one of these, may then be singled out for study. After a single pairing, or after repeated pairings of CS and UCS, the CS produces some, or at least segments of some, of the responses originally produced by the UCS. Fear/anxiety responses are of particular interest in this connection; they are frequently produced by noxious UCS's and are readily conditioned. These CR's may be similar to the original UCR's, but they need not be; under certain conditions they may in fact be the exact opposite. For example, in rats, shock (the UCS) produces parasympathetic responses, including heart rate decrement, but the $\overline{CS}$ produces sympathetic fear responses, including heart rate increment (Stern, J. G., & Ward, 1961, 1962; Fehr & Stern, 1965). However that may be, CS and $\overline{CS}$ acquire the function of signalling danger and coming pain, discomfort, fear, and annoyance; let us denote these nocive consequences as nocive or noxious responses (NR's).

Through the intermediacy of the UCS, the CS becomes associated with the NR's and signals their arrival to the organism. For reasons that will become obvious later, we prefer the term "NR" in this connection to the use of the terms "UCR" and "CR." It will be argued that the classical conditioning account, which is implicitly accepted when we use the classical terms, is somewhat deficient, and that a novel nomenclature will be useful in describing a theory that departs in some ways from the usual one. Each reinforcement (which may be defined as an NR following CS) increments the habit strength associating CS and NR; consequently each CS/UCS pairing serves to increment the CR. When we administer a $\overline{\text{CS}}$, however, classical theory assures us that this reinforcement is missing, and consequently extinction weakens the habit strength associating CR and NR.

It is here suggested that this account is partly erroneous. $\overline{\text{CS}}$, although unaccompanied by UCS or UCR, is in fact accompanied by CR. This CR is a partial, possibly weak, but real NR that is identical in many ways with the UCR, as already pointed out. Hence some reinforcement is provided, although perhaps so much weaker than that accompanying the UCS that its presence may not be very important under certain circumstances. Yet, in principle, it is always present; its presence would theoretically lead to a strengthening of the CS/NR bond, and hence to some form of incubation. What is being suggested, in other words, is that conditioning sets in motion a positive feedback cycle in which the CR provides reinforcement for the $\overline{\text{CS}}$. Usually the extinction process will be stronger than this form of reinforcement, leading to overall extinction, and making the action of CS/NR reinforcement unobservable. But under certain circumstances (e.g., when the UCS is exceptionally strong), the extinction process may be weaker than the CS/NR reinforcement process and observable incubation will result.

What is proposed, then, is this. As Kimble (1961, p. 426) points out,

> stimuli associated with painful events come, by a process of classical conditioning, to evoke fear. The status of fear as a motive is then inferred from the fact that it has the same properties as other motives, those of providing the basis for learning and of influencing the vigor of behaviour.

What we propose to add is that fear, so generated, is itself a painful event, and that stimuli associated with it (i.e., $\overline{\text{CS}}$) by classical conditioning, comes to evoke more fear, thus producing a positive feedback. This mechanism is well-known descriptively in psychiatric disorders; it resembles somewhat Seneca's famous saying about "having nothing to fear but fear itself." Take two clinical examples. Mr. X suffers from impotence on a particular occasion due to drink, fatigue, or illness; the CS's associated with the occasion produce fear/anxiety as a CR. On the next occasion these CR's follow upon the $\overline{CS}$ and cause reciprocal inhibition of sexual reflexes; this failure causes additional anxiety/fear CR's, which produce an even stronger reaction the third time, thus setting in motion a positive feedback circle which continues without the necessity of a new CS–UCS combination. Or consider a person unable to go to sleep because of overeating or noise; his failure (UCR) is associated with anxiety responses, which become conditioned to the CS's involved (bed, night, etc.). The next night the UCS is missing, but the $\overline{CS}$–CR association produces anxiety; the patient is worried that he may not be able to go to sleep, and now the worry keeps him awake. Thus his anxiety builds up by each repitition of the $\overline{CS}$. We now have a theory to account for the failure of many neurotic fears to extinguish *even though the usual conditions for extinction are present*. This theory not only rescues our model of neurotic disorder from failure, it also suggests a firm basis for certain phenomena associated with the growth of neurotic fears which otherwise would be difficult to understand.

Liddell (1944) and his collaborators have shown that even with the employment of very mild shocks it was possible to produce experimental neuroses. How is it possible that where the application of a series of mild shocks would only produce habituation and ultimately extinction, the use of CS in conjunction with these self-same shocks produces stronger and stronger reactions until finally a complete experimental neurosis is in evidence? The same kind of phenomenon is often observed in human neurosis; the UCR's involved may be rather mild, but the combination of CS and $\overline{CS}$ produces a final catastrophic breakdown.

These facts are difficult to understand in the absence of a theory of incubation; the cumulative addition of NR's produced by $\overline{CS}$ renders the growth in strength of anxiety reactions perfectly intelligible (Wolpe, 1958, p. 64). We must also bear in mind the important possibility that under certain circumstances, which might only too frequently occur in real-life conditioning situations, the $\overline{CS}$ is protected from extinction, unlike the UCR; Levis (1967) has provided experimental support for this view. Putting forward the view that in most situations the CS is not a single stimulus but a complex of stimuli, he pointed out that the CS may often take the form of a stimulus sequence, and that early members of this sequence will not be extinguished because of NR produced by later members of the sequence (to use our terminology). When sequential

CS's were actually employed in rat experiments, he was able to show that extinction was extremely slow, and proceeded very much according to theory. Clearly, whether or not these various theories are in accord with fact, the position of anxiety conditioning in real-life situations is much more complicated than the typical experimental single-stimulus conditioning setup; animal work will have to be designed in such a way in the future that these complications can be taken into account and evidence be secured regarding their adequacy or otherwise.

Disorders of the Second Kind

The theory of incubation may be important not only for giving a proper account of the development and preservation of neurotic anxiety in dysthymic patients, i.e., in cases of neurotic disorders of the first kind, but also in the development of disorders of the second kind. Consider the experimental studies of Rachman (1966) and Rachman and Hodgson (1968) of the origins of fetishistic sexual disorders; they showed that by pairing slides of shoes and nudes, physiological responses (penis plethysmograph) appropriate to the latter could be evoked by the former. While this is in line with a simple conditioning theory of the origins of fetishism, much is still left unexplained. In the typical fetishist, sexual responses to the fetishistic object are stronger than those to the sexual object itself, and may be indispensable for the occurence of any response to the primary sexual object; the simple conditioning theory does not account for these facts at all.

Now it may be suggested that sexual responses, like anxiety responses, have secondary drive properties as well as secondary reward properties; the physiological responses to the shoe slide are similar or identical with those to the slides of nudes, just as the physiological responses to the $\overline{CS}$ in the case of pain/anxiety are often identical with those to the primary UCS. (In fact, one might say that these drive and reinforcement properties are in fact tertiary, because responses to slides of nudes may be considered secondary, primary responses being to the actual touching of the genitals. These fine distinctions however, are probably not very relevant at this stage of theory construction.) Hence we may use our paradigm of incubation of fear and extend it to the incubation of sexual responses, and their enhancement upon the production of the appropriate $\overline{CS}$; in this way we can account for the observed facts of fetishistic behaviour. Clearly in doing so we are progressing to a more adequate but also a more complex model of conditioning, making use of Mowrer's "hope-relief" hypothesis (Gray, 1971, pp. 183–192).

If we consider the extinction of approach behaviour in passive avoidance learning as being based on the activity of the *punishment* mechanism (i.e., through the fear-frustrative nonreward hypothesis), so we may consider active avoidance learning and positive reward learning as being based on the activity of the reward mechanism. Mowrer called the activity in the reward mechanism produced by secondary rewarding stimuli "hope" and the activity caused by stimuli associated with non-punishment "relief;" hence Gray has called the compound theory the "hope-relief" hypothesis, to take its place beside the "fear-frustration" hypothesis. Such a hypothesis is of course closely linked with the neurological and physiological work by Olds and others on the reward (pleasure) and the punishment (pain) centres in the brain; Gray discusses these in some detail, a task not appropriate to the present report. He also adds the hypothesis that pleasure centres are more readily aroused in extraverts, pain centres in the introvert; such an hypothesis, while still lacking in experimental support, cannot be ruled out and might account to some degree at least for the observed differential susceptibilities of introverts and extraverts for disorders of the first and second kinds.

Gray and Smith (1969) have constructed a detailed model for conflict and discrimination learning that can be (and has been) tested experimentally; it is in terms of some such model that we ought to be thinking in trying to account for neurotic behaviour, bearing in mind the complex additional drive and reinforcement variables involved through the mechanisms of conditioning, extinction, and incubation.

TREATMENT OF NEUROTIC DISORDERS

Methods of treatment of neurotic disorders must of course take their place in the general scheme outlined previously. Clinicians are interested in the curative potential of these methods, and behaviour therapy has by now achieved an enviable record of clinical success (Rachman, 1971). However, psychologists are perhaps even more concerned with the light that therapy may throw on fundamental problems of anxiety extinction and preservation (Eysenck, H. J., &

Beech, 1971). These points of view are clearly antithetical in many ways; clinicians are apt to use any and every method they feel might benefit their patients, thus throwing away any possibility of controlled trials and cumulative knowledge gained by proper experimentation. Experimentalists are apt to prefer analogue studies, i.e., monosymptomatic phobias occurring in nonneurotic students; what is lost because these are not representative of typical psychiatric illnesses is gained because of the much greater experimental control which becomes possible with cases of this type. This natural divergence of interest is not in the best interests of the subject, but the possibility certainly exists of setting up properly controlled studies even within the purview of serious clinical neurosis. As an example, consider an experiment by Gillan (1971); her problem was the twofold one of (a) whether desensitization is more effective, less effective, or equally effective in the treatment of severely neurotic phobics suffering from complex disorders, as compared with psychotherapy, and (b) whether the employment of both hierarchies and relaxation procedures is mandatory in desensitization, or whether one or other of these two components is relatively inessential.

Four groups of randomly allocated and matched neurotic patients were treated (a) by densensitization, i.e., hierarchies plus relaxation; (b) hierarchies alone, i.e., without relaxation; (c) relaxation without hierarchies; and (d) psychotherapy. The first three types of therapy were carried out by Pat Gillan, the fourth by psychotherapists. Three types of criteria were set up: introspective (i.e., fear thermometer, self ratings), physiological (reactions to feared objects), and behavioural. In addition, the therapist rated the success of his or her treatment; an independent psychiatrist, unaware of the type of treatment the patient had received, also rated the degree of success of the treatment.

The results (some of which are shown in Table 3-2) clearly demonstrated the superiority of desensitization over psychotherapy; hierarchies without relaxation did almost as well as desensitization, while relaxation without hierarchies did almost as badly as psychotherapy. It is interesting to note that the various criteria were in good agreement, except for the psychotherapist, who rated his own success rather more highly than either the independent psychiatrist, or the patients themselves, or as appeared likely from the physiological and behavioural records of his patients. This fact is

Table 3-2.

Patients' Ratings

Type of therapy	Before treatment	After treatment	At follow-up
Total phobia			
Behaviour therapy	3.87	2.29	1.98
Hierarchies only	3.58	2.43	2.51
Relaxation with psychotherapy	3.67	3.34	3.04
Psychotherapy	3.77	3.14	3.13
Mean	3.72	2.80	2.66
Main phobia			
Behaviour therapy	4.36	2.35	2.13
Hierarchies only	3.91	2.48	2.38
Relaxation with psychotherapy	4.47	3.50	3.38
Psychotherapy	4.35	3.42	3.45
Mean	4.28	2.94	2.48

important—many studies of the effects of psychotherapy are based entirely on the ratings of the therapist himself, and it seems likely from these data that therapists may not be entirely objective in their assessment of their own efforts. Indeed, it would seem unreasonable to expect them to be, on psychological principles alone; the improvement of patients is the main reinforcement which the therapist receives for his efforts on their behalf, and one would not be surprised to see him try to maximise this reinforcement.

It is interesting to note that the patients in Gillan's study did not agree with the psychotherapist's exaggerated notions of effectiveness; their ratings agree better with outside assessments and objective physiological and behavioural records. This experiment is perhaps worthy of being regarded as a prototype of the sort of thing that should be done more frequently in this field; it gives us objective information about the relative effectiveness of different methods of therapy, and it also provides information about those parts of a given system of treatment (in this case desensitization) that carry the main burden of the work. Thus, it is clear that it is the hierarchies which are the most important; relaxation plays only a rather unimportant part in the procedure.

Flooding and Desensitization

The relative unimportance of relaxation also emerges from other studies (Rachman, 1968). It has been found, for example, that contrary to theory, it is possible to ask patients to actually innervate their muscles during desensitization, without impeding the success of the therapy (Nawas, Welsch, & Fishman, 1970). Other studies have shown that relaxation is not needed in order to produce therapeutic effects when patients are exposed to phobic imagery or situations (a list of these is given by Benjamin, Marks, & Husan, 1972). These authors also report a specific experiment in which they tried to obtain evidence regarding the adequacy of Wolpe's original "reciprocal inhibition" hypothesis as compared with the habituation theory of Lader and Wing (1966). They treated phobic patients by desensitization, using a cross-over design in which half the treatments used relaxation and the other half had simple viewing of neutral slides. No difference between conditions were observed, thus reinforcing the conclusion that relaxation is not an essential part of the procedure of desensitization. Skin conductance activity was significantly lower during relaxation than during observation of the neutral slides; this result gives no support to the Lader-Wing hypothesis. Is it possible that a simple extinction hypothesis, using the model of "flooding" research in the animal laboratory, could be adequate to not only for "implosion therapy," but also for "desensitization"?

This solution does not seem appropriate because there is a definite contradiction involved in the comparison between these two methods. Flooding involves the exposure of the patient to the highest degree of anxiety that can be elicited through exposure to the feared object/conduct, without preparatory exposure to lower degrees of anxiety ("hierarchies"). Wolpe, with respect to desensitization therapy, explicitly warns against such premature exposure, and evidence exists that such disregard of the hierarchy may produce severe setbacks in the patient's progress. This apparent conflict between two well-supported methods of treatment points up most clearly the need for theoretical considerations in regard to clinical methods; the clinician may well ask which of two apparently contradictory methods he should follow, seeing that both have behind them a solid amount of empirical support. The answer may be found in terms of the writer's theory of incubation (Eysenck, H.

J., 1968), which posits that exposure to the $\overline{CS}$ produces both enhancement and extinction of the CR, depending on various parameter values for the prediction of the final outcome. One of the most important of these parameter values is the duration of exposure; it is posited that short duration of exposure leads to greater enhancement (relative to extinction) of the CR, whereas long duration of exposure leads to greater extinction (relative to enhancement).

There is good experimental evidence from the animal laboratory for this generalization (Reynierse, 1966; Rohrbaugh & Riccio, 1970; Rohrbaugh, Riccio, & Arthur, 1972). Unpublished work from our laboratory, on human subjects, tends to support it also. In these terms we can find an easy rapprochement between the rival theories. In desensitization, accidental exposures to high anxiety $\overline{CS}$ are short; and they are terminated as soon as possible by the therapist. In "flooding" treatment, however, exposures are lengthy and likely to produce extinction rather than incubation. Thus, the two treatments retain their identity, and cannot be explained in terms of identical mechanisms; at the same time, we are no longer faced with the problems of apparent contradiction in empirical findings. Both methods may be said to rely on extinction; but Wolpe's method of desensitization is concerned with extinction of small portions of the total anxiety present, one at a time, whereas "flooding" attempts to extinguish large amounts of anxiety all at the same time. Relaxation apparently plays little part in desensitization, and can be disregarded. Similarly, the psychoanalytical mumbo-jumbo surrounding Stampfl and Levis' (1967) theory and practice of "implosion therapy" is clearly irrelevant to his successes. It is possible that, along these lines, associating theoretical concepts like "incubation of anxiety" with empirical animal work on parameters of the extinction and enhancement process, we may arrive at a better theoretical understanding of these methods of treatment.

Aversion Therapy

Most of the methods of treatment current at the moment are concerned with disorders of the first kind, i.e., the *removal* of anxiety; into this category come desensitization, flooding, modeling, negative practice, etc. The only methods that have been at all widely used for disorders of the second kind are operant conditioning (in particular the use of token economies, e.g., in the treatment of criminals), and aversion therapy (Rachman & Teasdale, 1969). Aversion therapy is of particular interest in this connection because it may be thought of as the creation, along experimental lines, of a neurosis, i.e., the *production* of anxiety in relation to a stimulus which to begin with is either neutral or actively pleasurable. The end result of a successful course of aversion therapy is not a neurosis because anxiety which is produced by the treatment is not maladaptive; it has the function of making the patient desist from conduct which previously he was unable to avoid, and which was socially undesirable and/or injurious in some way. But this important difference is irrelevant to the mechanism of anxiety induction; according to Mowrer's two-factor theory we would expect aversion therapy to mirror the genesis of a genuine neurosis in miniature. It would not be possible to review here all the work that has been done by experimentalists in an effort to test this hypothesis; the conclusion seems to be that, on the whole, there is little evidence of proper anxiety being produced by the aversion treatment, either as demonstrated by physiological measurement or by introspection (Hallam & Rachman, 1972).

In addition, there are certain highly specific factors in connection with aversion conditioning which are difficult to understand. Certain UCR's became more readily associated with certain types of CS. Thus, for instance, shock-induced aversion to alcohol seems to be less efficacious than aversion produced by emetic drugs (e.g., Hallam, Rachman, & Falkowski, 1972). This may be due to the fact that when X-ray irradiation and its consequences are employed as the UCS, Garcia and his associates have shown convincingly that rats will readily acquire aversions to gustatory stimuli while audiovisual and tactile stimuli do not provide cues readily made into CS. With shock as the UCS, however, aversions were rapidly acquired to audiovisual and tactile stimuli, but not to gustatory ones. (Garcia & Koelling, 1966; Garcia, Kovner, & Green, 1970; Garcia, McGowan, & Green, 1972). This specificity may have important corollaries for human aversion treatment (Wilson & Davison, 1969).

The situation or object that forms the target of the aversion procedures tends to lose its attractiveness, but it does not inspire fear and anxiety; it becomes neutral or mildly annoying, possibly because of such factors as the small number of repititions involved in the conditioning procedure, or the very mild UCS involved. Nevertheless, it is important to consider the alternative theory Hallam and

Rachman have put forward to account for the success of aversion therapy; this theory might also be applicable to some varieties of neurotic disorder and their development. The main novelty in the proposed theory is Hallam and Rachman's first law, which states that "during periods of heightened autonomic responsiveness the target behaviour is suppressed." Aversion therapy works by increasing autonomic responsiveness, and they have shown that success of the therapy is intimately linked with such increased autonomic responsiveness.

Personality Factors in Neurosis

Hallam and Rachman also postulate that "the increase and decline of responsiveness are related to personality characteristics"; specifically, "a combination of high introversion and high neuroticism will be associated with an easily obtained increase and a slow decline in responsiveness." This emphasis on the close relation between personality and the growth and extinction of anxiety and neurotic behaviour is, of course, in line with the view expressed at the beginning of this report (H. J. Eysenck, 1970b). It is curious that few therapists, and equally few experimentalists, have paid much attention to the personalities of their patients and subjects in this connection.

One study that has paid explicit attention to the personality of the patients is by DiLoreto (1971); it demonstrates very clearly the paramount importance of personality variables in interaction with type of therapy employed. He used three clearly defined types of therapy; viz., systematic desensitization (Wolpe), client-centered therapy (Rogers), and rational-emotive therapy (Ellis). Each type of therapy was represented by two therapists, and the target behaviour was social anxiety, with batteries of tests and highly reliable observational techniques being used to measure pretreatment and posttreatment status of objects. Subjects were divided into high and low E scorers, and various hypotheses were put forward regarding the expected interaction of personality type and type of therapy employed.

The outcome in DiLoretto's study was relatively clear-cut. Desensitization was the most effective treatment, being equally applicable to extraverts and introverts. Client-centered therapy was about $2\frac{1}{2}$ times more effective in reducing anxiety with extraverts than with introverts. Rational-emotive therapy was nearly 3 times more effective in reducing anxiety with introverts than with extraverts. On the whole, treatments produced better effects than placebo or no treatment, but extraverts showed about 5 times more spontaneous remission than introverts. It will be clear that outcome was very dependent on therapy-personality interaction; no simple averaging of results would have given meaningful results. It is apparent that choice of treatment depends very much on the personality type of the patient, and that comparisons between treatments are meaningless unless personality variables are taken into account. That this should be so follows from our general theory; future work on the growth and extinction of anxiety must pay attention to so fundamental a variable.

SUMMARY AND CONCLUSIONS

We are now in a position to summarize the contents of this whole argument. It is suggested that there now exists an adequate model of neurotic behaviour, based on the principles of learning theory. This model accounts for the major facts that have come to light concerning the growth and extinction of anxiety in the production and cure of neurotic disorders. It is suggested that this model is superior to the earlier "dynamic" one based on Freudian theories, and that experimental and observational research has strongly disproved the most vital deductions that had been made from the earlier model.

It is too early to come to any definitive conclusions about the learning theory model; clearly, it has considerable promise and has already given rise to methods of treatment which have proved their value. Critics of behaviour therapy have usually directed their barbs at imaginary and unreal deficiencies of this theory (Eysenck, H. J., 1970b). They are, of course, fully justified in pointing out the incomplete state of the theory and the existence of certain anomalies that are difficult to explain at the moment. Incompleteness and the existence of anomalies are, of course, the inevitable concomitants of any theory in the process of construction. Indeed, as Lakatos and Musgrave (1970) have shown, these are the characteristics of every scientific theory that has ever existed.

It is a peculiar feature of much controversy in psychology that critics seem to demand that a theory must be perfect in every detail before they consent to take it seriously. On those grounds, no scientific theory would ever have survived. Theories have their strong and weak points; it should be our task to retain the strong points and improve the weak ones. It may be suggested that the theory here outlined has sufficient positive features in its favour to make this task worthwhile. In due course we have the possibility of ending up with a proper theory of neurotic behaviour. This certainly seems to be a worthwhile prospect.

REFERENCES

Adelman, H. M., & Maatsch, J. L. Learning and extinction based upon frustration, food reward and exploratory tendency. *Journal of Experimental Psychology*, 1956, 52, 311-315.

Amsel, A., & Roussel, J. Motivational properties of frustration: 1. Effects in a running response of the addition of frustration to the motivational complex. *Journal of Experimental Psychology*, 1952, 43, 363-368.

Bandura, A. *Principles of behaviour modification.* New York: Holt, Rinehart, & Winston, 1969.

Bandura, A. Psychotherapy based upon modelling principles. In A. Bergin & S. Garfield (Eds.), *Handbook of psychotherapy and behaviour change.* New York: Wiley, 1971.

Bandura, A., & Walters, R. H. *Social learning and personality development.* New York: Holt, Rinehart, & Winston, 1963.

Benjamin, S., Marks, I. N., & Husan, J. Active muscular relaxation in desensitizations of phobic patients. *Psychological Medicine*, 1972, 2, 381-390.

Borgström, C. A. *Archiv Rassenbiologie*, 1939, 33, 334-343. (Quoted by Hutchings, 1972)

Brown, R. T., & Wagner, A. R. Resistance punishment and extinction following training with shock or non-reinforcement. *Journal of Experimental Psychology*, 1964, 68, 503-507.

Burt, C. Factorial studies of personality and their bearing on the work of the teacher. *British Journal of Educational Psychology*, 1965, 35, 368-378.

Campbell, P., Sanderson, R. E., & Laverty, S. G. Characteristics of a conditioned response in human subjects during extinction trials following a simple traumatic conditioning trial. *Journal of Abnormal and Social Psychology*, 1964, 68, 627-639.

Cattell, R. G. The interaction of hereditary and environmental influences. *British Journal of Statistical Psychology*, 1963, 16, 191-210.

Chodoff, P., & Lyons, N. Hyesteria: The hysterical personality and hysterical conversions. *American Journal of Psychiatry*, 1958, 114, 734-740.

Christiansen, K. O. Threshold of tolerance in various population groups illustrated by results from Danish criminological twin studies. In A. V. S. de Reuck & R. Carter (Eds.), *Ciba Foundation symposium on the mentally abnormal offenders.* London: Churchill, 1968.

DiLoreto, A. O. *Comparative psychotherapy.* New York: Aldine Atherton, 1971.

Dollard, J., & Miller, N. E. *Personality and psychotherapy.* New York: McGraw-Hill, 1950.

Eysenck, H. J. The inheritance of extraversion-introversion. *Acta Psychologica,* 1956, 12, 95-110.

Eysenck, H. J. (Ed.) *Behaviour therapy and the neuroses.* Oxford: Pergamon Press, 1960.

Eysenck, H. J. Behaviour therapy, spontaneous remission and transference in neurotics. *American Journal of Psychiatry,* 1963, 119, 867-871.

Eysenck, H. J. *The biological basis of personality.* Springfield, Ill.: Charles C Thomas, 1967.

Eysenck, H. J. A theory of the incubation of anxiety/fear responses. *Behaviour Research and Therapy,* 1968, 6, 309-321.

Eysenck, H. J. *Crime and personality.* London: Paladin Books, 1970. (a)

Eysenck, H. J. Psychological aspects of anxiety. *British Journal of Psychiatry,* Special Publication No. 3, 1970, 7-20. (b)

Eysenck, H. J. Behaviour therapy and its critics. *Journal of Behaviour Therapy and Experimental Psychiatry,* 1970, 1, 5-15. (c)

Eysenck, H. J. Hysterical personality and sexual adjustment, attitudes and behaviour. *Journal of Sexual Research,* 1971, 7, 274-281.

Eysenck, H. J. Genetic factors in personality development. In A. R. Kaplan (Ed.), *Human behaviour genetics.* In press, 1975.

Eysenck, H. J. Behaviour therapy: Present and future. In J. C. Bregelmann and W. Tunner (Eds.), *Behaviour Therapy.* München: Urban & Schwarzberg, 1973. (a)

Eysenck, H. J. Personality, learning and "anxiety." In H. J. Eysenck (Ed.), *Handbook of abnormal psychology* (2nd Ed.). London: Pitman, 1973. (b)

Eysenck, H. J., & Beech, H. R. Counter conditioning and related methods. In A. E. Bergin & S. L. Garfield (Eds.), *Handbook of psychotherapy and behavioural change.* London: Wiley, 1971.

Eysenck, H. J., & Eysenck, S. B. G. *The Eysenck personality inventory.* London: University of London Press, 1965.

Eysenck, H. J., & Eysenck, S. B. G. *Personality structure and measurement.* London: Routledge and Kegan Paul, 1969.

Eysenck, H. J. & Rachman, S. *The causes and cures of neurosis.* London: Routledge and Kegan Paul, 1965.

Eysenck, H. J., & Wilson, G. *The experimental study of Freudian theories.* London: Methuen, 1973.

Eysenck, S. B. G., & Eysenck, H. J. Scores on three personality variables as a function of age, sex and social class. *British Journal of Social and Clinical Psychology,* 1969, 8, 69-76.

Fehr, F. S., & Stern, J. G. Heart rate conditioning in the rat. *Journal of Psychosomatic Research,* 1965, 8, 441-453.

Festinger, L. *A theory of cognitive dissonance.* Stamford: University Press, 1957.

Freeman, H. L., & Kendrick, D. C. A case of cat phobia treatment by a method derived from experimental psychology. *British Medical Journal,* 1960, 11, 497-502.

Freud, S. Two short accounts of psychoanalysis (Trans. J. Strachey). London: Hogarth Press, 1962.

Garcia, J., & Koelling, R. Relation of cue to consequence in avoidance learning. *Psychonomic Science*, 1966, 4, 123-124.

Garcia, J., Kovner, R., & Green, K. Cue properties of flavors in avoidance learning. *Psychonomic Science*, 1970, 20, 313-314.

Garcia, J., McGowan, B., & Green, K. Biological constraints on learning. In A. H. Black & W. F. Prokasy (Eds.), *Classical conditioning II*. New York: Appleton-Century-Crofts, 1972.

Gillan, P. *An experimental investigation of behaviour therapy in phobic patients*. Unpublished doctoral dissertation, London, University of London, 1971.

Gray, J. *The psychology of fear and stress*. London: Weidenfeld & Nicolson, 1971.

Gray, J. A., & Smith, P. T. An arousal-decision model for partial reinforcement and discrimination learning. In R. M. Gilbert & N. S. Sutherland (Eds.), *Animal discrimination learning*. London: Academic Press, 1969.

Greenson, R. R. *The technique and practice of psychoanalysis*. New York: International University Press, 1967.

Hallam, R., & Rachman, S. Theoretical problems of aversion therapy. *Behaviour Research and Therapy*, 1972, 10, 341-353.

Hallam, R., Rachman, S., & Falkowski, W. Subjective attitudinal and physiological effects of electrical aversion therapy. *Behaviour Research and Therapy*, 1972, 10, 1-13.

Hayashi, S. In H. Mitsuda (Ed.), *Clinical genetics in psychiatry*. Osaka: Osaka Medical College, 1967.

Henderson, P. K., & Gillespie, R. D. *Textbook of psychiatry* (10th Ed.). London: Oxford University Press, 1969.

Herrnstein, R. J. Method and theory in the study of avoidance. *Psychological Review*, 1969, 76, 49-69.

Hinde, R. A. *Animal behaviour*. London: McGraw-Hill, 1966.

Hodgson, R. J., & Rachman, S. The effects of contamination and washing in obsessional patients. *Behaviour Research Therapy*, 1972, 10, 111-117.

Jinks, J. L., and Fulker, D. S. Comparison of the biometrical, genetical MAVA and classical approaches to the analysis of human behaviour. *Psychological Bulletin*, 1970, 73, 311-349.

Jones, M. C. A laboratory study of fear: The case of Peter. *Pedagogical Seminars*, 1924, 31, 308-315. (a)

Jones, M. C. The elimination of children's fears. *Journal of Experimental Psychology*, 1924, 7, 383-390. (b)

Jordan, B. T., & Kempler, B. Hysterical personality: An experimental investigation of sex-role conflict. *Journal of Abnormal Psychology*, 1970, 75, 172-176.

Kempthorne, O. *An introduction to genetic statistics*. New York: Wiley, 1957.

Kimble, G. *Hilgard and Marquis' conditioning and learning*. New York: Appleton-Century-Crofts, 1961.

Lader, M. H., & Wing, L. Physiological measures, sedative drugs and morbid anxiety. *Maudsley Monograph* No. 14, London: Oxford University Press, 1966.

Lakatos, I., & Musgrave, A. *Criticism and the growth of knowledge.* Cambridge: University Press, 1970.

Lange, J. *Verbrechen als Schicksal.* Leipzig: Thieme, 1929.

Lawrence, D. H., & Festinger, L. *Deterrents and reinforcement.* London: Tavistock, 1962.

Levis, D. J. Implosive therapy: Part 2. The subhuman analogue, the strategy and the technique. In S. C. Armitage (Ed.), *Behavior modification techniques in the treatment of emotional disorders.* Battle Creek, Mich.: V.A. Publications, 1967.

Lewis, A. J. Psychological medicine. In D. Hunter (Ed.), *Price's textbook of the practice of medicine.* London: Oxford University Press, 1956.

Liddell, H. S. Conditioned reflex method of experimental neurosis. In J. McV. Hunt (Ed.), *Personality and the behaviour disorders.* New York: Ronald Press, 1944.

Lorenz, K. Über die Bilding des Instinktbegriffes. In C. Schiller (Ed.), *Instinctive behavior.* New York: International University Press, 1957.

McAllister, D. E., & McAllister, F. J. J. Incubation of fear: An examination of the concept. *Journal of Experimental Research in Personality.* 1967, **2**, 180-190.

Mednick, S., & Freedman, J. Stimulus generalization. *Psychological Bulletin,* 1960, **57**, 169-200.

Miller, N. E. Liberalization of basic S–R concepts; extensions to conflict behaviour, motivation and social learning. In S. Koch (Ed.), *Psychology: A study of science,* Vol. 2. New York: McGraw-Hill, 1959.

Miller, N. E., & Dollard, J. *Social learning and imitation.* New Haven: Yale University Press, 1941.

Mowrer, O. H. On the dual nature of learning—a reinterpretation of "conditioning" and "problem solving." *Harvard Educational Review,* 1947, **17**, 102-148.

Napalkov, S. V. Information process of the brain. In N. Wiener & J. C. Schade (Eds.), *Progress in brain research,* Vol. 2. Amsterdam: Elsevier, 1963.

Nawas, M., Welsch, W., & Fishman, S. The comparative effectiveness of pairing aversive imagery with relaxation, neutral tasks and muscular tension in reducing snake phobia. *Behaviour Research and Therapy,* 1970, **8**, 63-68.

Nicholson, J. N. Some operant conditioning effects in children and their relation to personality and development. Unpublished doctoral dissertation, Oxford University, 1972.

Nicholson, J. N., & Gray, J. A. Behavioural contrast and peak shift in children. *British Journal of Psychology,* 1971, **62**, 367-374.

O'Neill, M., & Kempler, B. Approach and avoidance responses of the hysterical personality to sexual stimuli. *Journal of Abnormal Psychology,* 1969, **74**, 300-305.

Rachman, S. Sexual fetishism: An experimental analogue. *Psychological Research,* 1966, **16**, 293-296.

Rachman, S. The role of muscular relaxation in desensitization therapy. *Behaviour Research and Therapy*, 1968, 6, 159-166.

Rachman, S. *Phobias: Their nature and control.* Springfield, Ill.: Charles C Thomas, 1968.

Rachman, S. *The effects of psychotherapy.* Oxford: Pergamon, 1971.

Rachman, S. Clinical applications of observational learning, imitation and modelling. *Behavior Therapy*, 1972, 3, 379-397.

Rachman, S., & Hodgson, R. J. Experimentally induced "sexual fetishism." *Psychological Record*, 1968, 18, 25-27.

Rachman, S., & Teasdale, J. *Aversion therapy and behaviour disorders.* London: Routledge and Kegan Paul, 1969.

Reynierse, J. N. Effects of C.S. only trials in resistance to extinction of an avoidance response. *Journal of Comparative and Physiological Psychology*, 1966, 61, 156-158.

Rohrbaugh, M., & Riccio, D. Paradoxical enhancement of learned fear. *Journal of Abnormal Psychology*, 1970, 75, 210-216.

Rohrbaugh, M., Riccio, D. C., & Arthur, D. Paradoxical enhancement of conditioned suppression. *Behaviour Research and Therapy*, 1972, 10, 125-130.

Rosanoff, H. J., Handy, L. M., & Plesset, I. R. The etiology of child behaviour difficulties, juvenile delinquency and adult criminality with special reference to their occurrence in twins. *Psychiatric Monographs, No. 1.* Sacramento: Department of Institutions, 1941.

Savage, R. D., & Eysenck, H. J. The definition and measurement of emotionality. In H. J. Eysenck (Ed.), *Experiments in motivation.* Oxford: Pergamon Press, 1964.

Schulsinger, F. Psychopathy: Heredity and environment. In L. Erlenmeyer-Kimling (Ed.), Genetics and mental disorder. *International Journal of Mental Health*, 1972, 1, 190-206.

Shields, J. Personality differences and neurotic traits in normal twin school children. *Eugenics Review*, 1954, 45, 213-246.

Shields, J. *Monozygotic twins.* Oxford: Oxford University Press, 1962.

Shields, J. Psychiatric genetics. In M. Shepherd & D. L. Davis (Eds.), *Studies in psychiatry.* London: Oxford University Press, 1968.

Shields, J., & Slater, G. La similarite du diagnostic chez les jumeaux. *L'evolution psychiatrique*, 1966, 2, 441-451.

Slater, G., & Shields, J. Genetical aspects of anxiety. In M. H. Lader (Ed.), *Studies in anxiety. British Journal of Psychiatry*, Special Publication No. 3. Ashford: Headley, 1969.

Solomon, R. L., & Wynne, L. C. Traumatic avoidance learning: The principles of anxiety conservation and partial irreversibility. *Psychological Review*, 1954, 61, 353-385.

Stampfl, T. G., & Levis, D. J. Essentials of implosive therapy: A learning-theory-based psychodynamic behavioral therapy. *Journal of Abnormal and Social Psychology*, 1967, 72, 496-503.

Stern, C. *Principles of human genetics.* San Francisco: Freeman, 1960.

Stern, J. G., & Ward, T. J. Changes in cardiac response of the albino rat as a function of electro-convulsive seizures. *Journal of Comparative and Physiological Psychology*, 1961, 54, 385–391.

Stern, J. G., & Ward, T. J. Heart rate change during avoidance conditioning in the male albino rat. *Journal of Psychosomatic Research*, 1962, 6, 157–162.

Stumpfl, F. *Die Ursprünge des Verbrechans*. Leipzig: Thieme, 1936.

Tinbergen, N. *The study of instinct*. Oxford, University Press, 1951.

Turner, L. H., & Solomon, R. L. Human traumatic avoidance learning. Theory and experiments on the operant-respondent distinction and failures to learn. *Psychological Monographs*, 1962, 76, (Whole No. 559.)

Wagner, A. R. The rate of reinforcement and unreinforcement in an "apparent frustration effect." *Journal of Experimental Psychology*, 1959, 57, 130–136.

Wagner, E. R. Frustration in punishment. In R. N. Haber (Ed.), *Current research in motivation*. New York: Holt, Rinehart, & Winston, 1966.

Watson, J. B. *Behaviourism*. New York: Norton, 1924.

Watson, J. B., & Rayner, R. Conditioned emotional reactions. *Journal of Experimental Psychology*, 1920, 3, 1–14.

Wilson, G. T., & Davison, G. C. Aversion techniques in behaviour therapy: Some theoretical and metatheoretical considerations. *Journal of Consulting and Clinical Psychology*, 1969, 33, 327–329.

Wolpe, J. *Psychotherapy by reciprocal inhibition*. Stamford: University Press, 1958.

Yoshimasu, S. Co-operative psychiatric research on criminals and juvenile delinquents. Abstracted in English in *Exerpta Criminologica*, 1965, 5, 61–62.

4

RESEARCH ON ANXIETY AND PHOBIC REACTIONS

R. W. Ramsay

University of Amsterdam
Amsterdam, The Netherlands

In 1962 a chair of "Personality Theory" was created in Amsterdam to which Prof. Johan Barendregt was appointed. It was decided to concentrate on the clinical aspects of personality study; and within the extant tradition of clinical psychology, the activities of the department were to consist of diagnostic testing. The task set for the department was not simply to use a "package-deal" battery of intelligence, projective, etc. tests, but to choose tests appropriate for each particular patient or evolve new ones; to construct a theory concerning this person; and with the help of theory, to select the most appropriate therapy. Though this seemed like a sound approach, it proved to be impossibly time consuming, and we never got to the therapy part of the plan. A decision was made to curtail our research and therapy, and limit it to one class of anxiety reactions.

In clinical psychology, the typical approach is to work on a broad range of clinical problems from a single theoretical framework, be it behavioristic, psychoanalytic, or some other point of view. We chose to study one phenomenon, phobias, and to approach this problem from as many different angles as possible. Phobias were chosen because in this syndrome anxiety is most clearly seen; the syndrome can be easily defined (so we thought); an adequate form of therapy was available (behavior therapy); and with a minimum of training, students could become actively engaged in both research and therapy.

Thus, in 1966, Prof. Barendregt's "phobia project" was born. In describing this project, the writer wishes to give full credit to Prof. Barendregt for developing the phobia project and for the ideas and research the project has generated.

GOALS AND METHODS
OF THE PHOBIA PROJECT

The principle aims of the phobia project are teaching, research, and therapy. Students are expected to become familiar with one aspect of "disturbed" or abnormal behavior and the techniques for investigating this behavior. They are also expected to come to know the most important variables in the development and maintenance of phobias and to be able to use various techniques for bringing about changes in this behavior. In research, the phobic syndrome of anxiety reactions was to be investigated from both a theoretical and a practical point of view. In return for providing the research project staff with information about their anxiety reactions, patients were given therapy in the hope that their distress would be reduced.

In 1966, the staff of the phobia project consisted of four people. At the end of 1972 there were 25 staff members, not all full time, but all working on some aspect of phobias. In the area of physiology, students and staff are investigating cardiovascular reactivity in anxiety reactions, conditioning, and heart rate and autonomic response specifity to stress. Experimentation has also been carried out in electroencephalogram (EED) Alpha Conditioning (Driessen, 1971; Meeder, 1971) and autonomic reactivity under varying conditions of stimulation (Sierhuis & Swaab, 1970; van Wijk, 1971). In general, phobics adapt more slowly than normals, but why, under what conditions, and with what consequences?

There appears to be some correlation between the intensity of anxiety reactions and the menstrual cycle in females. This relationship and some other biochemical aspects of anxiety are being investigated (Duursma & Rooker, 1973; Rooker & Duursma, 1973).

Concerning perception and anxiety reactions, the influence on perception and signal detection of punishment, punishment avoidance, and reward have been investigated. We are working on the hypothesis that phobics see more of their phobic objects in the environment than do nonphobics, and that within the class of phobic objects there is little discrimination. For example, if you ask a dog phobic if there are any dogs around, his answer is; "Yes, thousands, they're on every street." A nonphobic would say there were a few dogs on the street, but not many. Ask a phobic to discriminate within the class "dogs"—old–young, safe–unsafe, gentle–savage—and he cannot do it. I recently asked a dog-phobic patient what is indicated when a dog wags his tail and he did not know! The implications for therapy are to give phobic patients a course in discrimination to help them learn to distinguish between safe and unsafe situations and objects.

In research on cognition and anxiety reactions, we have leaned heavily on the work of Schachter and his colleagues. Many of our clients seem to code their emotions incorrectly and therefore react inappropriately in numerous situations. The implications for therapy are either to give the client false feedback ragarding his physiological state (Bloemkolk, Defares, van Enkevort, & van Gelderen, 1971), a course in correct coding, or to reduce certain correlates of high arousal by means of beta-blocking medication.

Many of our patients seem to suffer from anxiety reactions due to difficulties in fulfilling the role they have to assume in their milieu. For such patients, a simple change in role can often work wonders. A traveling salesman with a travel phobia changed jobs to office work in the city and the phobia disappeared. Agoraphobic female patients live very much like the Pardah women in India (de Smet, 1969), except that in our society, the role of women is not to stay home but to go out each day for shopping and socializing. If the agoraphobic's role were changed to that of a Pardah woman, she would probably cease to experience anxiety reactions. Some North African men wear cloth masks over their faces. This mask, however, is not worn on all occasions but in precisely those situations that our blushing phobic patients report as difficult (Schutz, 1971). If the role of the blushing phobic were changed so that he could wear a mask over his face, he would probably cease to be phobic.

Recurrent strong anxiety reactions experienced by a patient will generally have repercussions on others in the environment. We are studying the relationship patterns, both verbal and nonverbal, of phobics and their partners (de Boom, 1970; Raapis Dingman, 1972; Zant, 1971). What role does the partner play in the development, maintenance, and eventual reduction of anxiety reactions? We have been astounded at the frequency with which the "healthy" partner breaks down as the "sick" partner recovers (Barendregt, 1969; Ramsay, 1971).

We have for a number of years carried out experimental analogue studies of phobias and other emotional reactions (Burgemeister, 1971; van Dam, Barendregt, & Kalsbeek, 1969; van Wijland, 1971). By means of hypnotic and posthypnotic suggestions, various emotions are induced and conditioned so that they are under the control of the experimenter. For example, a subject may be conditioned to respond with anger to a red light, feel happy when a blue light is turned on, become sexually stimulated when a buzzer is sounded, or become anxious when a green light is turned on. This subject may also be trained to respond with various intensities of emotions as the conditioned stimulus (CS) is varied in intensity—a green light at half intensity will evoke some but less anxiety. We can then take away the hypnotic and posthypnotic suggestions, and the subjects still respond to the various CSs. We never see anything resembling phobic reactions when "pure" emotions are evoked, but when incompatible emotions are aroused by, for example, a blue (anger) and a red (happy) light turned on together, the S becomes uncomfortable and we begin to see what looks like phobic behavior (Barendregt & van Dam, 1969). This work seems to agree with Izard's (1972) work on "mixed" and "pure" emotions.

There are a number of other research areas within the phobia project, but space does not permit me to go into these.[1] It should be obvious that we have set ourselves a big task in trying to understand this one syndrome of anxiety reactions. We have found that no single theory is sufficient, and the difficulty of the problem becomes more apparent when we come to therapy.

[1] The Department of Psychology of the University of Amsterdam produces a regular bulletin. Anyone interested in being placed on our mailing list should contact the writer. This bulletin provides a list of theses and literature surveys done within the department and summarizes some of the more interesting ones. Almost all theses are on stencil and can be bought for a small fee. A big problem, of course, is the language barrier—most theses are in Dutch.

THEORY AND THERAPY

When I read the literature on theoretical explanations of how anxiety reactions develop and on the practical outcomes of treatment, it all sounds so straightforward. But in my clinical practice it isn't straightforward at all. "Ah," I hear you say, "a muddle-headed practitioner!" But let us look at some of the theorizing.

The Eysenck & Beech (1971) account is probably the most up-to-date conditioning theory of neurosis. Their discussion of the genesis of neurotic disorders leans very much on conditioned emotional responses and secondary reinforcement through escape from anxiety-evoking situations. This is a clean, clear-cut theory of considerable scientific value. Eysenck and Beech admit that the theory does not encompass all observable phenomena, but is selective. The following reasons are given for being satisfied with this state of affairs: "A theory is not required to embrace all observations without careful selection. One of the main attributes of a good theorist is that he does not try to bring under one umbrella discordant and unrelated phenomena. . . ."

My patients do not seem to fit Eysenck's clear-cut and simple model. In some simple, monosymptomatic animal phobics, it is possible to trace the historical development of the neurotic behavior, and these cases fit quite well with Eysenck's model. The goodness of fit for complex agoraphobias, however, leaves much to be desired. Eysenck has the perfect right to select his observations so that his model will be a good one, but in doing so he detracts from the value it has for the practitioner who is faced with extremely complex material.

Eysenck states further that a restricted model can and should be expanded, and he has followed this rule in his own theorizing. For example, Eysenck first proposed a three-stage theory of the theoretical course of neurotic behavior (Eysenck & Rachman, 1965) and later expanded this to include the phenomenon of incubation (Eysenck, 1973). My point is not that model-building efforts, such as the work of Eysenck, lack merit, but rather that model building has not advanced enough to be of value to the practitioner. Phobic phenomena are too complex for a simple model to encompass.

As an example of trying to fit Eysenck's model, let us consider the case of a 28-year-old agoraphobic man who could remember exactly the situation in which he first became street-phobic. He was riding his motorcycle; and, at a particular corner, he suddenly started getting heart palpitations, felt faint, went into the nearest shop, rested for a time, and then called a cab and went home. As he described this I could visualize the subsequent development in terms of again approaching the same corner, CERs occurring, the beginning of avoidance of that corner, generalization taking place to other corners, etc. But no, he went on to describe how the next day he returned to the same corner to pick up his motorcycle and had no difficulties at all. Subsequent trips past that spot caused no problems. A few weeks later, however, while walking along another street he had a second panic attack. When questioned as to where he was going, he said that he did not know. The course of therapy tentatively indicated that there was a complex interaction of emotional difficulties with his girlfriend and the recent death of his father.

A three- or four-stage theory did not help much to understand this man's agoraphobic development. In fact, even though we routinely question our patients minutely about the beginnings of their phobias, it is rare that we can find processes that resemble Eynsenck's four-stage theory and then only in the case of simple phobias. We have to adopt other strategies to explain how complex anxiety reactions develop.

One strategy is to supplement a model such as Eysenck's with information from other fields, e.g., perception, cognition, motivation, social psychology, biochemistry. Indeed, information covering the whole broad field of psychology may be required to explain and treat a single case. This is a formidable task, and practitioners (e.g., Lazarus, 1970, 1971; Meyer, 1972) have expressed dissatisfaction with the help that theory lends to those in practice. Lazarus (1971) attempted to supplement the stimulus-response (S-R) models, but this effort has been described as "a mishmash of theories, a huggermugger of procedures, gallimaufry of therapies, and a charivaria of activities, having no proper rationale, and incapable of being tested or evaluated [Eysenck, 1970]." Clearly, theory and practice are not well developed, and attempts at development are often harshly discouraged.

Another strategy open to the practitioner is to change, chameleon-like, to fit the occasion. S-R theories deal with habits, and where this is applicable, the clinician espouses learning theory. Certain maladaptive habits need to be replaced by more adaptive habits. Other theories, employing different methods of sorting out and organizing facts, may become useful in some cases. Any one theory in itself is too narrow; therefore, the practitioner is forced to use a variety of models. The problem then is that he may mix incompatible theories, resulting, at best, in confusion for both therapist and patient.

Let us now look at some further theorizing and model building and applications to the clinical concept of neuroticism. Someone scoring high on this factor will have a predisposition to develop neurotic behavior patterns. We routinely test our patients and obtain an N score. But we *know*, almost without exception, that our patients score high on this factor. If we were in personnel selection, a knowledge of the N score would be of value, but as a research clinician interested in the *process* and development of what leads to scoring high on N, the theory and test results have not helped very much.

In primary school, Johnny gets all his sums right and Jimmy gets all his sums wrong. Both are tested, and it turns out that Johnny has a high IQ and Jimmy has a low IQ; the teacher is satisfied with this as an explanation of why one pupil can do the work and the other cannot. An orthopaedagogue, though, would want to know about the process of IQ formation for his particular client, Jimmy. It is possible, one of the multitude of possibilities, that Jimmy has always had slightly weak eyesight. Due to this, he has been limited in his perceptual abilities, which has led to not being able to study efficiently, and this has caused Jimmy to fall behind in his intellectual development. Giving Jimmy a pair of spectacles and a little remedial teaching would go a long way. Similarly, the clinician is fooling himself if the thinks that the N score gives him much information about a particular client; it does not tell him anything about the developments leading to a high N, nor of how to reverse these.

A possible explanation could be that a particular client with high N is genetically endowed with an overreactive nervous system which results in him being hurt often in the process of growing up. Consequently, he tends to withdraw from those around him, which leads to a deficiency in the learning of social skills and decreased ability in social interaction in later life. This results in approach-avoidance conflicts because he wants to be sociable but always fails, leading to much complaining behavior that is reflected in his answering "yes" to questions such as "Does your mood often go up and down?" and "Do you ever feel 'just miserable' for no good reason?" (Eysenck & Eysenck, 1964). Since the complaining behavior does not change anything, he becomes angry and bitter, and finally ends up sitting at home because he suffers panic attacks when he goes out onto crowded streets or into shops.

An alternative explanation is that the high N individual has a perfectly normal nervous system but, as he grows up, his eyes develop a slight malfunctioning in peripheral vision. Since his everyday functioning requires social contacts on busy streets he must be constantly aware of what is going on around him. He is therefore forced to constantly move his head backwards and forwards, and he begins to notice that in certain situations he is very tense and nervous, and can only relax at home. In avoiding certain situations in which he is tense, he finds himself cut off from normal social contacts and starts complaining about his lot, which is reflected in answering "yes" to certain questions. The complaining behavior does not change anything, etc.

Both cases end up in the clinician's office with exactly the same symptoms. Unfortunately, the theoretical background behind knowing the N scores does not tell me anything about the process leading to the high N scores. So we could go on hypothesizing developmental sequences for hearing deficiencies, overprotected children, underprotected children, etc. As for therapy for each individual, that will to a large extent depend on the developmental sequence and the reasons causing the high N score.

The point here is not whether the theoretical accounts of the development of neurotic behavior are either right or wrong, selected or all inclusive. It is simply that the clinician has to deal with complex material. He is fooling himself if he believes that hypothetical constructs such as neuroticism give an explanation of complex neurotic behaviors and lead to adequate therapeutic approaches.

MULTIPLE MODELS
ARE NECESSARY

To understand the factors involved in the development, maintenance, and treatment of anxiety reactions, the therapist cannot rely on simple S-R models. We hear time and again from our female agoraphobic patients that their problems began at the birth of the first child. Is this a biochemical factor or is it a dependency-relationship problem? We find in some of our patients that there is a strong correlation between menstrual cycle and severity of anxiety reactions, which would indicate that biochemical factors are important. Some of our patients respond well to antidepressant drugs without the need of other forms of therapy. Kelly, Guirguis, Frommer, & Mitchell-Heggs, (1971) report similar but more spectacular results. Other patients in our project recover from their anxiety reactions only when the relationship problems between husband and wife are resolved.

Some of our patients seem to suffer from perceptual deficits of various kinds. Barendregt & Bleeker (1973) describe the treatment of an agoraphobic who lost her phobic reactions after a visit to an oculist to remedy a slight visual defect. But the explanation was not as simple as that. It appears that her being able to attribute her dizziness and headaches to visual problems, and therefore adequately register them, was the main factor in reducing the anxiety reactions. Here it seems that a combination of perceptual and cognitive deficits led to the development of the anxiety reactions, and correction of these deficits resolved the problems.

Many patients seem to code their emotional reactions inadequately, which leads them to develop severe anxiety reactions, and such patients benefit from a course in coding emotions "correctly" (Bloemkolk et al., 1971). The role a person has to fulfill and the social milieu in which he operates also play a large part in the development and maintenance of anxiety reactions. These complexities are not taken into account by any simple model, nor does treatment for these problems necessarily follow from such a model. If practice is to influence theory building, as it should, the practitioner has the right to indicate some of the lacunae and shortcomings of the theoretician.

MOTIVATION AND THERAPY

In Holland, as in many other countries, there is a club for phobics. The Dutch club is run by an energetic ex-phobic who regularly sends out a printed bulletin. She also writes articles in the women's journals, gives newspaper interviews, organizes television and radio programs, and advertises the club extensively. There is little reason to believe that people suffering from anxiety reactions of a phobic nature would not know of the existence of this club. Furthermore, through the efforts of the leader of the phobia club and the cooperation of therapists, it was stated in the February 1973 issue of the club bulletin that anyone who wanted treatment could be accommodated. General practitioners and psychiatrists have been trained to recognize phobias and have been exposed to numerous articles that give hope for the treatment of phobic anxiety reactions; therefore, they can easily refer patients for treatment. Thus, it would seem that most people who suffer phobic anxieties would know that, in some way or another, they could do something about it.

How many phobics are there, and how many seek help? Marks (1969) quoted a study estimating that 0.22% of the population in one particular area suffered from phobias severe enough to be disabling. There is no reason to suppose that the Dutch population differs radically on this aspect from the Vermont population. Thus we may estimate that in Holland there are 16,000 adults disabled by phobic problems. Of this number about 8% join the phobia club, and those who are motivated to join the club are not all in therapy, even though therapy is generally available at a low cost to those who cannot afford it. To my mind, this shows a surprising lack of motivation on the part of phobics to take any steps to relieve their distress.

We did a small survey recently within the phobia club, which, remember, only covers 8% of the total phobic population. We sent a questionnaire to 199 randomly selected members of the club, and more than 80% returned the questionnaire. Of this number, 84.5% still suffer from severe problems; but of these, only 56% are now in treatment, despite the recent statement in the bulletin that any member could be placed in therapy. Thus, it seems evident that only a small percentage of the total phobic population seeks therapy.

People have a perfect right to choose not to go into therapy, and those who do not seek treatment present no immediate problem to me as a therapist. However, the low percentage from the phobic club who are in treatment tells us something about the motivation to change. Assuming that motivation to change is a continuum from very low to very high, most people suffering from anxiety reactions are so poorly motivated that they do nothing about it. Some phobics, of course, seek therapy without going via the club, but this number is not all that large and still does not vitiate my argument about the motivation of the phobic population to do something about their distress. In other words the whole continuum of motivation appears to be slanted towards the lower end, and many of those who come into therapy are only marginally motivated.

In phobias we find a prime and clearcut example of how anxiety can disrupt what might have been a happy and productive life. Behavior therapy is most advanced in the effective treatment of phobic behavior, and the success has been unparallelled in the history of therapeutic interventions. We have some powerful techniques, and these are constantly being refined and extended. Yet much of my clinical endeavor is not spent in using these techniques to quickly relieve the anxiety and pain. Most of the time is spent in constantly bolstering the motivation of the patient to stay in treatment so that the techniques can be given a chance to work.

The counterconditioning of anxiety can be quickly learned, is easy to apply, and seems to work even if applied in a "sloppy" manner (inverted or random hierarchies, short or long sessions—given by students, tape recorders, computers, etc.). Much of my work, and clinical skills, is devoted to strengthening marginal motivation and getting the patient to carry out the necessary program. I have not seen anything in the behavior therapy literature on this problem of motivation (or lack of it), and much more work is needed to tease out the intricate positive and negative reinforcement schedules involved in motivation.

The second big problem here concerns those who do not present themselves for treatment, or have dropped out before anything effective can be done. There is some evidence (Bandura, 1969; Marks, 1969) that phobic behavior is contagious in the form of being passed on from parents to children. For example, a young man in his 20's who is phobic for dogs can remember, from an early age, that every time he and his mother went out together and passed a dog on the street, he could feel his mother tense up and suck in her breath sharply. Not a word was ever said about dogs being dangerous, but he quickly learned to avoid all dogs. Another example: a young lady presented herself for therapy because of a fear of spiders, which severely curtailed her normal activities. In the family background the grandmother, mother, aunt, and sister were all phobic for spiders. The patient related that there was always a bell in the house and, whenever anyone discovered a spider, the bell was vigorously rung and everyone ran screaming out of the house. If most phobics remain phobic and pass on their phobias, there seems to be little chance of gradually reducing the incidence of the syndrome. We can do little preventive work when most severely disabled phobics are not motivated to seek or accept help, and therefore remain severely disabled. If preventive steps could be taken, it is possible that the phobic syndrome could become a rare event, caused by some unavoidable physical trauma, that can be easily and quickly dealt with.

MOTIVATION FOR CHANGE
OR MOTIVATION FOR THERAPY

In therapy, another major problem seems to lie in differences between the motivation of clients and the aims of the therapist. As a clinician I want to effect changes in the behavior of my client so that anxiety reactions are reduced to the point where he can function adequately within his or her milieu. In practice, however, I have been forced to accept the fact that these aims often do not coincide with the aims and motivations of my clients. Initially, I attempt to build a positive relationship with my client, or, to put it in another way, I establish a situation in which I am a dispenser of positive reinforcements for my client. This is done during the initial assessment and behavior analysis and is necessary to keep the client motivated enough to stay in therapy. Then I start applying various behavior therapy techniques, giving the client various (difficult) tasks to do, limiting the positive reinforcement and making it contingent on carrying out these tasks. In carrying out these assignments, the client's anxiety reactions seem to disappear—the client reinforces me—and our assessments show that we are progressing well. Some clients are a bit niggardly in dispensing positive reinforcement for the therapist, but, if the schedule drops too low, I, as therapist, drop out of therapy, and must chalk up a failure. So we play the game of mutual reinforcement while the objective assessments improve.

One may suppose that the positive reinforcement accruing from not being plagued by anxiety attacks and being free to maneuver in society, would in and of itself be strong enough for the client to take over as he or she masters the techniques of reducing the anxiety. The client would then warmly thank the therapist and free him from further efforts. So it would seem when I read the fantastic success rates reported in the literature and the beautiful diagrams of progress in therapy and at follow-up.

Some of my clients, though, do not play the game according to these rules. In fact, many of them do not. They are highly motivated for therapy and find it wonderful that, after 20 years of not being understood, let alone listened to, by husband/wife, friends, relations, general practitioner, psychiatrists, etc., finally some bright young person or one of his numerous bright young assistants is prepared to really do something. The trouble is that therapist and client mean different things by the words "do something." The game of mutually reinforcing each other works well, but often when the therapist starts suggesting that things are going so well that the client should soon be able to go it alone, the client has a major relapse. The therapist is adamant in not positively reinforcing relapse behavior, the client tries other tactics—new symptoms—but this also does not help. Consequently, the client goes back to "improving" and the therapist responds by adjusting his schedule of reinforcement such that the client reaches the originally agreed upon goals for ending therapy.

Within a year there is a relapse. Where have we as therapists gone wrong? We've played the game by the wrong rules. The psychoanalyst would immediately say that we have problems of not working through the transference. As a behavior therapist, however, I do not like the idea of having to switch therapeutic techniques in midstream and espousing an orientation that will be, at best, slow to produce results, in an attempt to prevent this relapse.

CLIENT-THERAPIST RELATIONSHIPS

In psychoanalytic therapy the concept of transference, which concerns the patient-therapist relationship, holds a central position. Early in the history of behavior therapy, Wolpe reported a case in which in the middle of a treatment, he, as therapist, went on holiday. The treatment was continued by an assistant, and the patient made progress under the guidance of the assistant. Thus, concluded Wolpe, the relationship between patient and therapist is not important.

While Wolpe's conclusion was drawn from an anecdote and therefore of questionable validity, this type of thinking has discouraged behavior therapists from studying relationship problems in therapy. Indeed, many investigators use tape recorders and computers to minimize the therapist effect; in some studies the relationship is specifically mentioned, (e.g., Wilson, Hannon, & Evans, 1968), but this factor tends to be ignored. The relationship factor is a significant topic that is ignored or neglected in behavior therapy, the therapy which has shown itself to be the most powerful in dealing with anxiety reactions. Because of this, behavior therapists are less effective than they could be.

The best method for reducing or eliminating anxiety reactions seems to be successive approximation in a graded fashion. This is most effective in vivo, with modeling for approaching the situation or object that elicits the anxiety. Prolonged exposure to the situation is required until the anxiety has extinguished and the client has learned to cope adequately with the situation in all its complexities. This approach can be applied to monosymptomatic phobias, social functioning in groups, adequate sexual behavior, marital harmony, obsessive-compulsive disorders, hysterical conversion disorders, and virtually to any case in which anxiety plays a part in disrupting behavior.

To put a therapy plan into action, the therapist first needs to build up a relationship of trust and confidence with his client. Without this relationship, it is often impossible to complete even the first successive approximation, because the client drops out of therapy. Usually there is little trouble with YAVIS clients (Goldstein, 1971) in establishing a relationship, using this relationship in the therapy, and then dissolving the relationship as therapy is no longer necessary. This occurs almost unnoticed—it is "natural" to a skilled clinician. It should be made explicit, however, so that the relationship can be used with maximum efficiency and relationship building can be taught to others. Such skills are not "natural" in the sense that they are instinctive. They are learned, follow the principles of learning with which we are familiar, and can be learned either well or poorly.

Some people are motivated for therapy, not motivated for change. Many patients seek therapy for reasons different from the therapists' reason for doing therapy. Many people want therapy in order to make their lives more interesting, or to feel that they are interesting to others. They do not want therapy in order to change. For this problem, I see no solution other than a sliding scale of fees, based on what the client can afford, that includes bonuses for being ahead of schedule, with fees geometrically progressing for extra time in therapy. My clients and colleagues find this recommendation hard to accept, and I must admit that it would be difficult to realize in practice.

Let me attempt to sum up this brief account of some of the problems we face in clinical work. It has become clear that the understanding and treatment of anxiety reactions is not a simple matter, and espousing any single theoretical approach is not sufficient. Prof. Barendregt has found it necessary to include in his phobia project not only the study of modern learning theories and behavior therapy techniques, but to supplement these with information from many areas of psychological enquiry. We hope to continue along these lines, because careful attempts at integration should do more justice to understanding the complexities of anxiety reactions than any one theoretical viewpoint can give.

SUMMARY

In this paper I have tried to give a brief review of one approach to research into one type of anxiety reaction -phobic disorders. Some of the problems of making use of psychological theory in clinical practice have been considered. I have also examined and commented on problems of the marginally motivated client and clients who want therapy but resist change.

REFERENCES

Bandura, A. *Principles of behavior modification*. London: Holt, Rinehard, & Winston, 1969.

Barendregt, J. T. An attempt at destruction of a proportionality. Symposium on Behavior Therapy, 19th International Congress of Psychology, 1969.

Barendregt, J. T., & Bleeker, A. A. M. Een geval van agorafobie by een esoforie. *De Psycholoog*, 1973, 8, 43–49.

Barendregt, J. T., & v. Dam, F. S. A. M. Experimental neurosis by control of emotions. Film presented at the 19th International Congress of Psychology, London, 1969.

Bloemkolk, D., Defares, P., v. Enckevort, G., & v. Gelderen, M. Cognitive processing of information on varied physiological arousal. *European Journal of Social Psychiatry*, 1971, 1, 31.

Boom, F. T. de. Kommunicatiepatronen binnen gezinsinterakties. Doctoraal scriptie, Univ. van Amsterdam, 1970.

Burgemeister, M. Het gebruik van hypnotische procedures by psychologische experimenten. Doctoraal scriptie, Univ. van Amsterdam, 1971.

Dam, F. van, Barendregt, J. T., & Kalsbeek, J. H. W. Uitlokken en doseren van emoties via hypnose, Ned. *Tijdschrift v.d. Psychol.*, Apr. 1969, 193.

Driessen, M. H. D. Operant conditioneren van het frontale alpha-ritme. Doctoraal werkstuk, Univ. van Amsterdam, 1971.

Duursma, N., Rooker, A. Onderzoek naar fluctuaties in lichamelijke en psychische klachten by fobicae in relatie tot de menstruele cyclus. Doctoraal werkstuk, Univ. van Amsterdam, 1973.

Eysenck, H. J. (Ed.) *Experiments in behaviour therapy*. New York: Pergamon Press, 1964.

Eysenck, H. J. A mish-mash of theories. *International Journal of Psychiatry*, 1970, 9, 140–146.

Eysenck, H. J. Anxiety and the natural history of neuroses. Paper presented at the Advanced Study Institute on Stress and Anxiety in Modern Life, June 1973. (See Chapter 3 of the present work.)

Eysenck, H. J., & Beech, H. R. Counter conditioning and related methods. In A. E. Bergin & S. L. Garfield (Eds.), *Handbook of psychotherapy and behavior change*. New York: Wiley, 1971.

Eysenck, H. J., & Eysenck, S. B. G. *Eysenck Personality Inventory*. London: University of London Press, 1964.

Eysenck, H. J., & Rachman, S. *The causes and cures of neurosis*. San Diego: Knapp, 1965.

Goldstein, A. P. *Psychotherapeutic attraction*. New York: Pergamon Press, 1971.

Izard, C. E. Anxiety: A variable combination of interacting fundamental emotions. In C. D. Spielberger (Ed.), *Anxiety: Current trends in theory and research*, Vol. 1. New York: Academic Press, 1972.

Kelly, D., Guirguis, W., Frommer, E., Mitchell-Heggs, N., & Sargant, W. Treatment of phobic states with antidepressants. *British Journal of Psychiatry*, 1970, 120, 387–398.

Lazarus, A. A. Behavior therapy. *International Journal of Psychiatry*, 1970, 9, 113–139.

Lazarus, A. A. *Behavior therapy and beyond*. New York: McGraw-Hill, 1971.

Marks, I. M. *Fears and phobias*. London: Heinemann, 1969.

Meeder, T. R. Ontwikkeling van de apparatuur en van een methode voor, alsmede een eerste poging tot, het conditioneren van het frontale EEG alpha ritme. Doctoraal werkstuk, Univ. van Amsterdam, 1971.

Meyer, V. The impact of research on the clinical application of behavior therapy. Paper presented at the International Symposium on Behavior Modification, Minneapolis, 1972.

Raapis Dingman, H. Communicatie en manipulatie-aspecten van symptomen. Doctoraal scriptie, Univ. van Amsterdam, 1972.

Ramsay, R. W. The social relations of phobics in behaviour therapy. 17th International Congress of Applied Psychology, 1971.

Rooker, A., & Duursma, N. Fysiologische en psychologische veranderingen gedurende de menstruele cyclus. Doctoraal scriptie, Univ. van Amsterdam, 1973.

Schutz, J. T. M. Gesluierde mannen. Doctoraal scriptie, Univ. van Amsterdam, 1971.

Sierhuis, F. A., & Swaab, H. E. Autonoom functioneren van fobische patienten by drie vormen van stimulatie. Doctoraal werkstuk, Univ. van Amsterdam, 1970.

Smet, H. de. Pardah en fobie. Doctoraal scriptie, Univ. van Amsterdam, 1969.

Wijk, L. J. van. Een nadere analyse van het materiaal uit "autonoom functioneren van fobische patienten by 3 vormen van stimulatie" met het oog op autonome respons specificiteit. Doctoraal werkstuk, Univ. van Amsterdam, 1971.

Wijland, A. J. M. van. Enige fysiologische correlaten van post-hypotische emotionele reacties. Doctoraal werkstuk, Univ. van Amsterdam, 1971.

Wilson, G. T., Hannon, A. E., & Evans, W. I. M. Behavior therapy and the therapist-patient relationship. *Journal of Consulting and Clinical Psychology*, 1968, 32, 103–109.

Zant, J. Reacties op inkonsistente kommunikaties of Het is om je ziek te lachen! Doctoraal scriptie, Univ. van Amsterdam, 1971.

II
EXPERIMENTAL RESEARCH ON ANXIETY AND FEAR

5

ANXIETY:
STATE-TRAIT-PROCESS

Charles D. Spielberger

University of South Florida
Tampa, Florida, United States

The hallmarks of a mature science are clearly defined theoretical constructs, widely adopted conventions for their operational measurement, and lawful empirical relationships that are precisely expressed in mathematical terms. In the physical sciences, finely calibrated instruments and detailed procedures for their use provide operational specification of all fundamental theoretical concepts.

Psychology, too, may point with pride to a few areas in which relationships among operationally defined concepts can be expressed in mathematical terms. Most psychologists would agree that Fechner's classical work in psychophysics has yielded conceptual definitions, operational procedures, and empirical laws that have remained

This chapter is based, in part, on the presidential address presented by the writer at the Annual Meetings of the Southeastern Psychological Association, New Orleans, April 1973. In conducting the research, I am greatly indebted to my graduate students and colleagues whose work is described herein. Some of the work was supported by grants from the National Institutes of Mental Health (OM-362; MH-7446) and Child Health and Human Development (HD-947), United States Public Health Service.

steadfast. In contrast, theory and research in the fields of human motivation and personality are relatively underdeveloped areas of psychological science. Yet, here too, in recent years there has been discernible progress.

As an observer of and contributor to research on personality over the past two decades, I am encouraged by recent developments and even optimistic about the future. In this chapter, I will endeavor to describe some of the insights and disappointments, promising leads and blind alleys, that my students and I have encountered in our efforts to clarify the nature and meaning of anxiety. In this research, we have investigated the effects of anxiety on learning and academic achievement, the arousal and induction of anxiety by different kinds of stress, and the effects of stress and anxiety on a variety of behaviors. On the basis of the evidence that has accumulated from our studies, we have developed a differentiated conception of anxiety as a transitory emotional state, as a relatively stable personality trait, and as a complex psychological process.

Let me begin by setting the scene with regard to the status of anxiety research, circa 1950. Then, as now, Freud's psychoanalytic conceptions provided the framework for most clinical interpretations of anxiety phenomena. Although early experimental work was also influenced by Freudian concepts, Hull's (1943) learning theory, as extended by Kenneth W. Spence and Janet Taylor, provided the conceptual framework that has related anxiety research to the mainstream of psychology.

FREUD'S CONCEPTION
OF ANXIETY

For Freud (1924), anxiety was "something felt," a fundamental, unpleasant affective (emotional) state or condition. This state, as Freud observed it in patients with anxiety neuroses, was characterized by apprehension or anxious expectation, "all that is covered by the word nervousness," and efferent discharge phenomena. The physiological symptoms of anxiety included heart palpitations, nausea, disturbances in respiration, sweating, muscular tension, tremor, and vertigo. Anxiety was distinguishable from other unpleasant affective states, such as anger or depression, by its unique combination of phenomenological and physiological qualities, which gave it a special "character of unpleasure [Freud, 1936]."

In his early theoretical formulations, Freud believed that anxiety resulted from the discharge of repressed, somatic sexual tensions, which he called libido. When libidinal energy was blocked from normal expression, it accumulated and was automatically transformed into anxiety, or into symptoms that were anxiety equivalents. Freud subsequently modified this view in favor of a conception of anxiety that emphasized its functional utility to the ego. In this later conceptualization, anxiety was regarded as an internal reaction or response that served as a *signal* to indicate the presence of a danger situation.

Freud also differentiated between *objective* and *neurotic* anxiety, a distinction based on whether the source of danger was from the external world or from the individual's own internal impulses. Objective anxiety, which was synonymous with fear, was a complex internal reaction to anticipated injury or harm from some *real* external danger. The intensity of objective anxiety was proportional to the magnitude of the external danger that evoked it.

Like objective anxiety, neurotic anxiety was a danger signal, but the source of the danger was the individual's own repressed sexual and aggressive impulses, not some external danger. These impulses were originally repressed because their expression in childhood had been associated with painful punishment. When a partial breakdown in repression led to the renewed perception of danger from one's own impulses, a neurotic anxiety reaction occurred which was experienced as "objectless" or "free-floating" because the memory of the original punishment remained repressed. Thus, neurotic anxiety is the end product of a complex process in which internal impulses evoke an anxiety reaction that signals the danger of further punishment if the impulses are expressed.

EXPERIMENTAL RESEARCH ON ANXIETY

In 1939, Mowrer published an article in the *Psychological Review* in which he formulated Freud's danger signal theory of anxiety in the terminology of stimulus-response (S-R) psychology. Translated into the concepts of S-R learning theory, Mowrer regarded anxiety and fear as synonymous, and defined fear as the conditionable portion of the pain reaction. Through a classical conditioning process in which a painful (unconditioned) stimulus was paired with any number of previously neutral stimuli, a wide range of objectively nondangerous circumstances could acquire the power to evoke conditioned fear reactions. Since these fear responses were intense and unpleasant experiences, they functioned as an acquired drive with the power to activate behavior and to reinforce the learning of new habits.

It was Pavlov who paved the way around the turn of the century for experimental research on fear and anxiety. His studies of experimental neurosis in animals stimulated numerous investigations of fear, frustration, and conflict, of which Gantt's (1942) dogs, Masserman's (1943) cats, and Liddell's (1944) sheep are perhaps best known. Before 1950, however, there was relatively little work on human anxiety. In commenting on this state of affairs, Mowrer is said to have remarked, "There is at present no experimental psychology of anxiety, and one may even doubt whether there will ever be [May, 1950, p. 99]." In a similar vein, and at about the same time, Hoch and Zubin (1950) introduced a symposium, sponsored by the American Psychopathological Association, with the following statement:

> Although anxiety is the most pervasive psychological phenomenon of our time and the chief symptom in the neurosis and in the functional psychoses, there has been little or no agreement on its definition, and very little, if any progress in its measurement [p. v].

The marriage between psychoanalysis and learning theory proposed by Mowrer was consummated by Dollard and Miller (1950), and the concept of anxiety soon found an honored and respected place within the psychological laboratory. In the field of animal behavior, the classical experiments conducted at Yale in the 1940's by Hovland, Miller, and others provided clear evidence that fear could be classically conditioned; these experiments also demonstrated that fear reduction provided sufficient motivation for the acquisition of many instrumental responses.

Janet Taylor (1951) extended experimental research on anxiety to human subjects. Taylor (1953) selected items from the Minnesota Multiphasic Personality Inventory for the construction of the Manifest Anxiety Scale (MAS) and then used the MAS as a measure of individual differences in motivation in her doctoral research on eyelid conditioning. By conservative estimate, the MAS (Taylor, 1953) has been employed in well over 2,000 studies since it first appeared (Spielberger, 1966a). In most of these studies, the scale was used as an operational measure of drive level (D) as this concept is employed in Hull's (1943) learning theory. It is generally assumed that subjects with high MAS scores are more emotionally reactive and, therefore, higher in D than persons with low scores.

The availability of the MAS contributed to the development of the Spence-Taylor theory of emotionally based drive (Spence, K. W., 1956, 1958; Taylor, 1956). This theory, which has come to be known as Drive Theory, proceeds from Hull's (1943) assumption that the strength of a given response is a multiplicative function of total effective drive state and habit strength. According to Drive Theory, the effects of high drive on performance in a learning task will depend on the number and the strength of the specific habit tendencies that are elicited in a given situation. The theory assumes that all habit tendencies evoked by a particular stimulus or situation are multiplied by D.

By the mid-1950's, there was considerable evidence of the construct validity of the MAS as an index of drive level and predictions derived from Drive Theory were supported with regard to the performance of high and low anxiety subjects in a variety of learning tasks. Individuals with high MAS scores consistently demonstrated superior performance on tasks, such as eyelid conditioning, in which there was a single dominant response. In complex learning tasks, in which strong error tendencies competed with the correct response, high anxiety subjects did more poorly than subjects with low anxiety. Thus, for simple learning tasks with relatively few competing response tendencies, high anxiety facilitated performance, whereas on complex tasks in which, presumably, a number of relatively strong competing error tendencies were elicited, high anxiety resulted in performance decrements.

Initiated in 1955, the research described in this chapter was guided by Spence-Taylor Drive Theory and by Freud's clinical concepts of anxiety. Our early work was concerned with investigations of the effects of anxiety on learning. As the research progressed, we became more aware of and sensitive to the critical role of stress in evoking anxiety reactions. Our more recent studies have investigated the effects of stress and anxiety on behavioral measures of learning. Since this work has spanned a period of nearly two decades, only the more important or representative findings are discussed. In describing the research, special emphasis is given to critical methodological issues and salient theoretical implications.

THE EFFECTS OF ANXIETY ON LEARNING

Our first study was stimulated by the clinical observation that anxious college students often "choke up" on examinations. In therapy sessions, these same students frequently report that they were unable to recall answers to test questions which they were reasonably certain they "knew." On the assumption that examinations in college courses are complex tasks, Drive Theory would predict that anxious students would have greater difficulty and perform more poorly that would nonanxious students on examinations in most college courses. However, on simple or easy items of an otherwise complex examination, Drive Theory would also predict that anxious students should perform better than nonanxious students. To explore these questions, we investigated the effects of anxiety on a laboratory task that embodied some of the important features of a classroom test.

Study I: The Effects of Anxiety on Recall

The materials that must be learned in preparation for an examination vary in complexity or difficulty, and the specific elements that need to be recalled on a test are not generally known beforehand. Therefore, we sought an experimental task that consisted of discrete scorable elements of varying levels of difficulty. We initially planned to use standard tests of memory or recall (e.g., Digit Span Test, Wechsler Memory Scale), but these did not seem suitable because the subject's attention is either directed to the specific material to be recalled (immediate memory) or to highly overlearned information often dating back into childhood (remote memory). The typical classroom test is comprised of multiple choice and/or short answer questions that generally require the student to recall unspecified elements from a larger body of materials learned in the recent past, rather than the immediate or remote past.

An experimental task that we had employed in an earlier study appeared to have many of the characteristics we were seeking (Goodstein, Spielberger, Williams, & Dahlstrom, 1955). This task consisted of a series of nine geometric designs (Bender, 1938) presented one by one in the same order to each subject. The subjects were required to copy each design within a 40-second time limit and were not told they would be asked to reproduce the design. Following the completion of an unrelated 6-minute interpolated task (Draw-A-Person), the subjects were told to reproduce as many of the designs as they could remember.

In the earlier study, difficulty of recall for each of the nine designs was influenced by two factors: the intrinsic complexity of the design based on its geometric properties and the serial position in which the design was presented during the copying phase of the task. In general, the findings indicated that when intrinsic complexity was counterbalanced, designs presented at the end of the series were recalled more often than those presented at the beginning. Consequently, by presenting the most difficult designs first and the easiest designs last, the range of difficulty of recall for individual designs could be maximized. On the basis of Drive Theory, it was predicted that high anxiety would facilitate the recall of the easy designs when presented at the end of the list and would lead to performance decrements for the more difficult designs presented at the beginning of the list.

The subjects in this study were 48 undergraduate college students selected on the basis of extreme scores on the MAS (Spielberger, Goodstein, & Dahlstrom, 1958). The high anxiety group had MAS scores of 19 and higher; the low anxiety group had scores of 7 or lower. The nine designs were presented (one by one in an order that maximized the range of recall difficulty) to each subject in individual testing sessions. After the brief interpolated task, the subjects were asked to reproduce as many designs as they could recall.

The performance of the high anxiety subjects was superior to that of low anxiety subjects in recalling the easier designs and inferior to low anxiety subjects in the recall of the more difficult designs. The facilitation of the performance of high anxiety subjects in the recall of the easy designs was consistent with the Drive Theory interpretation that high anxiety or drive activates correct response tendencies on tasks where they are dominant. Also, in accordance with Drive Theory, the performance decrements observed for high anxiety subjects on difficult designs can be attributed to the activation of competing error tendencies by high drive level on tasks for which the strength of the correct response tendency was relatively weak.

The results of this laboratory experiment suggested that the performance of high anxiety subjects on classroom tests might vary as a function of the difficulty level of individual test items. In subsequent discussions of test-taking problems with anxious students and in reviewing their responses to specific test items, it was observed that they did as well as other students on clearly worded items but had a great deal more difficulty on ambiguous items. The reason most frequently given by anxious students for their test-taking difficulties was that they "misinterpreted" or "misread" test items. Interestingly, the wrong answers given by anxious students to misinterpreted questions were often highly detailed and specific, suggesting that the student was reporting an overlearned response (error tendency) to an inappropriate stimulus. Put differently, misinterpretations of examination questions by high anxiety students appear to reflect a dynamic process in which high drive activates strong error tendencies on ambiguous (difficult) tasks, thereby contributing to performance decrements.

Study II: Anxiety and Academic Achievement

The findings in Study I suggested that the effects of anxiety on performance in a laboratory learning task depend on the complexity or difficulty of the task, which is determined by the relative strength of correct responses and error tendencies that are generated during the process of learning. Do these findings generalize to real-life learning situations? For example, what effects, if any, does anxiety have on academic achievement?

On the assumption that examinations in most college courses are relatively difficult for the average student, Drive Theory would lead us to expect that high anxious students would tend to do more poorly than low anxious students in classroom examinations and that high anxious students would earn lower grades. But learning materials that are moderate in difficulty level for the average student may actually be quite easy for the very bright students, whereas the same materials would be extremely difficult for students with limited ability. Thus, the difficulty of a given learning task depends not only on the characteristics of the materials to be learned, but also on the intellectual ability of the learner.

Accordingly, for a task that is moderately difficult for the average student, Drive Theory would predict that high anxiety would facilitate academic achievement for bright students while leading to performance decrements for low- and average-ability students. To test these predictions, the effects of anxiety on the academic achievement of college students who differed in intellectual ability was evaluated. The subjects in this study were male college students enrolled in introductory psychology. The MAS was used to measure anxiety. Ability was measured by the ACE Psychological Examination, a widely used test of scholastic aptitude.

The MAS was administered at the beginning of each semester, and data were collected over a period of six consecutive semesters. Grade-point averages (GPA's) were obtained for each student for the single semester during which he took the MAS. GPA was defined as the weighted average of the grades obtained in all courses taken by the student during the term in which he participated in the study, with 4 points credited for each hour of A, 3 points for B, 2 points for C, 1 point for D, and 0 for F. MAS scores, ACE scores, and GPA's were available for 140 high and 144 low anxiety students.

The students were divided into five levels of intellectual ability on the basis of their ACE scores, and the GPA's of high and low anxiety students at each level were compared. The grades of low-ability students (ACE scores in the lower 20%) were uniformly low irrespective of their anxiety level. For the three middle-ability groups (between 20th and 80th percentile on the ACE), students with high anxiety obtained consistently lower grades than did low anxiety students of comparable ability. For the high-ability students (upper 20% on the ACE), there was little difference in the academic achievement of the high and low anxiety students whose grades were uniformly high.

The performance decrements noted for high anxiety students in the broad middle range of ability were consistent with expectations based on Drive Theory, assuming that the academic task was moderately difficult for these average ability students. Failure to find any difference between the high and low anxiety students at the lowest level of ability was contrary to expectations and seemed to be due to a floor effect that resulted from university grading practices. Many of the students who participated in this study were juniors and seniors, and grades below C were relatively infrequent in upper-class courses. Another factor that may have contributed to the floor effect was that the low-ability students whose high anxiety was most detrimental to their academic performance had already dropped out of school because of academic failure and were therefore unavailable to participate in the study.

Failure to find differences between high and low anxiety students of high aptitude was also contrary to predictions from Drive Theory. It was expected that high anxiety would facilitate the performance of these bright students for whom college work was assumed to be relatively easy. While no differences were found in the academic performance of high and low anxiety students in the upper 20% of ability, greater variability in GPA was observed among high anxious students than for low anxious, high-ability students. This finding suggested that anxiety might indeed be facilitative for some of the high anxiety students within this group and detrimental to others. These possibilities were examined by further dividing the highest aptitutde group at the median ACE score for this group and comparing the grades of high and low anxiety students who were above and below the median.

The GPA's of the very brightest high-anxiety students (upper 10% on the ACE) were superior to the grades of low anxiety students of comparable ability. In contrast, bright high anxiety students who scored below the median for the high-ability group (between the 80th and 90th percentile on the ACE) had lower grades than their low anxiety counterparts. Thus, the facilitative effects of high anxiety predicted by Drive Theory for bright students were found, but only for students whose ACE scores placed them in the top 10% in scholastic aptitude.

A 3-year follow-up of the students who participated in this study revealed that more than 20% of the high anxiety students were classified as academic failures and did not complete their college education, as compared with fewer than 6% of the low anxiety students. Even for the lowest aptitude group, for whom no differences in GPA were found during the single semester in which they participated in this study, more than twice as many high anxiety, low-ability students were academic failures. When students from the lowest aptitude group (whose lack of ability contributed to their higher failure rate) were excluded from consideration, the percentage of high anxiety students who failed was nearly four times as great as the number of low anxiety academic failures.

The results of this study would appear to indicate that the effects of anxiety on academic achievement are cumulative and widespread. Through underachievement and academic failure, the full contributions of many able college students are diminished or lost because of anxiety. The findings of this study also helped to establish for us the importance of research on anxiety and the learning process and stimulated further investigation into the mechanisms that mediate the effects of anxiety on learning.

Study III: The Effects of Anxiety on Rote Learning

The two previous studies tested predictions from Drive Theory with regard to the effects of anxiety on learning *outcomes*. High anxiety led to performance decrements on difficult tasks and to the facilitation of performance on easy tasks. It was also demonstrated that task difficulty was a function of the intrinsic complexity of the learning materials, the manner in which the materials were presented, and the intellectual ability or aptitude of the learner. While these outcome results were generally consistent with Drive Theory, it should be noted that Drive Theory is more directly concerned with the learning process than with learning outcomes.

According to Drive Theory, high anxiety or drive will facilitate performance when a correct response is stronger than competing error tendencies, and high anxiety will lead to performance decrements when the error tendencies elicited by a learning task are stronger than correct responses. On many learning tasks, subjects are given a number of trials in which they are required to master the learning materials, along with feedback about their performance on each trial. Under these conditions, it would be expected that the relative strengths of correct responses would increase as learning progressed and that competing error tendencies would extinguish.

The goals of Study III (Spielberger, 1966b; Spielberger & Smith, 1966) were to investigate the effects of anxiety on a rote learning task that permitted a trial-by-trial analysis of the learning process. The learning task consisted of 12 Consonant-Vowel-Consonant (CVC) nonsense syllables to be learned by the serial anticipation method. This task was selected on the basis of evidence that the nonsense syllables were of moderate difficulty for college students (Montague, 1953). For these learning materials, it was expected that the performance of high anxiety subjects would be inferior to that of low anxiety subjects in the early stages of learning. In the later stages of learning it was expected that high anxiety would eventually facilitate performance as correct responses were strengthened and competing error tendencies were extinguished.

The subjects in this study were undergraduate males enrolled in an introductory psychology course who scored in the upper and lower 20% of the MAS. The high anxiety students had MAS scores of 21 or higher; low anxiety students scored 9 or lower. It was also determined that the high and low anxiety students were reasonably well matched in scholastic aptitude as measured by the ACE.

When presented the word list, subjects were given standard instructions for the serial anticipation method of verbal learning. Following six trials on an easy practice list, the test list was repeatedly presented until the subject attained the learning criterion of two successful perfect trials, or received a maximum of 25 trials. The results were disappointing in that no differences in the performance of high and low anxiety students were found at any stage of learning. Clearly, Drive Theory was not supported. Was the theory to be abandoned, or could some explanation be found for the failure to find drive differences for subjects who differed in anxiety?

One possible explanation of the failure to find any anxiety differences in the present study was suggested by K. W. Spence (1958). Spence originally assumed that people with high MAS scores were chronically higher in drive level than were persons with low scores; i.e., persons with high MAS scores were expected to manifest higher levels of anxiety or drive in all situations. On the basis of contradictory research findings reported in the literature, Spence reasoned that the anxiety measured by the MAS might be *reactive* rather than *chronic*. Spence's reactive hypothesis assumed that subjects with high MAS scores will respond with higher drive only in situations containing some degree of stress, but will not differ in drive level in nonstressful situations. Consistent with the reactive hypothesis, I. G. Sarason (1960) noted accumulating evidence that anxiety was differentially aroused in high and low anxiety subjects only in situations in which there was some form of "personal threat."

The results of Study III clearly did not support the view that MAS scores reflect chronic differences in drive level. But if the MAS measures reactive anxiety and if there was insufficient stress in the present experiment to evoke differential anxiety reactions in subjects with high and low MAS scores, no differences in the performance of these subjects would be expected.

It should be noted that there was no effort in this study to induce stress. In fact, the experimenter was exceedingly considerate of the needs of her subjects, and did everything conceivable to reassure them and make them feel comfortable while they participated in the study. She was also regarded by her peers as personally pleasant and nonthreatening. Thus, it seemed quite plausible that our experimental conditons were not sufficiently stressful to arouse differential drive levels in subjects with high and low MAS scores. The following study was designed to investigate serial rote learning under more stressful experimental conditions.

Study IV: Stress, Anxiety, and Rote Learning

In this study, the same experimenter and exactly the same learning task were employed as in the preceding study. The subjects were male college students selected on the same basis as in Study III. To make the experiment more stressful, the subjects were told that the goal of this study was to evaluate their intelligence (Spielberger, 1966b). Prior to the presentation of the serial learning task, a brief but relatively difficult concept formation task was administered (Denny, 1966), after which the following instructions were given:

> The part of the experiment which you have just completed is one measure of thinking and is related to one kind of intelligence. The rest of the experiment has to do with a somewhat different method of thinking in which your task is to memorize a list of nonsense syllables. We have done some research on the relationship between nonsense syllable learning and intelligence. Here is a graph of the relationship we found. ... You see, speed of learning increases with intelligence [Spielberger, 1966b, p. 385].

The subjects were shown a graph in which "number of correct responses" increased substantially as a function of "IQ." The practice and test lists were then presented exactly as they had been given in the preceding study.

As predicted by Drive Theory, the performance of the high anxiety subjects was inferior to that of low anxiety subjects in the early stages of learning, and high anxiety subjects did better than low anxiety subjects in the later stages of learning. The consistency of these findings was evaluated within the context of Drive Theory by dividing the 12-syllable CVC test list into two sublists of "hard" and "easy" words, defined in terms of the number of errors elicited by each syllable for the total sample of high and low anxiety subjects. To insure a clear separation between hard and easy words, the four words that elicited an intermediate number of errors were eliminated. The four syllables that individually elicited the fewest errors comprised the easy word list; the hard list consisted of the four syllables that elicited the largest number of errors.

The influence of anxiety on performance was found to differ for the hard and easy words at different stages of learning. On the initial block of 5 trials, the performance of high anxiety subjects was inferior to that of low anxiety subjects for both types of words. On the second and third trial blocks, the high anxiety subjects continued to do more poorly than low anxiety subjects on the hard words, but did better than the low anxiety subjects on the easy words. By the fourth trial block, the performance of the high anxiety subjects was superior to that of low anxiety subjects for both types of words, and this superiority was maintained on the final trial block. Support for Drive Theory was evident in the fact that anxiety began to facilitate correct responses for easy words at an earlier stage of learning than was the case for the hard or difficult words. The theory would predict that high drive would facilitate performance at an earlier stage of learning for tasks on which correct responses were stronger relative to competing error tendencies, as was true in the present experiment for the easy words relative to the hard words.

The results of this study were strikingly different from those obtained in Study III. Since the two experiments differed only in the instructions that were given to the subjects, it may be concluded that the stressful instructions in the present study, i.e., informing subjects that they were taking an intelligence test, induced differential levels of drive in the high and low anxiety subjects. The findings further suggested that the MAS measured reactive anxiety, i.e., individual differences in the disposition to respond to stress with more or less anxiety. It would appear that persons who score high on the MAS are more disposed to perceive stressful situations as personally dangerous for them, and to respond to such situations with increased anxiety and higher elevations in drive level than low anxiety subjects. The studies described in the next section were designed to evaluate the relationship between individual differences in anxiety and emotional reactions to stress.

STRESS AND ANXIETY

It is widely accepted that most people respond to stressful situations with increased anxiety and that anxiety reactions are characterized by feelings of apprehension, tension, and activation of the autonomic nervous system (e.g., Freud, 1924, 1936; Martin, 1961; Spielberger, 1966a). When anxiety reactions are experimentally induced by stressful stimulation, the particular index by which the strength of these reactions are to be evaluated must be specified. Changes in heart rate, blood pressure, muscle action potential, and galvanic skin response have been used as physiological indicants of anxiety. A number of self-report measures of apprehension and tension have also been developed to measure emotional reactions to stress (Spielberger, 1972a).

The fundamental question that was explored in the following studies was whether persons who differ in reactive anxiety, as measured by scales such as the MAS, would show differential emotional reactions to stress. On the basis of the findings in Study IV, it was expected that persons with high MAS scores would show greater increases in self-report and physiological measures of anxiety than would those with low MAS scores.

Study V: The Effects of Stress on the Galvanic Skin Response

The galvanic skin response (GSR) has been frequently employed as a measure of autonomic nervous system (ANS) activity, and ANS arousal is generally considered to be an important characteristic of anxiety (e.g., Malmo, 1957; Martin, 1961; Silverman, 1957). The two GSR measures that have been used most extensively to assess ANS arousal are the resistance of the skin to an externally applied current (basal resistance), and the amplitude of skin resistance to specific stimulation (GSR specifics). More recently, GSR nonspecific activity, defined as the frequency of measurable fluctuations in skin resistance that occur in the absence of specific stimulation, has also been used as a measure of arousal (Greiner & Burch, 1955; Silverman, Cohen, & Shmavonian, 1959). Both GSR nonspecifics and basal resistance have been shown to increase in response to stressful stimulation.

In his doctoral dissertaton, Katkin (1964, 1965) investigated the effects of threat of electric shock on GSR basal resistance and nonspecific responses. The subjects were undergraduate college males with scores in the upper and lower 20% of the MAS raw score distribution (scores of 19 or higher, or 7 or lower). The high and low anxiety subjects were assigned to stress and nonstress (control) experimental conditions. Baseline GSR measures were obtained during a 10-minute period in which subjects were instructed "to just sit back and relax for a while, as I measure some of your physiological reactions."

Following the baseline period, the subjects in the control condition were told "to continue resting just as you were for 10 more minutes." The instructions for the control group were designed to facilitate the relaxation of the subjects and to convince them that the experimenter was interested only in measuring physiological responses while they rested. As during the baseline period, GSR nonspecifics and basal resistance were measured continuously for the entire 10-minute experimental period.

Subjects in the stress condition were asked "have you ever had rheumatic heart disease? Buerger's disease? Raynaud's disease?" For all subjects, the answers to these questions were negative. The subjects were then told they would receive some strong electric shocks during the next 10-minute period and that the procedure "is safe if you are in good health." After the subject agreed to accept the shock, "dummy" electrodes were attached to the right ankle. The GSR was measured continuously as the subjects anticipated shock, but no shocks were actually delivered to any subject.

Both high and low anxious subjects showed increased autonomic arousal in the stress condition, but not in the nonstressful control condition. According to the reactive interpretation of MAS scores, the high anxiety subjects in the stress condition were expected to manifest greater increases in the GSR measures than low anxiety subjects. Contrary to expectation, however, no differences between high anxiety and low anxiety subjects were found for either GSR measure. Since the magnitude of the change in the GSR measures in response to the threat of shock was approximately the same for the high and low anxiety subjects, there was no evidence in this study that persons with high anxiety were more prone to demonstrate more intense emotional reactions to stress than were low anxiety subjects.

Study VI: The Effects of Stress on Heart Rate

Hodges and Spielberger (1966) evaluated the effects of threat of shock on heart rate (HR) using essentially the same experimental design employed by Katkin. The subjects were male college students with extreme scores on the MAS; the high anxiety subjects had MAS scores of 21 or higher, the low anxiety subjects scored 8 or lower. High and low anxiety subjects were assigned, in equal numbers, to either a stress or nonstress (control) experimental condition.

In addition to the MAS, the subjects in this study were given a "Fear of Shock Questionnaire" (FSQ). The FSQ consisted of a single item to which they responded, on a 5-point rating scale from "none" to "extreme," by indicating how much concern or apprehension they would feel about "participating in a psychology experiment in which you received electric shock." The MAS and the FSQ were both given about 2 months before the beginning of the experiment.

In the context of a verbal conditioning task (Spielberger, Southard, & Hodges, 1966), subjects in the stress condition were given the following instructions:

> That's fine. Now we want to see how a strong electric shock will effect the relationship between the verbal task and your blood pressure. During the remainder of the experiment you will receive electric shock. . . . Although the shocks you receive may be quite strong, they will not harm you. . . . After we attach these electrodes to your leg you will perform the same task as before [Hodges & Spielberger, 1966, p. 289].

Electrodes were then attached to the subject's left ankle. The subjects continued to work on the verbal conditioning task while they anticipated shock, but no shock was ever given. Heart rate, measured in beats per minute, was recorded continuously throughout the experiment.

In the nonstress condition, the experimenter paused for a period of time equivalent to that required to give the threat instructions, and subjects then resumed work on the experimental task. Immediately following completion of the verbal conditioning task, subjects in both the stress and control conditions were required to fill out the Zuckerman (1960) Affect Adjective Checklist (AACL), a self-report scale designed to measure fluctuations in subjective anxiety level. In responding to the AACL, subjects in the threat condition were instructed to report how they felt when they were first informed that they were going to receive the electric shock. Subjects in the nonstress condition were asked to indicate how they felt at the beginning of the experiment.

Both high and low anxiety subjects in the stress condition showed an immediate and substantial increase in HR in response to threat of shock, whereas subjects in the control group showed little or no change in HR as they continued to work on the verbal conditioning task. On the basis of a reactive anxiety interpretation of MAS scores, subjects with high MAS scores were expected to show a greater increase in HR than subjects with low MAS scores. Contrary to expectations, however, the increase in HR for both groups, from just before the stress instructions to the 30-second period immediately following these instructions, was approximately 15 bpm. Thus, as in Katkin's study, no differences in reactive anxiety were found for high and low anxiety subjects in response to the threat of electric shock.

Changes in HR in the stress condition were also evaluated for subjects with high and low scores on the FSQ. For this analysis, changes in HR for subjects who indicated little or no fear of shock were compared with HR changes for subjects who reported moderate to extreme fear of shock. The increase in HR was more than twice as great for subjects who reported moderate to extreme fear of shock than for subjects who reported little or no fear (23 bpm vs. 11 bpm).

The correlations in this study of self-report measures of anxiety with changes in HR were also of interest. For the stress condition, scores on the AACL correlated .49 with HR changes evoked by threat of shock, demonstrating that subjects who showed a greater increase in HR reported more subjective anxiety in the experimental situation. The correlation of FSQ scores with change in HR was .43. As previously noted, subjects who reported higher fear of shock responded to the threat of shock with greater increases in HR. In contrast, the correlation of MAS scores with change in HR was essentially zero, and MAS and FSQ scores were also un-correlated.

In summary, reactive anxiety as measured by the MAS and fear of shock appeared to be independent and unrelated personality traits. Only fear of shock predicted changes in ANS arousal in response to the threat of electric shock, suggesting that the amount of ANS arousal induced by a stress situation is determined by the subjects "cognitive appraisal" of the situation as more or less threatening for them (Lazarus & Opton, 1966).

Study VII: The Effects of Psychological and Physical Stress on the Arousal of Anxiety

The two preceding studies (V and VI) tested the hypothesis that persons with high anxiety, as measured by the MAS, would show greater physiological arousal in response to stress than persons with low MAS scores. Contrary to expectation, high and low anxiety subjects showed similar changes in GSR and HR in response to the threat of an electric shock. But subjects in Study VI who reported high fear of shock 2 months before the experiment responded to the threat of shock with a greater increase in HR than did subjects who previously reported little or no fear of shock. Furthermore, scores on the FSQ were unrelated to MAS scores.

Whether persons who are high or low in anxiety proneness, as measured by the MAS, respond to stress with differential elevations in anxiety or drive level would seem to depend on the nature of the stress situation. Performance differences for subjects who differ in anxiety are most often found under conditions of ego involvement (Spence, J. T., & Spence, K. W., 1966). This was true in Studies I, II, and IV, but not in Study III, in which there was little, if any, stress and no differences were found as a function of MAS scores. In stress situations that are characterized by physical danger (e.g., threat of shock), high and low anxiety subjects show similar increases in arousal. Thus, persons who differ in anxiety as measured by the MAS appear to respond to psychological stress with greater elevations in drive level, but do not manifest differential drive levels in nonstressful situations or in situations involving physical danger.

In his doctoral dissertation, Hodges (1966, 1968) evaluated the effects of psychological and physical stress on the anxiety reactions of subjects who differed in anxiety proneness as measured by the MAS. The subjects were male undergraduate college students enrolled in an introductory psychology course who were selected on the basis of extreme scores on the MAS (18 or higher, 11 or lower). The high and low anxiety subjects were randomly assigned in equal numbers to one of three experimental conditions: failure threat, shock threat, and no threat.

Subjects were tested individually. At the beginning of the experiment, each subject was told that the study was concerned with the relationship between performance on a verbal task and several physiological measures. The subjects were then instructed to relax while resting measures of HR were obtained. After the rest period, the subject was required to complete the AACL by checking words that described how he felt *at that moment*. The Wechsler (1955) Digits Backward Test was then given. After the subject's limit was determined, he was given instructions appropriate to the experimental condition to which he had been randomly assigned before reporting for the experiment. Heart rate was continuously recorded in all three experimental conditions.

Subjects in the failure-threat condition were told: "You're not doing too badly, but it seems to me that you could do better. In any case, most students I have had in the experiment were able to respond quicker [Hodges, 1968, p. 336]." The subjects were then given six additional series of digits, and told: "Try to concentrate harder so that you can repeat the digits as quickly as possible and still not make any mistakes." The AACL was then given with instructions to report how the subject felt while repeating the last series of digits.

Subjects in the physical stress (shock-threat) condition were threatened with pain while ego threat was minimal. They were told:

> You're doing very well, in fact better than most students. Now we are interested in the effects of a strong electric shock on your blood pressure. I am going to give you some items just as easy as the previous ones, but between some of your trials, you will receive one or more strong electric shocks. Although the shocks you receive will be quite strong, they will not harm you [Hodges, 1968, pp. 366–367].

Dummy electrodes were then attached to the subject's ankle, and six additional series of digits were presented. Except for the instructions and the attachment of the electrodes, the procedures for the shock-threat condition were exactly the same as for the failure-threat condition.

In the no-threat condition, the subjects were simply told: "You're doing very well, in fact better than most students. Now I'm going to give you some items just as easy as the previous ones [Hodges, 1968, p. 367]." Except for the instructions, the procedures for the no-threat condition were exactly the same as for the failure-threat condition.

The two stress conditions produced greater increases in both HR and AACL scores than did the no-threat control condition. The magnitude of the increase in AACL scores was greatest in the failure-threat (ego-threat) condition, whereas shock-threat produced the greatest increase in HR. High anxiety subjects responded to the failure-threat condition with a greater increase in the self-report measure of anxiety than did low anxiety subjects, but did not differ in their reactions to threat of shock. The high and low anxiety subjects showed similar changes in HR in both stress conditions.

The findings in this study would seem to indicate that *type of stress* must be taken into account in investigations of the effects of stress on anxiety or drive level. Consistent with the results of the two previous studies, physical stress (threat of shock) was not related to anxiety proneness as measured by the MAS. The results of this study suggested that the MAS reflects differences in anxiety proneness in situations that contain threats to self-esteem (ego threat) and that persons with high MAS scores are more disposed to respond to this type of psychological stress with greater elevations in anxiety or drive level.

STRESS, STATE–TRAIT ANXIETY, AND LEARNING

The series of studies reported in this chapter provide evidence of the utility of Drive Theory in predicting the effects of anxiety on performance in learning experiments. It should be apparent, however, that the nature of anxiety, as well as the relationship between anxiety and drive level, is more complex than was originally believed. The findings in these studies demonstrated that stress plays a critical role in evoking differences in drive level for persons who differ in anxiety proneness and that Drive Theory does not account for the effects of stress on anxiety arousal.

Before attempting to clarify the complex relationship between stress, anxiety arousal, and performance, it will be helpful to review and summarize the findings of the studies that were described in the preceding section of this chapter. The first two studies provided evidence that the effects of anxiety on performance on a learning task depended on the relative strength of correct responses and competing error tendencies that were elicited by the learning materials. High anxiety facilitated performance on easy tasks in which correct responses were dominant and led to performance decrements on difficult tasks in which error tendencies were stronger than correct responses.

The failure to find any anxiety differences in Study III suggested that the MAS measured anxiety proneness, i.e., reactive anxiety that was evoked by stress, rather than chronic differences in anxiety or drive level. The results in Study IV supported this reactive hypothesis while also providing evidence that anxiety influenced performance in different ways at different stages of learning. High anxiety led to performance decrements early in learning, when correct responses were relatively weak and error tendencies were strong, and to the facilitation of performance later in learning as correct responses became stronger and error tendencies were extinguished.

The effects of different kinds of stress on measures of ANS arousal were investigated in Studies V, VI, and VII. Stress induced by the threat of electric shock was expected to evoke greater changes in measures of ANS arousal for subjects who were high in anxiety proneness (as measured by the MAS) than in subjects who were low in anxiety proneness. Contrary to this expectation, while shock-threat evoked large changes in physiological indicants of anxiety in all three experiments, there were no differences in the reactions of subjects who were high and low in anxiety proneness. In Study VII, however, psychological stress in the form of negative feedback about performance evoked greater increases in a self-report measure of anxiety for subjects who were high in anxiety proneness than for low anxiety subjects. Thus, scores on the MAS seemed to reflect individual differences in the disposition to respond to threats to self-esteem (ego threats) with differential elevations in anxiety or drive level.

Much of the ambiguity and confusion in research on stress, anxiety, and learning seems to arise from the indiscriminant use of the term "anxiety" in at least two different ways. As I have previously noted:

Anxiety is perhaps most commonly used in an empirical sense to denote a complex reaction or response—a transitory state or condition of the organism that varies in intensity and fluctuates over time. But the term anxiety is also used to refer to a personality trait—to individual differences in the extent to which people are characterized by anxiety states and by prominent defenses against such states [Spielberger, 1966a, p. 12].

Anxiety as an emotional state (A-State) is characterized by subjective, consciously perceived feelings of tension, apprehension, and nervousness accompanied by or associated with activation of the autonomic nervous system (Spielberger, 1966a, 1972a). A-States may vary in intensity and fluctuate over time as a function of the stresses that impinge on the organism. The level of intensity of an anxiety state may be measured by self-report scales such as the Today form of the AACL or by changes in physiological measures that reflect activation of the autonomic nervous system. such as heart rate, blood pressure, and galvanic skin response.

Trait anxiety (A-Trait) refers to relatively stable individual differences in anxiety proneness, i.e., to differences among people in the disposition or tendency to perceive a wide range of situations as threatening and to respond to these situations with differential elevations in state anxiety. A-Trait dispositions are reactive and remain latent until activated by the stress associated with a specific danger situation. On the basis of the studies of stress, anxiety, and learning reported in this chapter, persons who are high in anxiety proneness are disposed to perceive greater danger in relationships with other people that involve threats to self-esteem and to respond to these ego threats with greater elevations in state anxiety or drive level than persons low in anxiety proneness. High and low A-Trait persons do not appear to differ in their reactions to threats posed by physical dangers.

It now seems apparent that the term "anxiety" is also used by a number of personality theorists to refer to a complex process. Consequently, anxiety as process needs to be added to the distinction between anxiety as a transitory state and as a relatively stable personality trait (Spielberger, 1972b). Anxiety as process refers to a complex sequence of cognitive, affective, and behavioral events that is evoked by some form of stress. This process may be initiated by a stressful external stimulus or by internal cues that are perceived or interpreted as threatening. An anxiety state is at the core of the anxiety process, which may also involve (*a*) cognitive appraisal of a stressful situation as personally threatening, (*b*) psychological defenses that are activated in an effort to reduce or alleviate intense and unpleasant anxiety states, and (*c*) behaviors that are motivated by intense levels of A-State.

The investigations described earlier in this chapter have important implications with regard to conceptualizations of anxiety as a transitory state, a relatively stable personality trait, and a complex cognitive-emotional-motivational process. For example, the subjects were selected in the first three studies on the assumption that persons with high scores on the MAS were more emotional and, consequently, high in drive level; i.e., subjects with high MAS scores were believed to be chronically higher in drive level than were people with low MAS scores. While the results in the first two studies were consistent with this assumption, the failure to find differences in performance attributable to drive level in Study III called attention to the importance of situational stress as a variable in research on anxiety and learning.

The introduction of stress as an experimental variable in Study IV led to results that were consistent with Drive Theory, and that supported the assumption that the MAS measures reactive rather than chronic differences in anxiety or drive level. These findings also served to focus our attention on the importance of the state-trait distinction in anxiety research by providing evidence that the MAS measured individual differences in anxiety proneness. Scores on the MAS appeared to be related to the level of intensity of state anxiety only when there was sufficient situational stress to evoke differential A-State reactions in individuals who differed in A-Trait.

In all seven studies described in the preceding sections, the MAS provided a measure of trait anxiety though we did not fully appreciate the state-trait distinction at the time the first three studies were conducted. In Studies I and II, differences in drive level were inferred from scores on the MAS, and the results were consistent with Drive Theory. Apparently, the learning tasks provided sufficient situational stress to evoke differential levels of A-State in persons who differed in anxiety proneness. In Study IV, state anxiety was manipulated by the explicit introduction of situational stress as an experimental variable. Stress was also experimentally manipulated in the last three experiments, and changes in state anxiety were inferred from physiological measures of ANS arousal and a self-report measure of feelings of tension, apprehension, and nervousness.

It should be apparent in all of these studies that we were concerned with a complex process through which different kinds of stress evoked increases in A-State in subjects who differed in anxiety-proneness. The anxiety process is extremely complex and involves a number of different measurable components. To use the term anxiety to refer to the entire process attempts to incorporate too much within a single concept. Anxiety-as-process definitions also run the risk of obscuring important components of this process, which should be independently conceptualized and operationally measured as critical variables in a state-trait theory of anxiety. I have previously noted that

> The concept of anxiety-as-process implies a theory of anxiety that includes stress, threat, and state and trait anxiety as fundamental constructs or variables. The development of a comprehensive theory to account for anxiety phenomena must begin with a definition of the response properties of anxiety states. After these properties are conceptually identified, appropriate procedures for measuring them must be constructed [Spielberger, 1972b, p. 489].

In the introduction to this chapter, it was suggested that a mature science requires clearly defined theoretical constructs, accepted conventions for their operational measurement, and lawful empirical relationships that can be expressed precisely in empirical terms. Recent developments in research on stress, anxiety, and learning have contributed to the clarification of anxiety as a psychological concept and to the development of measures of anxiety that are coordinated with theoretical advances (Spielberger, 1972a, 1972b). Future progress in anxiety research will be facilitated by the adoption of terminological conventions that permit more precise communication among investigators and by the construction of valid measures of state and trait anxiety.

Over the past 10 years, my students and I have been involved in the development of the State-Trait Anxiety Inventory (STAI). Originally constructed as a research instrument for investigating anxiety phenomena in normal adults, the STAI has proved useful in the measurement of state and trait anxiety in high school and college students and in neuropsychiatric, medical, and surgical patients (Spielberger, Gorsuch, & Lushene, 1970). The STAI A-Trait scale has been employed as a research tool for selecting subjects who vary in the disposition to respond to psychological stress with different levels of A-State intensity. It has also proved effective in screening students and patients for anxiety proneness. The STAI A-State scale has been used extensively in laboratory studies to determine the level of A-State intensity induced by stressful experimental procedures and as an index of drive level, as this concept is defined by Hull (1943) and K. W. Spence (1958). The A-State scale has also served as a sensitive measure of changes in the transitory anxiety experienced by medical and surgical patients and by clients in counseling, psychotherapy, and behavior therapy.

SUMMARY AND CONCLUSIONS

The experiments on stress, anxiety, and learning reported in this chapter were stimulated by Spence-Taylor Drive Theory and by Freud's clinical conception of anxiety. In general, the results of these studies have provided additional empirical support for Drive Theory and contribute to clarification of the nature of anxiety as a psychological concept. This research has also contributed to the extension of Drive Theory to incorporate individual differences in intelligence or learning aptitude and has stimulated the construction of new self-report measures of state and trait anxiety. On the basis of the empirical findings, we have attempted to formulate a State-Trait Theory of Anxiety that specifies the conditions in which threats to self-esteem or ego threats evoke differential levels of state anxiety in persons who differ in anxiety proneness.

In the aggregate, the research findings reported in this chapter would seem to have important implications for the formulation of an adequate theory of stress, anxiety, and learning. The research evidence suggests that a comprehensive theory must take all of the following factors or variables into account: (*a*) the nature and magnitude of situational stress, (*b*) the measurement of the level of intensity of state anxiety evoked by situational stress, (*c*) the measurement of individual differences in anxiety proneness, (*d*) the availability of appropriate behavior for coping with anxiety states aroused by situational stress, (*e*) clarification of the influence of psychological defenses used by subjects in learning experiments to reduce state anxiety, (f) specification of the relative strength of correct reponses and competing error tendencies evoked by a learning task, and (g) measurement of the intelligence or learning aptitude of subjects who participate in learning experiments.

REFERENCES

Bender, L. A. *A Visual Motor Gestalt Test and its clinical use.* New York: American Orthopsychiatric Association, 1938.

Denny, J. P. Effects of anxiety and intelligence on concept formation. *Journal of Experimental Psychology*, 1966, 72, 596-602.

Dollard, J., & Miller, N. E. *Personality and psychotherapy.* New York: McGraw-Hill, 1950.

Freud, S. *Collected papers.* Vol. 1. London: Hogarth Press, 1924.

Freud, S. *The problem of anxiety.* New York: W. W. Norton, 1936.

Gantt, W. H. The origin and development of nervous disturbances experimentally produced. *American Journal of Psychiatry*, 1942, 98, 475-481.

Goodstein, L. D., Spielberger, C. D., Williams, J. E., & Dahlstrom, W. G. The effects of serial position and design difficulty on recall of the Bender Gestalt Test designs. *Journal of Consulting Psychology*, 1955, 19, 230-234.

Greiner, T. H., & Burch, N. R. Response of human GSR to drugs that influence the reticular formation of brain stem. *Federation Proceedings; Federation of American Societies for Experimental Biology*, 1955, 14, 346.

Hoch, P. H., & Zubin, J. (Eds.) *Anxiety.* New York: Grune & Stratton, 1950.

Hodges, W. F. The effects of success, threat of shock, and failure on anxiety. Unpublished doctoral dissertation, Vanderbilt University, 1966.

Hodges, W. F. Effects of ego threat and threat of pain on state anxiety. *Journal of Personality and Social Psychology*, 1968, 8, 364-372.

Hodges, W. F., & Spielberger, C. D. The effects of threat of shock on heart rate for subjects who differ in manifest anxiety and fear of shock. *Psychophysiology*, 1966, 2, 287-294.

Hull, C. L. *Principles of behavior.* New York: Appleton-Century-Crofts, 1943.

Katkin, E. S. The relationship between self-report and physiological indices of anxiety during differentially stressful conditions. (Doctoral dissertation, Duke University) *Dissertation Abstracts*, 1964, 64, 5596.

Katkin, E. S. Relationship between manifest anxiety and two indices of autonomic response to stress. *Journal of Personality and Social Psychology*, 1965, 2, 324-333.

Lazarus, R. S., & Opton, E. M. The study of psychological stress: A summary of theoretical formulations and experimental findings. In C. D. Spielberger (Ed.), *Anxiety and behavior.* New York: Academic Press, 1966.

Liddell, H. S. Conditioned reflex method and experimental neurosis. In J. McV. Hunt (Ed.), *Personality and the behavior disorders.* New York: Ronald Press, 1944.

Malmo, R. B. Anxiety and behavioral arousal. *Psychological Review*, 1957, 64, 276-287.

Martin, B. The assessment of anxiety by physiological behavioral measures. *Psychological Bulletin*, 1961, 58, 234-255.

Masserman, J. H. *Behavior and neurosis: An experimental psychoanalytic approach to psychobiological principles.* Chicago: University of Chicago Press, 1942.

May, R. *The meaning of anxiety.* New York: Ronald Press, 1950.

Montague, E. K. The role of anxiety in serial rote learning. *Journal of Experimental Psychology*, 1953, 45, 91-96.

Mowrer, O. H. A stimulus-response analysis of anxiety and its role as a reinforcing agent. *Psychological Review*, 1939, 46, 553-565.

Sarason, I. G. Empirical findings and theoretical problems in the use of anxiety scales. *Psychological Bulletin*, 1960, 57, 403-415.

Silverman, R. E. The manifest anxiety scale as a measure of drive. *Journal of Abnormal and Social Psychology*, 1957, 55, 94-97.

Silverman, A. J., Cohen, S. I., & Shmavonian, B. M. Investigation of psychophysiologic relationships with skin resistance measures. *Journal of Psychosomatic Research*, 1959, 4, 65-87.

Spence, J. T., & Spence, K. W. The motivational components of manifest anxiety: Drive and drive stimuli. In C. D. Spielberger (Ed.), *Anxiety and behavior.* New York: Academic Press, 1966.

Spence, K. W. *Behavior theory and conditioning.* New Haven: Yale University Press, 1956.

Spence, K. W. A theory of emotionally based drive (D) and its relation to performance in simple learning situations. *American Psychologist*, 1958, 13, 131-141.

Spielberger, C. D. Theory and research on anxiety. In C. D. Spielberger (Ed.), *Anxiety and behavior.* New York: Academic Press, 1966. (a)

Spielberger, C. D. The effects of anxiety on complex learning and academic achievement. In C. D. Spielberger (Ed.), *Anxiety and behavior.* New York: Academic Press, 1966. (b)

Spielberger, C. D. Anxiety as an emotional state. In C. D. Spielberger (Ed.), *Anxiety: Current trends in theory and research.* Vol. 1. New York: Academic Press, 1972. (a)

Spielberger, C. D. Conceptual and methodological issues in research on anxiety. In C. D. Spielberger (Ed.), *Anxiety: Current trends in theory and research.* Vol. 2. New York: Academic Press, 1972. (b)

Spielberger, C. D., Goodstein, L. D., & Dahlstrom, W. G. Complex incidental learning as a function of anxiety and task difficulty. *Journal of Experimental Psychology*, 1958, 56, 58-61.

Spielberger, C. D., Gorsuch, R. L., & Lushene, R. E. *Manual for the State-Trait Anxiety Inventory.* Palo Alto, Calif.: Consulting Psychologist Press, 1970.

Spielberger, C. D., & Smith, L. H. Anxiety (drive), stress, and serial-position effects in serial-verbal learning. *Journal of Experimental Psychology*, 1966, 72, 589-595.

Spielberger, C. D., Southard, L. D., & Hodges, W. F. Effects of awareness and threat of shock on verbal conditioning. *Journal of Experimental Psychology*, 1966, 72, 434–438.

Taylor, J. A. The relationship of anxiety to the conditioned eyelid response. *Journal of Experimental Psychology*, 1951, 41, 81–92.

Taylor, J. A. A personality scale of manifest anxiety. *Journal of Abnormal and Social Psychology*, 1953, 48, 285–290.

Taylor, J. A. Drive theory and manifest anxiety. *Psychological Bulletin*, 1956, 53, 303–320.

Wechsler, D. *Manual for the Wechsler Adult Intelligence Scale*. New York: Psychological Corp., 1955.

Zuckerman, M. The development of an Affect Adjective Check List for the measurement of anxiety. *Journal of Consulting Psychology*, 1960, 24, 457–462.

6

A PERSON-SITUATION
INTERACTION MODEL
FOR ANXIETY

Norman S. Endler

Department of Psychology
York University
Toronto, Ontario, Canada

One of the important issues regarding personality in general, and anxiety in particular, is the controversy as to whether *traits* or *situations* are the major source of behavioral variance. Clinicians (Rapaport, Gill, & Schafer, 1945) and personologists (Cattell, 1946, 1950; Cattell & Scheier, 1961; McClelland, 1951; Murray, 1938) have contended that traits (personality variables) manifested in terms of cross-situational consistencies are the major determinants of behavior. This viewpoint emphasizes intrapsychic or dispositional constructs. Social psychologists and sociologists (Cooley, 1902; Cottrell, 1942 a, b; Dewey & Humber, 1951; Lindesmith & Strauss, 1949; Mead, 1934) have assumed that situations, and the meanings these situations have for individuals in terms of cultural rules and roles, are the major determinants of behavior.

A modified version of this paper was presented at the NATO Advanced Study Institute on "Stress and Anxiety in Modern Life" in Murnau Am Staffelsee, West Germany, June 10-16, 1973. The study was assisted under Grant 391 of the Ontario Mental Health Foundation. Canada Council (S73-0543) provided the travel funds to attend this conference. The assistance of Marilyn Okada is appreciated.

Mischel (1968, 1969, 1971) and Vernon (1964) have criticized the trait approach to personality. Whereas both contend that the empirical evidence does not support the "personologists" position of cross-situational consistency, Mischel (1971) emphasized that "a person will behave consistently across situations only to the extent that similar behavior leads, or is expected to lead, to similar consequences across these conditions [p. 74]." To the contrary, Alker (1972) recently claimed "that personality variables can explain people's behavior even though that behavior varies from situation to situation [p. 1]."

The cross-situational consistency (continuity) versus the situational specificity (change) controversy is an important and complex issue for social psychology and personality in general, and for anxiety in particular. Although no one would deny the existence of continuity and stability, there is substantial evidence from various domains of behavior to indicate the existence of situational specificity and personality change. In fact, the justification of psychotherapy is predicted in large part on the notion of personality change, and most therapists specifically aim at reducing (changing) the level of anxiety.

Although there is some evidence of *intellectual* and *cognitive* transituational consistency and stability over time (Mischel, 1969) with respect to *noncognitive personality dimensions* and *social behavior*, the evidence supports a behavioral specificity interpretation. Mischel (1968) summarized the evidence in favor of *situational specificity* for such character traits as aggression, rigidity, dependency, attitudes to authority, and other noncognitive personality variables. Endler (1966) and Endler and Hoy (1967) provided evidence of the importance of situational factors in social conformity; and Argyle and Little (1972) reviewed the evidence bearing on the importance of situational factors with respect to person perception, social behavior, and social response questionnaire studies.

Endler (1973), Endler and Hunt (1969), Hunt (1965) and Mischel (1968, 1969) reported validity coefficients for measures of personality traits that typically range from .20 to .50 with a median of about .30, thereby accounting for a trivial 9% of the relevant variance. Endler and Hunt (1969) analyzed self-report anxiety data for 22 samples of males and 21 samples of female subjects, including subjects varying in age, social class, educational level, geographical location, and mental health. They found that, on the average, individual differences contributed only 4.44% of the variance for males and 4.56% of the variance for females, but the results for situations were also not encouraging. Situational variance accounted for 3.95% of the variance for males and 7.78% of the variance for females. In contrast, *each* of the two-way interactions (subjects by situations, subjects by modes of response, and situations by modes of response) accounted for about 10% of the total variance. That is, each of the interactions accounted for more of the total variance than either persons or situations.

Bowers (1972) summarized nine articles published since 1959 that deal directly with the situation-versus-person controversy. His review includes data on self-report measures (e.g., anxiety and hostility), self-ratings based on real situations (feelings of trust, affiliation, etc.), and actual behavior or observed behavior in specific situations (talking, smoking, honesty, hyperaggressive behavior). He found that person-by-situation *interactions* accounted for more variance than either persons (individual differences) *or* situations in 13 of 16 possible comparisons. Furthermore, these interactions accounted for more variance than the *sum* of the main effects in 8 out of the 16 comparisons. Bowers (1972) reported that the average variance in these studies due to persons, situations, and person-by-situation interactions were 12.69%, 7.86%, and 19.72%, respectively. Argyle and Little (1972), in their review of person perception and social behavior studies, concluded that although situations accounted for more variance than did persons, "Person X Situation Interaction accounts for more variance than either Situations or Persons alone [p. 16]."

Endler (1973) and Endler and Hunt (1966) previously suggested that the person-versus-situation issue may be a pseudo-issue. This does not mean that persons and situations are unimportant sources of behavioral variance; rather, it suggests that the question has been inappropriately phrased and may well have led to much misguided research. It is inappropriate to ask whether situations *or* persons are the major source of behavioral variance, or whether persons *plus* situations are the major sources of behavioral variance (Endler, 1973). The appropriate question is, "*How* do individual differences and situations *interact* in determining behavior?" While this question has relevance for personality in general, this study focuses on an interaction model for anxiety in which the multidimensional nature of the construct is emphasized.

THE NATURE OF ANXIETY

The construct of anxiety has great theoretical and practical importance. It has generated voluminous research, differing methodological formulations, and some attempts at comprehensive theories; but there is more heat than light and little consensus as to exactly what anxiety is and how it can be reliably measured. Anxiety has been conceptualized as a stimulus for behavior, as a learned drive, as a personality variable, and as a complex response. Put differently, anxiety has been conceptualized as an independent variable (stimulus), an intervening variable (drive, personality trait), and as a dependent variable (response). Here, we focus primarily on the response and personality aspects of anxiety and on the situations that evoke it. Spielberger's (1966, 1972) state-trait theory of anxiety is examined, and it is compared and integrated with the Endler and Hunt (1966, 1968, 1969) person-by-situation interaction model of anxiety.

State Anxiety Versus Trait Anxiety

Cattell and Scheier (1958, 1961), through factor analysis, identified two distinct anxiety factors: *trait* or chronic anxiety, which they defined as a relatively permanent and stable characteristic of people, and *state* or acute anxiety, which they defined as a transitory condition which varies from moment to moment and from day to day. Examples of trait anxiety include factor loadings on characterological variables such as tendency to embarassment, ego weakness, and guilt proneness. Physiological variables such as systolic blood pressure and respiration rate have high loadings on the state anxiety factor, and the variables covary over periods of measurement. The instruments used by Cattell and Scheier to measure these state and trait anxiety factors did not relate these anxiety indicators to specific situations.

Spielberger (1966, 1972) suggested that much of the conceptual and empirical confusion with respect to anxiety results from the failure to distinguish between trait and state anxiety. Spielberger defined state anxiety (A-State) as an emotional reaction "consisting of unpleasant, consciously-perceived feelings of tension and apprehension, with associated activation or arousal of the autonomic nervous system [1972, p. 29]." Trait anxiety (A-Trait), according to Spielberger, refers to individual differences in anxiety proneness, i.e., the tendency to respond with A-State under stress. Spielberger (1972) states that since high A-Trait people are self-deprecatory and concerned with "fear of failure," they should, therefore, be more likely to perceive situations that are ego involving as more threatening than would low A-Trait individuals. That is, high A-Trait persons will manifest more intense levels of A-State arousal in ego-threatening situations than will low A-Trait individuals. Under neutral or nonthreatening conditions, the level of A-State arousal should be equivalent for both high and low A-Trait people.

According to Spielberger (1972), research on the state-trait anxiety theory should investigate and specify the stressful stimuli that elicit differential levels of A-State for high and low A-Trait people. Rappaport and Katkin (1972), O'Neil, Spielberger and Hansen (1969), and others have found that high A-Trait individuals in *ego-threatening conditions* or *situations* manifest greater changes in A-State than do low A-Trait individuals. For *physical danger situations*, however, high A-Trait individuals do not show greater increases in A-State than do low A-Trait individuals. For example, Katkin (1965) and Hodges and Spielberger (1966) found that threat of shock produced increases in A-State, but that the observed changes were not related to A-Trait level, as assessed by the Taylor (1953) Manifest Anxiety Scale (MAS). Spielberger, Gorsuch, and Lushene (1970) and Auerbach (1973) reported similar results. Hodges (1968) reported a positive relationship between level of A-Trait and changes in A-State under ego threatening conditions, but no relationship between A-Trait level and changes in A-State under physical threat conditions. Most of these studies used the Taylor (1953) MAS or the A-Trait scale of the State Trait Anxiety Inventory (STAI) (Spielberger et al., 1970) as the measure of trait anxiety.

Endler and Shedletsky (1973) used the S-R Inventory of Anxiousness (Endler, Hunt, & Rosenstein, 1962) as a measure of trait anxiety and the STAI A-State scale as a measure of state anxiety. They found that both threat of failure (ego threat) and threat of shock (physical threat) evoked A-State arousal, but changes in A-State were unrelated to level of A-Trait under ego-threat situations. In the physical-threat condition, changes in A-State were related to A-Trait level in that high A-Trait subjects showed greater A-State arousal than did low A-Trait subjects. Differences between the Endler and Shedletsky (1973) and Hodges (1968) results may be due to differences in the S–R Inventory and the STAI as A-Trait measures. It is also possible that there was an ego-threat component in the Endler and Shedletsky (1973) physical-threat condition and/or their ego-threatening condition may not have been sufficiently intense to produce differential A-State arousal for high and low A-Trait subjects. It seems most likely, however, that the discrepancy was due to the fact that Hodges (1968), Spielberger et al. (1970), and Rappaport and Katkin (1972) assessed A-Trait via the Taylor MAS and the STAI, which are unidimensional, whereas Endler and Shedletsky (1973) assessed A-Trait via the multidimensional S–R Inventory of Anxiousness (Endler et al., 1962). Endler and Shedletsky (1973) contended that both the STAI and MAS measure primarily ego-threat or interpersonal trait anxiety and that ego-threatening situations interact with interpersonal A-Trait (STAI or MAS) to elicit differential A-State changes for high and low interpersonal A-Trait subjects, and that when a physical danger threat situation interacts with the interpersonal A-Trait (MAS or STAI) no differential changes in A-State occur. The S–R Inventory of Anxiousness, which is multidimensional, enables one to obtain measures of A-Trait associated with interpersonal (ego threat), physical danger, and ambiguous (both ego threat and physical danger) threat situations. A-Trait measures based on the S–R Inventory of Anxiousness would reflect potential interpersonal (ego threat) and physical danger anxiety and may possibly account for A-Trait interacting with physical danger in evoking differential A-State changes. The Endler and Shedletsky (1973) failure to find a similar interaction for the ego-threatening situations is not readily apparent.

Supporting evidence for the assumption that the STAI A-Trait scale measures primarily A-State proneness to interpersonal or ego threat comes from the findings of Hodges and Felling (1970) and Spielberger et al. (1970). They found that the correlations between the STAI A-Trait and STAI A-State scores were higher in ego-threatening situations than in physical danger situations. Further evidence for this is the finding by Shedletsky (1972) that the correlations of STAI A-Trait scores were significantly higher with the interpersonal situation scale than with the physical danger or ambiguous threat scales of the S–R Inventory of Anxiousness.

While Spielberger's (1966, 1972) state-trait theory accurately describes the relationship between A-State, type of threat, and

A-Trait, the STAI A-Trait measure is restricted to interpersonal trait anxiety and ignores other aspects of the domain of trait anxiety. The Endler and Shedletsky (1973) results indicate that the S–R Inventory provides a valid anxiety measure of individual differences in responding to physical danger, and Endler and Hunt (1966) provided evidence that the S–R Inventory is also a valid anxiety measure of individual differences in responding to interpersonal threat situations. Trait anxiety is multidimensional, and this must be taken into account when examining the person (trait)-by-situation interaction.

Person-Situation Interactions and Anxiety

The Endler and Hunt (1966, 1968, 1969) interaction model of anxiety provides a basis for expanding the Spielberger (1966, 1972) state-trait anxiety theory which allows us to examine the nature of person-by-situation interactions. In effect we are attempting to integrate the state-trait model and the Endler-Hunt interaction model of anxiety within a broad methodological framework for anxiety research. The interaction model is basically derived from both the rationale and research regarding the S–R Inventory of Anxiousness (Endler et al., 1962).

Endler et al. (1962) suggested that the degree of expression of a personality trait is dependent on a number of factors, such as the proportion and types of situations in which certain responses are exhibited; the number, type, intensity and duration of these responses; and the relative provocativeness of the situations in arousing specific responses. Therefore, adequate assessment of a trait such as "anxiousness" must consider both the responses that characterize this trait and the appropriate evocative situations.

The S–R Inventory of Anxiousness sampled responses, situations, and individual differences (persons) separately to determine the relative variance contributions of each of these factors individually and in interaction with one another. As indicated earlier (Endler & Hunt, 1969), the percentage of variance attributed to situations (about 8%) and individual differences (about 5%) was relatively small, whereas the interaction of persons with situations contributed more of the total variance (about 10%) than did either main effect. About 30% of the total variance was due to the simple two-way interactions among subjects, situations, and modes of response. Therefore, Endler and Hunt (1966) suggested that personality description and assessment would be improved by describing the kinds of responses that people make in a variety of different situations.

The Endler-Hunt (1969) results have implications for trait and state anxiety and especially for A-Trait assessment. Neither trait nor state anxiety scores provide adequate information about anxiousness, unless there is also information about the evocative situations. Omnibus measures of A-Trait that do not take situations into account do not usually provide accurate behavioral predictions, since individual differences account for only about 5% of the total anxiety variance.

To fully understand trait anxiety (and also state anxiety), it is necessary to be cognizant of the *evocative situations* and the situation-by-person interactions (Endler & Hunt, 1969). Since the STAI A-Trait scale is a measure of A-Trait or anxiety proneness in social or interpersonal situations, the relationship between A-Trait, A-State, and type of threat, as suggested by the Spielberger (1966, 1972) trait-state anxiety theory, may be restricted to interpersonal or ego-threatening situations. Therefore, in examining the relationship between trait and state anxiety, it is necessary to assess the various aspects of multidimensional anxiety.

Multidimensional Measures of Trait Anxiety

In the past we have classified people into high and low A-Trait on the basis of total anxiety scores, using the multidimensional S–R Inventory of Anxiousness (Endler et al., 1962; Endler & Shedletsky, 1973). This practice may be misleading, however, in that it confounds interpersonal trait anxiety, physical danger trait anxiety, and ambiguous trait anxiety. In other words, individual differences in trait anxiety can occur in at least three domains: interpersonal, physical danger, and ambiguous (Endler et al., 1962).

A more appropriate procedure for measuring trait anxiety would be to obtain *three* separate measures of trait anxiety: interpersonal anxiety scores (summing across specific interpersonal situations), physical danger anxiety scores (summing across specific physical danger situations), and ambiguous anxiety scores (summing across specific ambiguous situations). Depending on the nature and purpose of an investigation, one could then use any one of these measures to classify individuals into high and low trait anxiety. For example, if one were interested in assessing the interactive effects of an interpersonal threatening situation and trait anxiety on state anxiety, persons could be classified into high and low A-Trait on the basis of their interpersonal trait anxiety scores (sum of the interpersonal situation scores) of the S-R Inventory of Anxiousness. Similarly, for physical threat situations, subjects could be classified on the physical danger component of A-Trait.

In order for Person (A-Trait) × Threatening Situation interactions to induce differential changes in A-State, the dimension of A-Trait classification should be congruent with the threatening situation. This suggests the need for multidimensional rather than unidimensional (global) measures of A-Trait. People who are high on interpersonal A-Trait are not necessarily higher on either physical danger A-Trait or ambiguous A-Trait.

THE S-R INVENTORY OF
GENERAL TRAIT ANXIOUSNESS

The measurement of multidimensional trait anxiety by summing across specific situations of the S-R Inventory of Anxiousness has certain limitations. It assumes that summing across specific situations within a factor domain provides some degree of generality. Furthermore, since the S-R Inventory has more than 150 items, it may be too long. Therefore, we have attempted to develop a general measure of A-Trait for each factor category and to devise scales with fewer items.

The multidimensional S-R Inventory of General Trait Anxiousness (S-R GTA) (Endler & Okada, 1974) was developed with the purpose of maximizing the effects of individual differences and minimizing the effects of situations. The inventory consists of four general situations and nine modes of response for each situation, thus yielding a 36-item scale. The first three general situations, based on the three situational anxiety factors (interpersonal, physical danger, and ambiguous) identified by Endler et al. (1962), were as follows: "You are in situations involving interaction with other people," "You are in situations where you are about to or may encounter physical danger," and "You are in a new or strange situation." The fourth general situation was designed to measure anxiety in innocuous, daily routines and stated, "You are involved in your daily routines."

Nine modes of response, based on the three mode-of-response factors (distress-avoidance, autonomic-physiological, and exhilaration-approach) found by Endler et al. (1962), were defined as follows: seek experiences like this, perspire, have an "uneasy feeling," feel exhilarated and thrilled, get fluttering feeling in stomach, feel tense, enjoy these situations, heart beats faster, and feel anxious. Each item employed a 5-point scale, ranging from "not at all" to "very much." Subjects were required to indicate the felt intensity of their own responses to the situation in question.

Subjects and Method

The S–R GTA was administered to samples of normal high school students, (182 males, 204 females), college students and adults (150 males, 197 females), and neurotic (34 males, 91 females) and psychotic (35 males, 10 females) adults. Means, standard deviations, standard error of mean scores, and alpha reliability coefficients were computed for the four situation scores and the nine mode-of-response scores for the various samples. Mean scores and standard deviations appear in Tables 6-1 and 6-2. In addition, *t* tests were calculated comparing situational scores for the various samples. In addition, one adult sample was also given the Taylor MAS and the Spielberger et al. STAI-Trait scale, and the STAI-Trait was also administered to a high school sample.

Results

Let us summarize some of our preliminary results for the S–R GTA.

Age and Sex Differences

Except for the general physical danger situation where normal adults are more anxious than normal youth (for both males and females), there were no other reported age differences regarding anxiety. The neurotic and psychotic samples consist of adult *S*s only, and therefore, no age group comparisons were possible. Of the normal youth, females were more anxious than were males, but only for the physical danger and ambiguous situations. For the normal adult sample, females scored higher than males for the physical danger situation. There were no reported sex differences for the neurotic or psychotic samples.

Table 6-1

Mean Scores and Standard Deviations for Normal Adult and Normal Youth Samples for the S–R Inventory of General Trait Anxiousness

Source of scores	Normal adults				Normal youth			
	Mean		Standard deviation		Mean		Standard deviation	
	Males (N = 150)	Females (N = 197)	Males (N = 150)	Females (N = 197)	Males (N = 182)	Females (N = 204)	Males (N = 182)	Females (N = 204)
Total inventory	95.21	99.77	17.15	15.65	93.65	99.49	15.16	16.77
Situation:								
1. Interaction with others	21.77	21.34	5.80	6.14	21.31	22.18	5.46	5.86
2. Encounter physical danger	30.89	34.69	7.06	7.08	28.34	32.56	7.37	7.28
3. New or strange situation	24.16	25.79	6.03	6.98	23.71	25.50	5.58	7.07
4. Involved in daily routines	18.89	17.96	5.85	4.51	20.29	19.26	5.00	5.48
Mode of response:								
1. Seek experiences like this	11.97	11.76	2.27	2.42	11.99	12.00	3.15	2.71
2. Perspire	9.66	9.85	3.01	3.14	9.11	9.31	3.93	3.12
3. Have an "uneasy feeling"	10.06	10.71	2.55	2.44	10.13	10.75	5.31	2.85
4. Feel exhilarated and thrilled	12.55	12.78	2.81	2.77	13.16	13.14	3.25	2.98
5. Get fluttering feeling in stomach	9.42	10.40	3.22	2.89	9.04	10.66	3.80	3.13
6. Feel tense	10.33	11.21	2.82	2.92	10.48	11.12	5.93	3.04
7. Enjoy these situations	11.33	11.57	2.69	2.66	11.71	11.87	3.02	2.69
8. Heart beats faster	9.99	10.36	2.69	2.64	9.35	10.21	3.11	2.95
9. Feel anxious	10.20	11.15	2.76	2.64	10.09	10.42	6.15	3.10

Source: Adapted from Endler and Okada (1973).

Table 6-2

Means Scores and Standard Deviations for Neurotic and Psychotic Samples
for the S-R Inventory of General Trait Anxiousness

Source of scores	Neurotic		Psychotic	
	Mean	Standard deviation	Mean	Standard deviation
	Males and females ($N = 125$)	Males and females ($N = 125$)	Males and females ($N = 45$)	Males and females ($N = 45$)
Total inventory	118.79	24.32	100.04	25.11
Situation:				
1. Interaction with others	24.74	8.51	23.20	7.18
2. Encounter physical danger	34.86	7.88	29.38	8.54
3. New or strange situation	30.74	7.98	26.47	7.29
4. Involved in daily routines	24.95	8.36	21.00	7.94
Mode of response:				
1. Seek experiences like this	13.47	3.33	11.89	3.49
2. Perspire	11.60	4.30	10.18	3.92
3. Have an "uneasy feeling"	13.71	3.65	10.98	3.84
4. Feel exhilarated and thrilled	14.15	3.27	13.11	3.80
5. Get fluttering feeling in stomach	12.54	4.28	9.36	4.11
6. Feel tense	13.98	3.79	10.67	4.17
7. Enjoy these situations	13.99	3.43	12.16	4.02
8. Heart beats faster	11.80	3.88	9.80	3.94
9. Feel anxious	13.01	3.83	11.91	4.57

Source: Adapted from Endler and Okada (1973).

Population Differences

1. *Normal adults versus neurotics.* Neurotic males were significantly more anxious than normal adult males for the interpersonal, ambiguous, and innocuous situations of the S-R GTA. Similarly, neurotic females were significantly more anxious than were normal adult females for all situations, except for the physical danger situation where there was no difference.

2. *Normal youth versus neurotics.* Whereas the neurotic males were more anxious than the normal youth males for the interpersonal and ambiguous situations only, neurotic females were

more anxious than were normal youth females for all four situations.

3. *Normal adults versus psychotics.* There were no situational anxiety differences between normal adult and psychotic males. Normal adult females were significantly more anxious than were psychotic females for the ambiguous situation only.

4. *Normal youth versus psychotics.* Normal youth and psychotic males did not appear to differ in anxiety on any of the four situations of the S–R GTA. Psychotic females, however, were more anxious than were normal youth females for the ambiguous situation only.

5. *Neurotics versus psychotics.* Neurotics were significantly more anxious than were psychotics on all four situations.

Situational Differences

From Tables 6-1 and 6-2 it is apparent that for the normal adult, normal youth, neurotic, and psychotic samples, subjects responded differentially to the four situations. The most anxiety-provoking situation was the physical danger one, followed by the ambiguous situation, then the interpersonal one, and finally, the innocuous situation. This same pattern emerged for all four samples.

Reliability

The coefficient alpha reliabilities (Cronbach, 1951) for the four situations of the S–R GTA appear in Table 6-3. From these results, it appears that the inventory is a reliable measure of trait anxiety.

Intercorrelations of Situations

Intercorrelating the four situations with one another for normal adult and normal youth samples combined, the neurotic sample, and the psychotic sample, yielded the results in Table 6-4. Because the intercorrelations for the normal adult and youth samples combined appeared to be relatively low, this may indicate that for normal subjects the situations are relatively independent of one another. This may provide additional evidence for the multidimensional nature of the S–R GTA. For the neurotic and psychotic samples the intercorrelations were somewhat higher, especially for the psychotics, and may indicate that abnormals are anxious about a greater proportion of situations than normals are, and are less capable of making appropriate perceptual differentiations.

Table 6-3

Coefficient Alpha Reliabilities for the Four Situations of the
S-R Inventory of General Trait Anxiousness for the Normal
Adult, Normal Youth, Neurotic and Psychotic Samples

Situation	Normal adults		Normal youth		Neurotic	Psychotic
	Males	Females	Males	Females	Males and females	Males and females
1. Interaction with others	.80	.82	.71	.74	.83	.76
2. Encounter physical danger	.83	.83	.80	.80	.82	.83
3. New or strange situation	.80	.86	.69	.83	.83	.75
4. Involved in daily routines	.75	.62	.64	.73	.84	.85

Table 6-4

Intercorrelations of the Four Situations of the
S-R Inventory of General Trait Anxiousness

Situation	Situation 1	Situation 2	Situation 3	Situation 4
Normal adult and youth samples combined, $N = 750$				
Situation 1	—	.11	.38	.24
Situation 2		—	.30	.01
Situation 3			—	.08
Situation 4				—
Neurotic sample, $N = 125$				
Situation 1	—	.32	.58	.35
Situation 2		—	.28	.17
Situation 3			—	.27
Situation 4				—
Psychotic sample, $N = 45$				
Situation 1	—	.47	.66	.73
Situation 2		—	.70	.30
Situation 3			—	.46
Situation 4				—

Factor Structure

A factor analysis of the four situations of the S–R GTA for normal subjects yielded two significant factors accounting for 40.27% and 26.49% of the variance, respectively. These two factors were a physical danger-ambiguous factor and an interpersonal-daily routine factor. The factor loadings for the four situations were .40, .80, .76, and –.14, respectively, for the first factor and .69, –.15, .30, and .83, respectively, for the second factor. There was only one significant situational factor for both the neurotic and psychotic samples. A factor analysis of the modes of response for the normal subjects yielded two significant response factors: physiological-distress and approach. These data provide further evidence for the multidimensional nature of trait anxiety.

Intercorrelations of S–R GTA, STAI-Trait, and MAS

Each of the four situations of the S–R GTA was correlated with the STAI A-Trait scale and the MAS for a sample of adults ($N = 64$). Both the STAI A-Trait scale and the MAS were more highly correlated with the interpersonal situation of the S–R GTA (.41 and .30, respectively) than with the physical danger (.23 and .24, respectively) or ambiguous (.20 and .19, respectively) situations, thus providing further evidence for the notion that the STAI-Trait and MAS focus primarily on interpersonal ego-threatening anxiety.

Sources of Anxiety Variance

Endler (1973) administered the S–R GTA to samples of high school students, university students, and adults attending an evening college. A variance components analysis indicated that individual differences for this multidimensional measure of trait anxiety accounted for less than 5% of the variance, situations accounted for 18%–28%, and person-by-situation interactions accounted for 17%–20% of the variance. For neurotic patients, individual differences accounted for 12% of the variance and for psychotic patients about 19% (Endler, 1973). For these two abnormal samples, situations accounted for 5%–6% of the variance, and person-by-situation interactions 22.08% for neurotics and 8.28% for psychotics. When these normal and abnormal samples were combined, Endler (1973) found that for this heterogeneous group, individual differences accounted for 9.66% of the variance, situations 16.11%, and person-by-situation interactions accounted for 18.24%, which was more than either main effect. These data provide further evidence of the importance of person-by-situation interactions and question the concept of a unidimensional or global measures of trait anxiety. Individual differences per se contribute very little to anxiety variance!

The findings for abnormals (neurotics and psychotics) that situations contributed very little to anxiety variance (5%–6%) and that there was only one situational factor on the S–R GTA, suggests that these subjects have difficulty in making appropriate perceptual differentiations; this may well be an imporant source of their pathology.

The fact that subjects respond differentially to different general situations, is one source of evidence that trait anxiety is multidimensional (i.e., it has interpersonal, physical danger, ambiguous, and innocuous components) and not unidimensional. The alpha coefficients indicate that the four situational scales of the inventory are each reliable measures of the different multidimensional aspects of trait anxiety; and the low intercorrelations of the situations indicate that, for normal subjects at least, the situations are relatively independent of one another. Further evidence of the multidimensionality of the inventory is from the factor structure—e.g., a physical danger-ambiguous factor and an interpersonal-innocuous factor were obtained. From the variance components analyses, the fact that the person-by-situation interactions accounted for more variance than either of the main effects is further evidence of the importance of the Person X Situation interaction and questions the concept of a unidimensional or global measure of trait anxiety.

PERSON-SITUATION INTERACTIONS AND STATE-TRAIT ANXIETY

As indicated earlier, Spielberger's (1966, 1972) conceptualization of the relationship between A-Trait, A-State, and type of threat appears to be restricted, since it encompasses only one aspect of trait anxiety (primarily interpersonal or ego-threatening) within the person-by-situation interaction anxiety model. Endler and Hunt (1969), in discussing their interaction model, suggested that both trait and state anxiety are multidimensional. A multidimensional trait anxiety measure such as the S–R GTA enables us to extend the state-trait theory to physical danger A-Trait and to ambiguous A-Trait personality dimensions.

To assess the joint effects of personality (A-Trait) and threatening situations on A-State, it is necessary for the A-Trait measure to be congruent with the threatening situation (Shedletsky & Endler, 1974). That is, if one wants to examine the interaction of physical threat and A-Trait on state anxiety, it is necessary to assess physical danger A-Trait independent of other facets of A-Trait. To assess the effects of interpersonal or ego threat and trait anxiety on state anxiety it is necessary to obtain a measure of interpersonal A-Trait.

Situational factors are important for A-State in that people respond differentially in threatening and nonthreatening situations. However, situational factors are equally important for A-Trait, and it is our contention that A-Trait is multidimensional rather than unidimensional. One would expect that persons differing in interpersonal A-Trait would respond differentially in A-State arousal to an ego-threatening situation but not necessarily respond differentially to a physical threat situation. Analogously, people differing in physical danger A-Trait should respond differentially to a physical threat situation. The model proposed in this paper would predict an interaction between *interpersonal* or *ego threat* (a situational factor) and level of interpersonal A-Trait (a personality factor) but no interaction between interpersonal threat and physical danger A-Trait. Behavioral consistency is predicted under similar or congruent evocative situations, but is not predicted where the evocative situations differ from one another (Endler, 1973; Mischel, 1969). When designing experiments, investigators must take into account the congruence between the evocative situation and the facet of the personality trait they are investigating.

The relationship between trait and state anxiety is certainly more complex than that suggested by the Spielberger (1966, 1972) state-trait anxiety model, but is also probably more complex than that initially suggested by the person-situation interaction model (Endler & Hunt, 1969). The field of anxiety is a highly complex one, and investigators have to be willing to tolerate a great deal of ambiguity, even if it does increase *their* anxiety levels! We have still not isolated the basic variables. However, we would agree with McGuire, who, in discussing the complexity of the personality and social influence susceptibility relationships, has suggested that even if we were cognizant of the basic parameters, "the interactional approach would still be more attractive from the theoretical viewpoint, since multifactorial designs would offer the economy of testing predictions and specifying parameters not only on main effects of the separate variables but on the interaction between them [McGuire, 1968, p. 1176]."

REFERENCES

Alker, H. A. Is personality situationally specific or intrapsychically consistent? *Journal of Personality*, 1972, 40, 1–16.

Auerbach, S. M. Trait-state anxiety and adjustment to surgery. *Journal of Consulting and Clinical Psychology*, 1973, 40, 264–271.

Argyle, M., & Little, B. R. Do personality traits apply to social behavior? *Journal for the Theory of Social Behavior*, 1972, 2, 1–35.

Bowers, K. S. Situationism in psychology: On making reality disappear. Department of Psychology Research Report No. 37, University of Waterloo, Ontario, Sept. 1972.

Cattell, R. B. *The description and measurement of personality*. New York: World Book, 1946.

Cattell, R. B. *Personality: A systematic theoretical and factual study*. New York: McGraw-Hill, 1950.

Cattell, R. B., & Scheier, I. H. The nature of anxiety: A review of 13 multivariate analyses comparing 814 variables. *Psychological Reports*, Monograph Supplement, 1958, 5, 351–388.

Cattell, R. B., & Scheier, I. H. *The meaning and measurement of neuroticism and anxiety*. New York: Ronald, 1961.

Cooley, C. H. *Human nature and the social order*. New York: Scribner's, 1902.

Cottrell, L. S., Jr. The analysis of situational fields. *American Sociological Review*, 1942, 7, 370–382. (a)

Cottrell, L. S., Jr. The adjustment of the individual to his age and sex roles. *American Sociological Review*, 1942, 7, 618–625. (b)

Cronbach, C. J. Coefficient Alpha and the internal structure of tests. *Psychometrika*, 1951, 16, 297–334.

Dewey, R., & Humber, W. J. *The development of human behavior*. New York: Macmillan, 1951.

Endler, N. S. Conformity as a function of different reinforcement schedules. *Journal of Personality and Social Psychology*, 1966, 4, 175–180.

Endler, N. S. The person versus the situation—A pseudo issue? A response to Alker. *Journal of Personality*, 1973, 41, 287–303.

Endler, N. S., & Hoy, E. Conformity as related to reinforcement and social pressure. *Journal of Personality and Social Psychology*, 1967, 7, 197–202.

Endler, N. S., & Hunt, J. McV. Sources of behavioral variance as measured by the S-R Inventory of Anxiousness. *Psychological Bulletin*, 1966, 65, 336–346.

Endler, N. S., & Hunt, J. McV. S-R Inventories of Hostility and comparisons of the proportions of variance from persons, responses, and situations for hostility and anxiousness. *Journal of Personality and Social Psychology*, 1968, 9, 309-315.

Endler, N. S., & Hunt, J. McV. Generalizability of contributions from sources of variance in the S-R Inventories of Anxiousness. *Journal of Personality*, 1969, 37, 1-24.

Endler, N. S., Hunt, J. McV., & Rosenstein, A. J. An S-R Inventory of Anxiousness. *Psychological Monographs*, 1962, 76, (17, Whole No. 536), 1-33.

Endler, N. S., & Okada, M. An S-R Inventory of General Trait Anxiousness. *Department of Psychology Reports*, York University, Toronto, 1974, No. 1.

Endler, N. S., & Shedletsky, R. Trait vs. state anxiety, authoritarianism, and ego threat vs. physical threat. *Canadian Journal of Behavioural Science*, 1973, 5, 347-361.

Hodges, W. F. Effects of ego threat and threat of pain on state anxiety. *Journal of Personality and Social Psychology*, 1968, 8, 364-372.

Hodges, W. F., & Felling, J. P. Types of stressful situations and their relation to trait anxiety and sex. *Journal of Consulting and Clinical Psychology*, 1970, 34, 333-337.

Hodges, W. F., & Spielberger, C. D. The effects of threat of shock on heart rate for subjects who differ in manifest anxiety and fear of shock. *Psychophysiology*, 1966, 2, 287-294.

Hunt, J. McV. Traditional personality theory in the light of recent evidence. *American Scientist*, 1965, 53, 80-96.

Katkin, E. S. The relationship between manifest anxiety and two indices of autonomic response to stress. *Journal of Personality and Social Psychology*, 1965, 2, 324-333.

Lindesmith, A. R., & Strauss, A. L. *Social psychology*. New York: Dryden, 1949.

McClelland, D. C. *Personality*. New York: Wm. Sloane Assocation, 1951.

McGuire, W. J. Personality and susceptibility to social influence. In E. F. Borgatta & W. W. Lambert (Eds.), *Handbook of personality and social research*. Chicago: Rand McNally, 1968.

Mead, G. H. *Mind, self and society*. Chicago: University of Chicago Press, 1934.

Mischel, W. *Personality and assessment*. New York: Wiley, 1968.

Mischel, W. Continuity and change in personality. *American Psychologist*, 1969, 24, 1012-1018.

Mischel, W. *Introduction to personality*. New York: Holt, Rinehart, & Winston, 1971.

Murray, H. A. *Explorations in personality*. New York: Oxford University Press, 1938.

O'Neil, J. F., Spielberger, C. D., & Hansen, D. N. The effects of state anxiety and task difficulty on computer-assisted learning. *Journal of Educational Psychology*, 1969, 60, 343-350.

Rapaport, D., Gill, M., & Schafer, R. *Diagnostic psychological testing*. Chicago: Year Book, 1945. 2 Vols.

Rappaport, H., & Katkin, E. S. Relationships among manifest anxiety, response to stress, and the perception of autonomic activity. *Journal of Consulting and Clinical Psychology*, 1972, 38, 219–224.

Shedletsky, R. Trait vs. state anxiety and authoritarianism-rebelliousness. Unpublished doctoral dissertation. York University, Toronto, 1972.

Shedletsky, R., & Endler, N. S. Anxiety: The state-trait model and the interaction model. *Journal of Personality*, 1974, 42, (in press).

Spielberger, C. D. The effects of anxiety on complex learning and academic achievement. In C. D. Spielberger (Ed.), *Anxiety and behavior*. New York: Academic Press, 1966.

Spielberger, C. D. Anxiety as an emotional state. In C. D. Spielberger (Ed.), *Anxiety: Current trends in theory and research*. Vol. 1. New York: Academic Press, 1972.

Spielberger, C. D., Gorsuch, R. L., & Lushene, R. E. *Manual for the State-Trait Anxiety Inventory*. Palo Alto, Calif.: Consulting Psychologists Press, 1970.

Taylor, J. A. A personality scale of manifest anxiety. *Journal of Abnormal Psychology*, 1953, 48, 285–290.

Vernon, P. E. *Personality assessment*. London: Methuen, 1964.

7

TEST ANXIETY, ATTENTION, AND THE GENERAL PROBLEM OF ANXIETY

Irwin G. Sarason

University of Washington
Seattle, Washington, United States

The original aims of this report were to present a review of existing research on test anxiety, a consideration of the historical and conceptual contexts in which test anxiety came to be studied, and suggestions concerning the bridges that must be built between the study of specific anxieties such as test anxiety and pervasive general anxiety. In the course of attempting to achieve these aims, several basic issues continually came to the fore. These included the perennial problem of the relationship between anxiety and fear, the therapeutic approaches to disabling high levels of anxiety, and—the biggest issue of all—the conceptualization of anxiety. As it turns out, then, this paper addresses itself to the specific topic of test anxiety that stimulated it and also to several general theoretical issues concerning anxiety.

I am indebted to Professor Ronald E. Smith for reading an earlier draft of the manuscript. His criticisms were incisive, his suggestions helpful, and both were conveyed with verve and tact. I am most grateful to him.

THE MATRIX OF RESEARCH
ON TEST ANXIETY

For many years, theories of anxiety were rooted primarily in the experiences of the clinical worker and the insights of the sensitive observer of people as they go about their day-to-day activities. Important scientific papers appeared during the 1930's and 1940's when increasing efforts were made to study the problem of anxiety from an experimental perspective. Psychologists were in the forefront of these efforts that often took the shape of analogues of psychoanalytic concepts. During the 1950's, psychological researchers took another step forward in their attempts to assess anxiety quantitatively. Although some work along these lines had been done earlier, the 1950's saw a flowering of anxiety scales, questionnaires, and measures. (A few observers of the psychological scene noted this flowering of indexes of anxiety with not a little bit of alarm, arguing that the garden was infested with too many weeds.)

The Manifest Anxiety Scale (MAS), soon after its publication, became the most widely used measure of anxiety (Taylor, 1951, 1953). Both the construction and use of this instrument were somewhat anomalous. Although the word "anxiety" appears in its title, the MAS was constructed as a measure of drive—Hull's D, to be specific. However, the 50 true-false statements of the MAS were selected by asking clinical psychologists to judge which items of the Minnesota Multiphasic Personality Inventory (MMPI) reflected Norman Cameron's definition of anxiety. Despite the perhaps too subtle or fuzzy logic of this procedure (what does Cameron's definition of anxiety have to do with Hull's D?), the fact that the MAS's items did appear to deal with anxieties, worries, and reactions to stressful situations led to its incorporation into many research designs and even into clinical batteries.

A growing number of researchers in recent years have focused their attention on specific sources of anxiety, such as social anxiety, anxiety over public speaking, and test anxiety, because these sources are of considerable intrinsic interest themselves and also because of the, at times, nebulous character of the concept of general anxiety. Test anxiety has been the most widely studied of these specific anxieties, and there are now available a number of indexes of a person's anxiety over being examined and having one's performance evaluated. Among the more widely used instruments are the Test Anxiety Scale for Children (TASC), the Test Anxiety Scale (TAS) for use with high school and college students, and the School Anxiety Scale (SAS).

Phillips, Martin, and Meyers (1972), in their comprehensive review of the literature, pointed out that research on test anxiety has dealt with a wide variety of topics. These include the relationship between test anxiety and academic performance; the antecedants, particularly within the family, and the correlates of test anxiety; its concomitants, including physiological ones; and the reduction in students of high levels of test anxiety. Research on test anxiety has not grown out of a monolithic theory. Empirical studies of test anxiety have grown out of motivational and cognitive as well as habit and drive theoretical orientations. Nevertheless, much of the research derived from these orientations has employed similar operations and comparable tasks.

At this point, it would seem useful to describe a few of the widely used independent and dependent variables in experiments that deal with test anxiety. There are two reasons for doing so and for focusing on experimental studies. First, it is necessary to characterize the methodology of a field if one is to deal with theoretical issues in an informed way. Second, a number of the theoretical issues to be discussed later concern the results of experimental studies.

Experimental Studies

Since a person's level of test anxiety reflects his concerns over being evaluated, the creation, experimentally, of situations that arouse, exacerbate, or reduce the potency of these concerns is of major importance. A substantive body of literature now exists that bears on these experimental efforts. The following tacks have been taken in efforts to create conditions that bear on the experience of test anxiety.

1. *Achievement-orienting instructions.* The instructions administered prior to performance can potently influence performance. Achievement-orienting instructions direct the attention of the subject (*S*) to evaluations that will or might be made of the subject's performance. "The task, on which you are about to perform measures a component of intelligence" and "Do your work carefully because your score will reflect your level of intelligence" are the types of comments the experimenter (*E*) might make to the *S* in an experiment on test anxiety. Achievement-orienting instructions stress the test-like, evaluational aspects of experimental tasks on which *S*s perform. Their effects are usually contrasted with those of neutral or control instructions. Neutral or control instructions focus on the task-orienting character of the task on which the person is

asked to perform. Evaluation of *S*s' performance level is usually not mentioned.

2. *Reassuring instructions.* Less widely used than achievement-orienting instructions, reassuring instructions are, however, at least as intriguing. Rather than being part of an effort to arouse concern over adequacy of performance, they are employed to allay anxieties. For example, "The task on which you are going to perform is very, very difficult, and no one will successfully complete very many of the problems. So don't worry about how well you are doing. In this experiment the emphasis will be primarily on the characteristics of the task."

3. *Task characteristics.* Independent of which sort of orienting communications are given to the individual, the task will by itself exert an influence over his performance. Reassuring instructions administered prior to taking a vocabulary or analogies test may not be effective if *S* knows or believes that the task on which he is performing is a measure of his intelligence. Thus both the nature of the task (its complexity, its level of difficulty) and the face validity of the task for the person play roles in influencing his performance. The task and how it is introduced to *S* combine in determining performance level.

4. *Time pressure.* One popular way of heightening tension in performance is to stress the limited time available to *S* in working on the task at hand. The stress can be created either through direct comments by *E* or, somewhat more subtly, through the presence of stimuli indicative of performance evaluation. A stopwatch resting on the desk can be a potent factor in shaping *S*'s interpretation of the experimental situation. It is important to note that this can occur regardless of the researcher's interest. If test anxiety is not *systematically* included in an experimental design, it may nevertheless interact with a condition such as the presence of a stopwatch and thus represent an uncontrolled source of variation in behavior.

5. *Performance reports.* A paradigm that has been employed in studies on anxiety involves performance on two tasks, often with the researcher primarily interested in performance on the second one. Interspersed between the two tasks (the two tasks

might or might not be similar) is a report to S about the level of his performance on the first task. The report could simply be communication to S of his actual score on that task or it could be communication of a fiction: "Your performance was much poorer than the other students who participated in this experiment" or "You did very well on that task."

6. *Social learning variables.* A realistic account of most performance situations usually requires attention to interpersonal factors. There have been ample demonstrations of the interactions between these factors and performance so that ignoring their existence becomes a serious hazard to the researcher. This is true whether or not one's hypothesis involves interpersonal variables because there is always some form of relationship formed between E and S. Consider an investigator who is interested in paired-associates learning. Even though social variables may in no way be implicated in the formulation that gave rise to his experiment, the attitude of E toward S may color S's situational anxiety and consequently his performance. Although some of the findings of research on experimenter variables have aroused controversy, the fact remains that E's aims, expectations, hypotheses, and numerous subtle behaviors can, by themselves and in interaction with S's characteristics, constitute potent variables requiring at least assessment by the researcher (Sarason, I. G., 1972a).

One experimental manipulation in research on anxiety that has grown out of social learning theory involves giving S an opportunity to observe someone else (a model) perform in a situation similar to the one in which he will be expected to perform. The purpose of this sort of manipulation could be to orient S to what will be expected of him in the experiment. But beyond simply demonstration, the model's behavior could be orchestrated so as to influence S's expectations and attitudes. For example, a model who fails (or who is made to appear to have failed) might well differentially affect high and low test anxious students and perhaps even different types of high anxiety Ss.

Another social condition that can differentially influence the performance of Ss differing in test anxiety is the presence of an audience during performance. Yet another condition is created when

E makes an effort to establish rapport with *S*. What is the effect on *S*s differing in test anxiety of having a social contact with *E* prior to performing the experimental task? There is evidence that when this occurs, the opportunity for the social contact interacts with *S*'s personality (Sarason, I. G., Kestenbaum, & Smith, 1972).

Test anxiety and all other personality variables grow out of a social learning matrix. This matrix can be approached developmentally (e.g., "What roles do family attitudes play in the child's level of test anxiety?") or experimentally, ("In what ways is the individual influenced by opportunity to observe a model cope either adaptively or maladaptively with a testing situation?") Social learning operates both over long periods of time and in discrete situations. It seems likely that in the future its contributions to behavior will be more systematically explored than they have been in the past.

Findings of Experimental Studies

There is considerable evidence in support of the conclusion that high test anxious *S*s are deleteriously affected by conditions (such as achievement-orienting instructions and failure reports) that stress the evaluative implications of task performance. On the other hand, when an effort is made to create a neutral context for performance, differences between extreme test anxiety groups are smaller or, as has been found in several investigations, nonexistent. Under reassuring or task-orienting conditions, a few studies have reported superiority in performance of high to low test anxious groups (Sarason, I. G., 1972b).

Table 7-1 presents the results of an experiment in which *S*s learned a set of difficult serial learning items (Sarason, I. G., 1972b). High and low test anxiety groups (assessed by the TAS) were divided into five groups representing experimental conditions. Under the control condition, *S*s simply performed the serial learning task. The achievement-orientation instructions described the serial learning task as an intelligence test. In the reassurance condition, *S*s were given preperformance anxiety-allaying instructions. The following instructions constituted the motivating-task-orientation condition:

> This is an experiment concerning the shape of learning curves. Some people learn at a more rapid rate than do other people. Some people learn more during a given period of time

than do others. I am really not interested in either of these aspects of learning. My concern is exclusively with the shape of the learning curves for certain types of tasks. What would help me the most would be for you to think of the task on which you are to perform as an opportunity to get practice in memorizing different sorts of material. You won't get to try out all of the tasks, but you will find your task interesting and food for thought. I think you will find working on this task worthwhile.

The task-orienting condition informed S that the experiment was being conducted to shed light on the task rather than on the performance level of individuals.

Table 7-1 shows that the two test anxiety groups performed comparably under the control or neutral condition. However, the low TAS group gave significantly more correct responses under achievement orientation. Under the reassurance and task-orientation conditions, the high TAS means were somewhat greater than the low TAS means. The two test anxiety groups performed comparably under the motivated-task-orientation condition. These results indicate that personal threat, in the form of an evaluational emphasis, has a decidedly deleterious effect on high TAS Ss and that reassurance and task orientation have a more favorable influence on high than low TAS Ss. Thus preperformance communication to Ss interacts with test anxiety.

Table 7-1

Number of Correct Responses for Final Trial Block on Serial Learning Task (Material Low in Meaningfulness)

Conditions	High test anxiety	Low test anxiety
Control	47.83	46.67
Achievement orientation	34.08	65.08
Reassurance	58.75	42.24
Motivating task orientation	65.33	59.67
Task orientation	50.00	38.25

Source: Sarason, I. G., 1972b, p. 389.

The fact that these generalizations are supported by empirical evidence should not lead us to gloss over the importance of several categories of variables that may, under appropriate circumstances, interact with test anxiety and the experimental conditions. One such category consists of task variables. There is evidence that anxiety and task characteristics (type of task, its difficulty, complexity, familiarity) do combine in influencing performance. Another potentially confounding category is the interpersonal dimensions of the psychological experiment. The experimenter's personal characteristics (e.g., sex, anxiety level, expectancies, the stake he has in getting positive results) can significantly modify the effects of other variables (e.g., achievement-orienting instructions) on S's performance (Sarason, I. G., 1972a, 1972b).

The role of social learning variables in research on test anxiety has become more clear in recent years. Sarason, I. G., Pederson, and Nyman (1968) suggested that high TAS Ss benefit more from the opportunity to observe a model perform a task similar to the one on which they will perform than do low TAS Ss. I. G. Sarason (1972c) reported two experiments in which high, middle, and low TAS Ss performed on a serial learning task after receiving one of several types

Table 7-2

Mean Number of Correct Responses
in Experiment on the Serial Learning
Task (List S)

Text anxiety	Number of correct responses
High	
Model	221.11
Model fails	170.13
Control	166.31
Middle	
Model	201.54
Model fails	210.14
Control	174.55
Low	
Model	193.44
Model fails	232.11
Control	176.32

Source: Sarason, I. G., 1972c, p. 412.

Table 7-3

Mean Time Scores of Solution of 10 Anagrams

Test anxiety	Condition			
	Performance only	Performance-verbalization	Performance-verbilization-principles	Control
High TAS[a]	1989.33	1909.40	1670.27	2090.40
Low TAS	1860.67	1789.80	1890.93	1816.20

Source: Sarason, I. G., 1973.
[a]TAS = Test Anxiety Scale.

of observational opportunities. In the first experiment, Ss observed a model who engaged in self-derogation concerning her performance. The three TAS groups did not differ under this condition. In the second experiment, the situation was arranged so that the model did not make self-derogatory comments, but was given a failure report by E. That is, after the model had performed (according to a previously determined program of responses), E commented that her (the model's) performance had been very poor and represented a failure to attain a level that might be expected of college students. The experiment also included a modeling condition in which S simply observed a modeling demonstration of how one works on a serial learning task.

Table 7-2 summarizes the results of the experiments, which also included a control (no model) condition. The table reveals that for the "model fails" condition there was a negative relationship between test anxiety and performance. This relationship was positive for the model (demonstration) condition. The three TAS groups performed comparably under the control condition. These results suggest that when a person observes failure in another person, his reaction will depend upon his own test anxiety level. The high TAS observer performs at a relatively low level, whereas the low TAS observer may become more highly motivated to perform well—perhaps so as to avoid failing himself.

Table 7-3 illustrates the role of modeling in performance on a task other than serial learning (Sarason, I. G., 1973). The task consisted of a series of anagrams, with high and low TAS groups assigned to a particular preperformance condition. Under the performance-only condition, S watched as E worked sample anagrams. Under performance-verbalization, E also described verbally the steps he was going through in solving the anagrams. The performance-verbalization-principles condition involved the same procedure except for the addition of one element, E's statement of problem-solving principles applicable to successful anagram solution. Table 7-3 summarizes the results for the three experimental and the control groups. The best mean solution time was obtained by the high TAS group that observed a verbalizing model who also enunciated problem-solving principles. This experiment adds to our knowledge of the role of the personality variable of test anxiety in what might be called cognitive modeling. It suggests the possibility of using an observational learning paradigm in teaching people to more effectively think through problems, more effectively employ symbolic coding, and anticipate potential consequences of their behavior. Meichenbaum's (1972) (see also Meichenbaum & Goodman, 1971) valuable experiments have been a major contribution to the experimental exploration of cognitive modeling.

If, as appears to be true, high test anxious persons are deleteriously affected by personal threats such as those posed by achievement-orienting conditions, it is reasonable to speculate about ways in which this effect might be reduced. Sarason, I. G., et al. (1973) carried out a serial learning experiment in which Ss participated in what might be viewed as a rapport-building device, an interview with E. One group of Ss participated in an interview during which E focused on testing situations and examination anxieties; another group talked with E about various aspects of current topics of interest in the sphere of campus life. Whereas the test anxiety interview had a deleterious effect, the campus interview had a somewhat salutary effect on the serial learning of high TAS Ss. Apparently the test anxiety interview served to exacerbate worries of high TAS Ss over being evaluated.

The studies described previously were experimental explorations. The scope of empirical investigations of test anxiety extends far beyond that domain. For example, recent years have seen an increase of therapy studies aimed at determining how the undesirable consequences of test anxiety can be reduced or eliminated. Systematic desensitization has received especially intensive study that has yielded encouraging results (Osterhouse, 1972). Other behavior therapy tactics involving techniques such as reinforcement and modeling are good candidates for inclusion in the therapist's armamentarium (Rachman, 1972). Further exploration is needed also into more traditional therapeutic approaches, such as counseling, and into novel and improved educational methods, such as programed instruction and performance contracts.

Another flourishing and important area concerns the antecedents of test anxiety in terms of a person's specific life histories, family dynamics, and incidence of traumatic experiences in school (Phillips et al., 1972; Sarason, S. B., Davidson, Lighthall, Waite, & Ruebush, 1960). We need to know both how to treat anxiety and where it comes from. Information about these domains will ultimately contribute to gains in prevention; individualization of classroom instruction; and the development of educational philosophies, practices, and materials that place a realistic emphasis on the personalities of the people engaged in the educational enterprise.

A Learning—Attentional Theory of Test Anxiety

There is no single interpretation of the results mentioned previously that is superior in all respects to alternative conceptions. What follows is a theoretical formulation that seems to be consistent with the data, reasonably parsimonious, and provocative in planning directions for future research.

Our behavior is determined in part by the information available to us. Information at our disposal is, in turn, influenced by whether we attend to it. Attention, of course, is shaped in many ways by environmental events such as loud noises, directions, and entreaties. Over 75 year ago, William James commented upon the role played in attention by personality variables such as dispositions, attitudes, and preoccupations.

In my view, a person's level of test anxiety is, to a significant degree, a product of experiences that influence what he attends to in himself and in the world. The highly test anxious individual is one who is prone to emit self-centered interfering responses when confronted with evaluative conditions. Two response components have been emphasized by writers who espouse this view. One is emotional and autonomic reactivity—sweating, accelerated heart rate, etc. The other concerns cognitive events—e.g., saying to oneself while taking a test, "I am stupid," "Maybe I won't pass." It seems reasonable that saying such things to oneself during a test might interfere considerably with the task at hand, be it one that requires the acquisition of a new skill (e.g., learning to drive a car) or figuring out the answers to certain questions (e.g., items on an income tax form). Recent evidence suggests that these cognitive events may exert a more consistent negative influence on performance than does emotionality (Doctor & Altman, 1969; Morris & Liebert, 1969, 1970). A study by Doris and Sarason (1955) has provided evidence indicating that when asked about the reason why they failed a test, low test anxious college students tend to blame external factors ("It was a bad exam") and high test anxious tend to blame themselves ("I got confused").

How are these interfering responses learned? The responses occur as part of a process of heightened attention to oneself. Worry is an attentionally demanding cognitive activity. Unless one is especially adept at doing several things simultaneously, time spent in worrying about one's level of adequacy can be expected to interfere with task performance. From this point of view, a score on a measure such as the TAS reflects proneness to respond to evaluative cues, such as those given by achievement-orienting instructions, with self-attentional responses. The responses may vary quite a bit from person to person. Examples of self-preoccupying behaviors that are elicited by evaluative cues are fear of competition and of failure and ambivalence over achievement. The latter might occur in a student who responds to tests with anger and with annoyance over his parents' unreasonably high (in his view) academic standards.

This theory is consistent with the results of studies of the reactions of groups differing in test anxiety to achievement-orienting conditions. They are also consistent with the findings concerning performance under neutral and reassuring conditions. In the absence of explicit evaluative cues, differences between anxiety groups are either smaller than under achievement-orienting conditions or nonexistent. Interestingly, some of the data suggest that the performance of low test anxious persons is deleteriously affected by reassuring instructions that emphasize the nonevaluative aspect of work on a particular task. Perhaps a certain level of self-preoccupation must occur among persons who are usually low in anxiety in order to attain an optimal level of performance. In any event, conditions that are facilitative for high may be detrimental for groups low in test anxiety.

The studies relating test anxiety and modeling indicate that although high scorers have a tendency to become self-centered under evaluative stress, the direction of their attention is not completely one sided. Except perhaps for the most extreme of pathological withdrawal, persons—even those described here as being self-centered—attend both to internal and external stimuli. Available evidence indicates that when evaluative cues are not emphasized, the high test anxious individual learns quite a bit from observing a model demonstrate an adaptive approach to a task. However, when these cues are present, and when the model appears to have failed, the interfering effects of anxiety come to the fore. Though test anxiety would appear to be a type of trait anxiety, the balance in a given case between an inner-directed preoccupation with oneself and sensitivity to external cues such as the behavior of a model can be expected to vary with the level of evaluative stress, task characteristics, and the interpersonal dimensions of the setting in which performance takes place.

As a person's anxiety level increases, it is understandable that he should both worry and search the environment for helpful cues. Conditioning studies of verbal behavior have shown that reinforcement by E of S's verbal responses has its greatest effect among high test anxious persons who are experiencing evaluative stress (Sarason, I. G., & Ganzer, 1963). The fact that the high test anxious person is, at least consciously, desirous of performing at an acceptable level suggests that observational opportunities and reinforcement may be worthwhile vehicles in helping him to approach an optimal level of performance. Wine (1971) and Meichenbaum (1972) presented thoughtful contributions to our knowledge of how to redirect the attention of persons whose problems include maladaptive coping responses (as, for example, self-preoccupation while taking a test).

Wine (1971) recently presented a valuable review of the test anxiety literature from the standpoint of selective attention. She has pointed out that a large portion of the research on test anxiety scales has focused on the cues to which high scorers respond with personalized, task-irrelevant responses. This preoccupation with variables and conditions that deleteriously influence the high test anxious individual has resulted in insufficient emphasis on the positive side of attention processes. Research on perceptual, situational, and cognitive factors that influence how information is interpreted and used, as well as on the effects of the information on behavior, is needed to fill gaps in knowledge that exist at present. This information is of considerable general importance to students of test anxiety and other dimensions of personality (Easterbrook, 1959;

Egeth, 1967; Mandler, 1959). Wine (1970) reported the results of a provocative study of attentional training as a means of reducing the negative effects of test anxiety. Her approach included instructions to S to attend to task-relevant cues and practice on tasks with special emphasis on the emission of task-relevant behavior. Her findings indicated that highly test anxious persons were helped by the training they received. Meichenbaum (1972) also carried out research aimed at training test anxious people to gain better control over their attentional processes. His work suggests that covert behavior (e.g., private speech) obeys the same psychological laws as does overt behavior. It would seem that we are in the early states of developing effective methods of strengthening adaptive self-guidance systems.

I have argued that test anxiety can be viewed as a maladaption of attention which is stimulated by evaluative cues. According to the theory presented here this maladaptive situation (too great a self-deprecating preoccupation with oneself) is a product of experience that in turn conditions our reactions to other experiences. Although more information is needed concerning the developmental antecedents of proneness to respond with anxiety to tests, experimental approaches have much to contribute to an understanding of the conditions that exacerbate and diminish anxiety reactions to evaluative situations. Test anxiety may be as much a product of lack of practice in focusing on tasks as it is of psychodynamics. In this regard it is significant that socioeconomic differences have been uncovered by a number of investigators (Phillips et al., 1972). The higher levels of test anxiety reported by students with lower socioeconomic backgrounds may be related importantly to deficiencies in their attentional training or to low expectancies of success. There probably is no single route to the "achievement" of high test anxiety. In one case it may be due to ambivalence over being in school; and in another, the test anxiety might be secondary to inadequate training in how to approach situations from a task-oriented perspective.

TEST ANXIETY, GENERAL ANXIETY, AND FEAR

Test anxiety is one of a group of specific anxieties that include social anxiety, speech anxiety, and even teaching anxiety (Parsons, 1973). Though it is important to determine empirically the interrelationships among anxieties that become manifest in different types of situations, it is of some moment also to consider the relationship of specific anxieties to the concepts of general anxiety and of fear. Is test anxiety similar to general anxiety, albeit on a smaller scale? Or is it primarily a fear response? Students of test anxiety quite understandably might speculate about whether test anxiety is simply a fear response that has been conditioned to testing situations or a pervasive anxiety reaction to the anticipation of a negative evaluation of one's work. The questions that have been raised cannot be answered without considering the conceptualizations of anxiety and fear. Let us turn now to some of these conceptual problems and later return to the topic of test anxiety.

Anxiety and Fear

Virtually every undergraduate learns that anxiety is general, vague, and pervasive, whereas fear is specific and evoked by an identifiable stimulus. Epstein (1972) considered the possibility that perhaps anxiety and fear are identical except for the ease with which the evoking stimuli can be identified. If so, Epstein argues, one term should suffice in discussions of what are now called anxiety and fear. Other writers, conceding that anxiety and fear do share elements in common, have stressed the cognitive dimensions of anxiety (Lazarus & Averill, 1972; Spielberger, 1972). Whereas fear might be explicable in terms of the acquisition of emotional responses, these writers emphasize anxiety as a product of a series of cognitive steps, an important one of which is the person's appraisal of sources of personal threat in his environment.

I believe that there is a difference between anxiety and fear and that important clues concerning the nature of this difference may be uncovered in investigations of attentional processes. Let us now explore anxiety and fear from the perspective of what the person attends to.

Fear possesses a tangible quality in that its source is identifiable. The source might be a snake, a doctor's appointment at 3 o'clock, or the necessity to walk at night through the streets of a teeming slum. There is a compelling environmental immediacy to fear. Common to these examples is that the fearful individual's attention is focused on an environmental event or possible event that has distinctly noxious qualities. There may, actually, be more than one noxious stimulus, but the number is typically small. Removal of the noxious stimulus results in a drastic reduction of fear. That is, the person's apprehension, tenseness, and emotional arousal decline. These decrements, of course, will also follow from the individual's acquisition of an adaptive coping response.

The problem of anxiety seems to be more complex than that of fear. But this fact should not lead us to neglect the complexities of fear reactions and the possible role seemingly isolated fear responses can play in the development of anxiety states. For example, fears of various types characterize the periods of childhood. The reaction of parents to each particular fear may exert a significant influence beyond simply the matter of the probability of occurrence of the fear response to which they react. The child whose fear of the dark is treated exclusively with effusive expressions of affection by his mother receives not only information about what happens when he expresses fear of the dark but also a clue to the reaction other fears might elicit. If parental reinforcement of expressions of fear occurs often enough it is not inconceivable that the experience of apprehension and tenseness would become a relatively stable state of the individual. That is, fearfulness comes to occupy an increasingly significant role in the life of the person.

The end product might be an anxiety state that does not seem explicable in terms of identifiable noxious, frightening stimuli. The transition from relatively isolated fear to pervasive anxiety can come about in many ways. I have mentioned the child who receives affection after he expresses fear; but equally apt (perhaps more so) would be the child who is treated with contempt for expressing his fears. In this case, because the child is blamed for being afraid he comes to focus his attention increasingly on himself and to become more self-preoccupied ("What is wrong with me?"). The effects of these divergent parental reactions (from effusiveness to contempt) to fear will depend on many variables one of which is the importance in the life of the individual of the persons who respond in extreme ways to his fears. For example, the physically handicapped child whose social contacts are limited may be more susceptible to attention from his parents than is the normal child.

The metamorphosis from fear to anxiety can be viewed in terms of the language of observational learning. Children experience fears of their own; in addition, they observe fear and anxiety reactions in others. When the child observes the behavior of significant others, most notably his parents, he acquires normative information about what the world is like and how to respond to it. A perpetually fearful or anxious parent is, in effect, telling his child that the variety of ways of coping with fears is quite limited. The child observes the reactions of others to the avoidance responses and apprehensions of the fearful adult and thereby acquires clues as to how he might cope—either adaptively or maladaptively—with the dangers and threats of life. The observation of models and reinforcements meted out to the child provide the child with information to which he attends and which, in all likelihood, will influence his attention to events in the world about him and within himself.

Thus, both fear and anxiety may be viewed as outcomes of social learning; there is a stronger cognitive component in anxiety than in fear; and under certain circumstances a metamorphosis from fear to anxiety takes place. Fear and anxiety differ in the focus of attention. The fearful person is reacting to "it" out there; the anxious individual is preoccupied with "me." One reason anxiety is a more complex phenomenon than fear, is that developmentally the anxious person has been forced to adapt to multiple, perhaps simultaneous, fears. Another reason is that the worries of the anxious person are not subjected to consensual validation to the extent typical of most of us. The child who is told "There is no reason for you to be afraid of the dark," may become more self-preoccupied because he devotes much time to worrying about why he is different from everyone else, why he is afraid of the dark. In this way parents who dismiss or display rejection or contempt for the child's fears not only are not helping him but, on the contrary, may be strengthening his self-centered focus. The anxious individual must cope with compelling immediate fear-arousing situations. His level of adaptation to them is hindered by anticipations of danger that are caused more by internal preoccupations than by external factors. In making suggestions about the development of anxiety, I am aware that in all likelihood there is more than one road to anxiety. However, since there is a limit to the number of stimuli to which someone can attend (that limit, however, probably varies widely from person to person), it is not surprising that the anxious person is relatively ineffective in coping with many of the realities of life.

Anxiety is marked by diffuse emotional reactions, feelings of uncertainty, and helplessness. The anxious person seems to be afraid of unspecified correlates or consequence of unspecified noxious stimuli. Beyond the cognitive features of anxiety already noted, two features that have been implied should be made explicit. Another aspect of anxiety not dealt with thus far should also be brought into the picture. The implied features are the multiplicity of apprehensions that beset the anxious individual and semantic generalization. Someone whose only significant fear is that he might get bitten by a snake is living a comparatively simple life (at least in so far as fears are concerned). Someone who is afraid of snakes and is also afraid of women, and the anger he feels towards them, is required to devote more time to the tasks of (a) weighing the relative intensities of these fears—particularly when the feared events occur simultaneously—and (b) planning his behavior on the basis of the weights assigned. Thus, in anxiety there are multiple threats and dangers to be attended to. Some of these may not be pointable but rather may be response tendencies of which the person either is ashamed or is ambivalent. This is illustrated by someone who struggles to control his anger for fear of overreacting and thus letting the world in on his heretofore encapsulated fantasy life.

The multiplicity of fears that pervade the life of the anxious person leads us to a point not made thus far. It has to do with the roles of conflict and values in the experience of anxiety. In addition to having to worry about *more* things than does the less anxious individual, the anxiety-ridden person is beset by the need to consider their priorities and conflicts *among* them. Conflicts over priorities and deciding which apprehensions are most pressing add to the self-preoccupying character of anxiety and, in addition, heighten the emotional state of the person. Existential writers have stressed the fact that man has to cope with the experiences of the moment and the need for students of man's behavior to recognize the central role played by personal values and conflicts among them. In anxiety, we see not only tendencies toward avoidance responses, but also tendencies toward approach responses which, however, pose conflicts of values for the individual. Anxiety is a potent influence in life, not only because of the situations we seek to avoid, but also because of the people and situations we desire to influence. In some situations we may become more anxious over something we want to do to someone else than over what someone else might do to us. In other situations both of these tendencies may occur simultaneously.

It is tempting to think of fear, anxiety, and conflict as always being above the threshold of awareness. It is tempting also to do the same in thinking about attentional processes. The fact, so clearly recognized by Freud, is that this is often more a heuristic paradigm than a reality. As the concentration of fear responses culminates in anxiety, the person becomes, as we have pointed out, more self-preoccupied. These preoccupations will vary from anxious person to anxious person, but one commonality is *self-centering*—focusing attention on one's feelings, thoughts, and inability to cope with the problems of life. Important parameters in the psychological study of anxiety are the degree to which the individual can articulate for himself and for us the causes and content of his self-preoccupations.

Test Anxiety or Fear over Taking Tests?

The question of whether test anxiety is a relatively circumscribed problem or merely a manifestation of a more generalized condition is a logical outgrowth of the preceding discussion. If a person becomes worried about and reacts emotionally toward testing situations, should we describe him as being fearful or anxious? To the extent that eliminating the threat of having to take a test resembles removing a snake from a room, it would seem reasonable to view test anxiety and a snake phobia as being comparable.

This, of course, is not true because it would be relatively easy to live in a snake-free environment, but it is difficult to conceive of a test-free modern world. The snake phobic individual can live in cities (at least, the big ones) from which most big snakes have been eliminated. But there is no comparable place of refuge for the highly test anxious student who is afraid of being evaluated.

Even if there were such an evaluation-free refuge, the student would still have to deal with his ambivalences over being evaluated. Taking and passing evaluational hurdles is correlated with most measures of success in our competitive, industrialized society. Although some people enjoy taking evaluational hurdles, most of us take tests because they are necessary steps toward life goals. This being the case it is perhaps not a misnomer to speak of test anxiety rather than fear of taking tests.

Perhaps also there are two types of test anxiety, that occurring within a context of generalized anxiety and that occurring as a relatively circumscribed problem. In Test Anxiety Type A, a person gets upset before, during, and after tests because of relatively isolated unfortunate experiences (for example, a traumatizing teacher in the third grade). Test Anxiety Type B is characterized by (*a*) anxiety and worry in other areas and (*b*) conflict and ambivalence over achievement and being evaluated. An example of the second type would be the test anxious student who is worried about his social adjustment, preoccupied with the state of his health, and several other indicators of generalized anxiety. In addition, this student might be ambivalent over whether he really wants to become a successful lawyer. At the same time, he may feel anger toward his parents who, he believes, are more interested in his scholastic and occupational successes than in him as an individual. In short, he experiences conflict over his own attitudes and those of his parents.

It seems that research into the problem of test anxiety has not yet examined in sufficient detail the several types of test anxiety. This problem is important both theoretically and therapeutically. With regard to therapeutics, it makes intuitive sense to think that Type A and Type B Test Anxiety respond differently to particular therapeutic approaches. The relatively focalized Test Anxiety Type A might respond positively and quickly to a relatively focalized treatment such as systematic desensitization. The more general Test Anxiety Type B might, on the other hand, require a searching inquiry into the person's values and conflicts and the interrelatedness of his many worries. A study by McMillan and Osterhouse (1972) is interesting in regard to this suggested distinction. These researchers used desensitization as a treatment for test anxiety with two groups of high test anxious college students, those who were or were not high in general, free-floating anxiety (as inferred from scores on the MAS). McMillan and Osterhouse found that their high test anxiety group that was low in general anxiety responded more positively to desensitization than did their high test anxiety, high general anxiety group. Mitchell and Ng (1972) showed that for certain groups of high test anxious college students, a multifaceted treatment program yields superior results to desensitization alone.

Although the numbers are small, recent evidence gathered at the University of Washington Counseling Center are consistent with the findings of McMillan and Osterhouse.[1] Students at this center can avail themselves of a desensitization program designed to reduce test anxiety. It was possible to identify 11 students in the test anxiety desensitization program for whom scores on the writer's TAS and on

[1] I am indebted to Professor John Broedel for providing some of the data required for the comparisons presented here.

the General Anxiety Scale (GAS) were both available (Sarason, I. G., 1972b). In each of the 22 cases the therapist categorized each student at the end of the program as being either improved or not improved. The question of interest was whether general anxiety is related to improvement or nonimprovement. Using local norms, it was found that one of the six students judged to have shown improvement had a score in the upper 25% of the GAS distribution. On the other hand, four of the five students judged not improved had scores in the upper 25% of the GAS distribution.

Not only were the Ns for this comparison very small, but the clinical judgments concerning improvement were also quite subjective. (The judgments, however, were made without knowledge of the GAS scores). Nevertheless, the results are suggestive. It may be that desensitization is the method of choice primarily for focalized fears. The work of Gelder, Marks, and Lader supports consideration of this possibility (Gelder, Marks, & Wolff, 1967; Lader, Gelder, & Marks, 1967). Other approaches, perhaps involving a counseling effort to achieve cognitive change, may be required when a characteristic such as test anxiety is part of a picture of general anxiety. The findings of Katahn, Strenger, and Cherry (1966) suggest that this might well be true.

In this report, I have tried to approach test anxiety within the larger context of the problem of general anxiety. Test anxiety may not simply be an occasional affliction of the student. Even after leaving school, each of us frequently experiences evaluations of our work. Further inquiry is needed into the possible role general anxiety might play as a moderator variable relevant to the effects of test anxiety. While test anxiety is a subjective experience, it does have measurable consequences and, as the research I have reviewed here indicates, it can fruitfully be approached experimentally. An important next step suggested by the theoretical perspective I have presented here is the determination of the personality profiles of people differing in test anxiety and their relationship to behavior under experimental and clinical conditions. A further needed step concerns the social comparison process. The anxious person, as I have suggested, is preoccupied with himself. Research is needed to determine the degree to which this self-centering is a result of social comparisons (with parents, with teachers, with peers) that result in self-devaluation.

REFERENCES

Doctor, R. M., & Altman, F. Worry and emotionality as components of test anxiety: Replication and further data. *Psychological Reports*, 1969, 24, 563–568.

Doris, J., & Sarason, S. B. Text anxiety and blame assignment in a failure situation. *Journal of Abnormal and Social Psychology*, 1955, 50, 335–338.

Easterbrook, J. A. The effect of emotion on cue utilization and the organization of behavior. *Psychological Review*, 1959, 66, 183–201.

Egeth, H. Selective attention. *Psychological Bulletin*, 1967, 14, 41–57.

Epstein, S. The nature of anxiety with emphasis upon its relationship to expectancy. In C. D. Spielberger (Ed.), *Anxiety: Current trends in theory and research*. Vol. 2. New York: Academic Press, 1972.

Gelder, M. G., Marks, I. M., & Wolff, H. H. Desensitization and psychotherapy in the treatment of phobic states: Controlled inquiry. *British Journal of Psychiatry*, 1967, 113, 55–73.

Katahn, M., Strenger, S., & Cherry, N. Group counseling and behavior therapy with test-anxious college students. *Journal of Consulting Psychology*, 1966, 30, 544–549.

Lader, M. H., Gelder, M. G., & Marks, I. M. Palmar conductance measures as predictors of response to desensitization. *Journal of Psychosomatic Research*, 1967, 11, 283–290.

Lazarus, R. S., & Averill, J. R. Emotion and cognition: With special reference to anxiety. In C. D. Spielberger (Ed.), *Anxiety: Current trends in theory and research*. Vol. 2. New York: Academic Press, 1972.

Mandler, G. Stimulus variables and subject variables: A caution. *Psychological Review*, 1959, 66, 145–149.

McMillan, J. R., & Osterhouse, R. A. Specific and generalized anxiety as determinants of outcome with desensitization of test anxiety. *Journal of Counseling Psychology*, 1972, 19, 518–521.

Meichenbaum, D. H. Cognitive modification of test anxious college students. *Journal of Consulting and Clinical Psychology*, 1972, 39, 370–380.

Meichenbaum, D. H., & Goodman, J. Training impulsive children to talk to themselves: A means of developing self-control. *Journal of Abnormal Psychology*, 1971, 77, 115–126.

Mitchell, K. R., & Ng, K. The effects of group counseling and behavior therapy on the academic achievement of test-anxious university students. *Journal of Counseling Psychology*, 1972, 19, 491–497.

Morris, L. W., & Liebert, R. M. Effects of anxiety on timed and untimed intelligence tests. *Journal of Consulting and Clinical Psychology*, 1969, 53, 240–244.

Morris, L. W., & Liebert, R. M. The relationship of cognitive and emotional components of test anxiety to physiological arousal and academic performance. *Journal of Consulting and Clinical Psychology*, 1970, 35, 332–337.

Osterhouse, R. A. Desensitization and study-skills training as treatment for two types of test-anxious students. *Journal of Counseling Psychology*, 1972, 19, 301–307.

Parsons, J. S. Assessment of anxiety about teaching using the teaching anxiety scale: Manual and research report. Paper presented at the 1973 Annual Meetings of the American Educational Research Association.

Phillips, B. N., Martin, R. P., & Meyers, J. School-related interventions with anxious children. In C. D. Spielberger (Ed.), *Anxiety: Current trends in theory and research*. Vol. 2. New York: Academic Press, 1972.

Rachman, S. Clinical applications of observational learning, imitation and modeling. *Behavior Therapy*, 1972, 3, 379-397.

Sarason, I. G. *Personality: An objective approach*. (2nd ed.) New York: Wiley, 1972. (a)

Sarason, I. G. Experimental approaches to test anxiety: Attention and the uses of information. In C. D. Spielberger (Ed.), *Anxiety: Current trends in theory and research*. Vol. 2. New York: Academic Press, 1972. (b)

Sarason, I. G. Test anxiety and the model who fails. *Journal of Personality and Social Psychology*, 1972, 22, 410-413. (c)

Sarason, I. G. Test anxiety and cognitive modeling. *Journal of Personality and Social Psychology*, 1973, 28, 58-61.

Sarason, I. G., & Ganzer, V. J. Effects of test anxiety and reinforcement history on verbal behavior. *Journal of Abnormal Social Psychology*, 1963, 67, 513-519.

Sarason, I. G., Kestenbaum, J. M., & Smith, D. H. Test anxiety and the effects of being observed. *Journal of Personality*, 1972, 40, 242-250.

Sarason, I. G., Pederson, A. M., & Nyman, B. A. Test anxiety and the observation of models. *Journal of Personality*, 1968, 36, 493-511.

Sarason, S. B., Davidson, K. S., Lighthall, F. F., Waite, R. R., & Ruebush, B. K. Anxiety in elementary school children. New York: Wiley, 1960.

Spielberger, C. D. (Ed.) *Anxiety: Current trends in theory and research*. Vol. 2. New York: Academic Press, 1972.

Taylor, J. A. The relationship of anxiety to the conditioned eyelid response. *Journal of Experimental Psychology*, 1951, 41, 81-92.

Taylor, J. A. A personality scale of manifest anxiety. *Journal of Abnormal and Social Psychology*, 1953, 48, 285-290.

Wine, J. Investigations of an attentional interpretation of test anxiety. Unpublished doctoral dissertation, University of Waterloo, 1970.

Wine, J. Test anxiety and direction of attention. *Psychological Bulletin*, 1971, 76, 92-104.

8

CONDITIONED FEAR
AND ANXIETY

H. D. Kimmel

University of South Florida
Tampa, Florida, United States

It is traditional and even sometimes useful to begin presentations of this type by "defining" the more critical concepts to be elaborated, especially those whose names appear in the title. On the premise that a more generous and understanding attitude may be fostered among listeners and potential readers, even though you and they will soon discover that what will be suggested deviates substantially from tradition, a few introductory remarks regarding the present use of "conditioned fear" and "anxiety" may be appropriate. Whether these will serve as acceptable "definitions" must be judged in the context of what is done with them in the following discussion.

"Conditioned fear" is a term that came into vogue in the heyday of Hullian psychology in the United States, principally through the research and writing of Mowrer and N. E. Miller (e.g., Miller, N. E., 1948, 1951; Mowrer, 1939, 1940). Put as simply as possible, "conditioned fear" referred to the emotional component of the unlearned reaction to a painful stimulus, such as an electric shock, which could be conditioned in Pavlovian fashion to a previously indifferent stimulus, such as an innocuous sound or light. For Miller, the fear component was probably part of the total unlearned reaction to pain, i.e., originally part of the unconditioned response. For Mowrer, the fear component was not necessarily already present in the unconditioned pain reaction, but was more likely the anticipatory version of it. Both Miller and Mowrer struggled with the orthodox Hullian dogma, which conceptualized the Pavlovian fear-conditioning process in terms of drive reduction; and both finally shifted to the view that temporal contiguity alone, and not drive reduction, was the essential factor in the acquisition of conditioned fear.

The Hullians were hard pressed in those days to resolve what was called the "avoidance paradox" without at the same time applying the coup de grace to the drive-reduction theory itself. How could drive reduction explain the maintenance of a response such as running from one side to the other of a shuttle box, in the complete absence of the electric shock which presumably had provided the original motivation and reinforcement for the response? By treating the conditioned fear reaction as a *drive* (Miller, N. E., 1951), the Hullians found it logical to appeal to secondary reinforcement (or secondary drive reduction) via removal of the fear stimulus. Thus, the two-factor theory of avoidance learning came into existence and was maintained. (One might almost say that fear was conditioned in the Hullians by virtue of the close temporal contiguity of a stimulus—*the reliable observation of shuttle-box avoidance*—and a strongly established painful stimulus—*empirical jeopardy to Hull's drive-reduction theory*—and this conditioned fear was reduced by the invention of the two-factor theory, which also, then, reinforced and maintained the theory). In any case, Miller's subsequent experimental demonstration that conditioned fear has arousal properties, generating escape from the fear stimulus; that its reduction can motivate the learning of new responses, e.g., wheel-turning in the shuttle box; and that it could provide unique internal stimuli for differential responding, just as could primary drives such as hunger and thirst, firmly and definitively established the conceptualization of conditioned fear as a *state* rather than, say, merely a conditioned response, such as salivation. Vestiges of this tendency are apparent even today, as may be noted elsewhere in this volume.

Almost at the same time that conditioned fear, elicited by a previously innocuous stimulus by repeated pairing with a painful stimulus, was conceptualized as a motivational *state*, a reanalysis of the traditional concept of "anxiety" in terms of the organism's past experience with painful stimuli was also suggested by Mowrer (1939) and others. Mowrer's seminal paper on this subject proposed quite directly that "all anxiety reactions are probably learned," and he based his own position largely on a stimulus-response translation of Freud's treatment of anxiety. Because its influence was so great, and because it will be argued below that it was essentially incorrect in substance, albeit not in spirit, Mowrer's summary of his version of Freud's anxiety hypothesis deserves quotation.

A so-called "traumatic" ("painful") stimulus (arising either from external injury, of whatever kind, or from severe organic need) impinges upon the organism and produces a more or less violent defense (striving) reaction. Furthermore, such a stimulus-response sequence is usually preceded or accompanied by originally "indifferent" stimuli which, however, after one or more temporally contiguous associations with the traumatic stimulus, begin to be perceived as "danger signals", i.e., acquire the capacity to elicit an "anxiety" reaction. This latter reaction, which may or may not be grossly observable, has two outstanding characteristics: (i) it creates or, perhaps more accurately, consists of a state of heightened tension (or "attention") and a more or less specific readiness for (expectation of) the impending traumatic stimulus; and (ii), by virtue of the fact that such a state of tension is itself a form of discomfort, it adaptively motivates the organism to escape from the danger situation, thereby lessening the intensity of the tension (anxiety) and also probably decreasing the chances of encountering the traumatic stimulus. In short, *anxiety (fear) is the conditioned form of the pain reaction*, which has the highly useful function of motivating and reinforcing behavior that tends to avoid or prevent the recurrence of the pain-producing (unconditioned) stimulus [Mowrer, 1939, pp. 554–555, italics in original].

Although Mowrer indicated his awareness of the fact that psychoanalytic writers differentiate between anxiety and fear in terms of whether a consciously perceived object can be identified, and that this distinction may sometimes be useful, he explicitly decided to treat them as synonymous. Behavioristic writers have opted for synonymity of anxiety and conditioned fear ever since (e.g., Brown, 1961; Dollard & Miller, 1950). There are good reasons, however, to reexamine this decision. Most obvious among these is the well-known fact that conditioned fear extinguishes very rapidly when the unconditioned stimulus is removed. In fact, when the galvanic skin response of humans is employed in the study of conditioned fear, merely informing the subject that no more shocks will be administered may suffice to eliminate the conditioned response immediately and totally (Mandel & Bridger, 1973). Whatever "anxiety" actually is, it surely is not so easily dispelled, nor does its repeated elicitation in the absence of painful stimulation result in rapid extinction.

FEAR CONDITIONING AS THE MODEL OF ANXIETY

Even if it were possible to overcome the problem of rapid extinction of conditioned fear responses, for example, by postulating some kind of "anxiety conservation" hypothesis (Solomon & Wynne, 1954), by emphasizing the possibility of broad and relatively flat gradients of generalization of conditioned fear responses, or by assuming a history of extremely intense unconditioned stimuli, there are two lines of argument and evidence which, in my opinion, lead inexorably to the conclusion that conditioned fear, as it is ordinarily construed, cannot serve as an adequate model for either the acquisition of anxiety or for its most commonly described characteristics. First, peripheral autonomic indexes of conditioned fear reactions are not *persistent* even with continued reinforcement. Second, even current trait-state conceptualizations of anxiety appear to require longer term changes in state anxiety than are seen typically in conditioned fear reactions, the latter usually *lasting only a few seconds*. These two issues will be treated separately here.

Conditioned Fear Reactions Are Not Persistent

Research on the acquisition of conditioned fear invariably is built around a Pavlovian (classical) conditioning procedure. One of the principle reasons for this has been the persistent, albeit false, belief that autonomically mediated behavior cannot be modified in any other way (e.g., by instrumental conditioning) (Kimble, 1961; Skinner, 1938, 1953). Basically, the classical method for fear conditioning involves the paired presentation of an initially innocuous stimulus (the conditioned stimulus) with a painful, or at least unpleasant, electric shock (the unconditioned stimulus). The conditioned stimulus typically is turned on shortly before the unconditioned stimulus, and both stimuli terminate together. With human subjects, this procedure rapidly transforms the initially indifferent conditioned stimulus into one capable of eliciting strong sympathetic reactions, such as digital vasoconstriction, decreased skin resistance, pupillary constriction, cardiac acceleration (possibly followed by deceleration, or sometimes deceleration alone), altered respiration rate and pattern, and blood pressure changes, etc. The previously neutral conditioned stimulus produces freezing and cessation of food-motivated lever pressing, interruption of exploration, etc., when it is introduced in previously "safe" environments of subhuman mammals. Eyeblinks and other simple skeletal reactions of humans and subhumans alike, elicited in the presence of conditioned fear stimuli, are intensified.

An essential feature of the classical conditioning procedure is that the experimental subject is unable to influence the likelihood of occurrence of the unconditioned stimulus by making or withholding a response. As Seligman, Maier, and Solomon (1971) have shown, this "uncontrollability" (i.e., the probability of receiving an unconditioned stimulus is identical whether or not a response is made) is a sufficient condition for the development of a behavioral adjustment which they call "learned helplessness." Subjects given preliminary exposure to a series of uncontrollable shocks, during which they gradually cease responding violently to the shocks and begin to assume a supine posture with noticeable muscular flaccidity, show great impairment in their subsequent capacity to acquire an adaptive instrumental avoidance response, when this is made possible. The learned helplessness effect and later inability to learn to prevent controllable shocks are obtained whether or not the shocks are "predictable," as in classical fear conditioning. Even when the presentation of the conditioned stimulus is a "perfect" predictor of the forthcoming unconditioned stimulus, in the sense that the latter is never administered unless preceeded by the former and the former is always followed by the latter, the subject can do nothing to control the occurrence of the unconditioned stimulus.

Learned helplessness is not the result of an acquired skeletal response pattern, since Overmier and Seligman (1967) have demonstrated that preliminary uncontrollable shocks result in impairment in subsequent acquisition of shuttle-box avoidance even when the subjects are completely paralyzed by curare during the preliminary shock session and, therefore, cannot either make or learn to make any kind of skeletal adjustments. What appears to happen is that the subject's capacity to be motivated by conditioned fear (or the conditioned fear itself) is somehow attenuated as a result of the uncontrollability of the shock in the first part of these experiments, so that fear reduction is not available for reinforcement of an avoidance response later on. Even when an occasional successful avoidance occurs, the subject tends not to shift to this adaptive pattern thereafter, but more often returns to helplessness on subsequent trials. This loss of the subject's capacity to come under aversive control has been demonstrated interestingly by A. Amsel (personal communication, 1973), in an experiment in which initial uncontrollable shock was followed by continuously reinforced acquisition and extinction of a straight runway response, with food as reinforcement. The animals that had received preliminary uncontrollable shocks learned the food-motivated runway response quite readily (they were, if anything, easier to handle than control animals) and were *more* resistant to extinction. Amsel interprets this increased resistance to extinction as indicating that the cues of anticipatory frustration (a "cousin" of conditioned fear) are deficient in producing avoidance of the nonreinforced goal box, presumably as a result of the initial series of uncontrollable shocks. Following the runway extinction session, shuttle-box escape avoidance was attempted; but the experimental animals were helpless.[1]

A possible mechanism for the development of learned helplessness in simple classical fear-conditioning situations, based in part upon the combined influence of perfect predictability and complete uncontrollability, has been suggested in some of the work of my students and myself on classical galvanic skin response conditioning in humans (Kimmel, H. D., 1963, 1966, 1971). We have found that repeated, regular pairing of an invariant conditioned stimulus and

---

[1] Amsel also reports a subsequent inability to replicate the avoidance-interference effect in rats that have been shipped by air (inoculation?), suggesting that further study of this phenomenon is needed.

unconditioned stimulus (electric shock) results in initial augmentation of the galvanic skin response to the conditioned stimulus, followed, after only a few such incremental trials, by a decline in the magnitude of both the anticipatory conditioned response and the unconditioned response to the shock. We have called this attenuation of the conditioned galvanic skin response following early acquisition trials "management of fear" (Kimmel, H. D., 1963) and the related reduction of unconditioned response (UCR) strength is referred as "UCR diminution" (Kimmel, H. D., 1966). Subjects given only 16 paired trials following the largest of their acquisition conditioned responses also show extremely rapid extinction compared with subjects whose acquisition is terminated immediately following a reliable indication that the peak conditioned response has been attained. Furthermore, fear management as indexed by UCR diminution is absent in classical autonomic conditioning when predictability is less than perfect, as when a partial reinforcement schedule has been used (Fitzgerald, 1966), or when controllability is made possible, as in autonomic avoidance conditioning of the galvanic skin response (Kimmel, H. D., 1965).

Rather than building up an ever increasing tendency for the conditioned stimulus to evoke strong conditioned autonomic reactions, the classical fear-conditioning procedure provides only a brief, initial opportunity for the impending danger of the unconditioned stimulus to be anticipated emotionally via rapid acquisition of a conditioned fear response. But almost as quickly, the subject adjusts to the uncontrollability of the perfectly predictable shock by ceasing to react autonomically to the conditioned stimulus and even by reducing the vigor of the autonomic reaction to the unconditioned stimulus. This is certainly not the metaphor for the "expecation of trauma" that Freud (1936) thought anxiety is, by means of which a person may ". . . act as if it [the trauma] were already present as long as there is still time to avert it [pp. 149–150]." In classical fear conditioning, in fact, there may be "time" to avert the shock, but the subject is without the behavioral means to do so.

Even if the conditioned fear response is experimentally instrumentalized, following classical fear conditioning, so that its occurence terminates the presumably aversive conditioned stimulus (Kimmel, H. D., & Lucas, 1973), it tends to extinguish just as rapidly as does the conditioned fear response of classically conditioned subjects receiving normal extinction. The only difference between the extinction performances of Kimmel and Lucas' experimental and control groups was that the experimental group tended to make more responses to the *offset* of the conditioned stimulus, but this difference is easily explainable in terms of orienting reactions to the unexpected alterations in duration of the stimulus in the experimental group. In other words, once the classical fear conditioning paradigm has been used, the tendency toward fear management may be so great as to lead inexorably to reduced autonomic responding.

When no response is available to control the occurrence of the unconditioned stimulus, the "perfect predictability" of classical fear conditioning results instead in "manageability" of the conditioned fear reaction (and of the unconditioned reaction as well). It should not be surprising that the mammalian nervous system is capable of so subtle an adaptive adjustment, first, because the energy expenditure associated with making an essentially futile emotional reaction in advance of an uncontrollable electric shock is biologically uneconomical and, second, because the conditioned fear reaction is itself aversive and, solely on this basis, should not persist. Only if the fear response can eventuate in prevention of the impending aversive *unconditioned stimulus*, either directly, as in autonomic avoidance conditioning, or indirectly, by motivating an effective skeletal avoidance response, is there any reason to expect it to endure. Persistent anxiety reactions can hardly be the *direct* result of classical fear conditioning, unless one assumes that an instrumental contingency (resulting in prevention or substantial attenuation of the original unconditioned stimulus) is also somehow involved.

Conditioned Fear Reactions Last Only Briefly

In recent years there has been a growing tendency to distinguish between relatively stable individual differences in anxiety proneness (trait anxiety), measured by a variety of paper-and-pencil and other tests, and the anxiety condition itself (state anxiety), measured by paper-and-pencil tests and/or autonomic indexes (Spielberger, 1972). In my opinion, this movement has had a highly beneficial effect to the extent that it has clarified both semantic and substantive differences between the chronic long-term condition and the acute temporary one. The present discussion is offered in somewhat the same spirit, in the sense that it speaks to still more detailed analysis of the temporal dimensions of emotional reactions. According to

Spielberger (1972), "The term state anxiety is most often used to describe an unpleasant emotional state or condition which is characterized by subjective feelings of tension, apprehension, and worry, and by activation or arousal of the autonomic nervous system [p. 482]." The difficulty here for the classical fear-conditioning model is that even temporary "state" anxiety has a time course far exceeding that of *any* conditioned fear reaction.

When a conditioned fear stimulus is presented, the subject may display a variety of sympathetically mediated autonomic reactions. Although these tend to be considerably "slower," i.e., longer in latency, duration, and recovery time, than skeletal reactions, the entire constellation probably lasts no longer than 10–15 seconds, even when the conditioned stimulus is protracted. A state of relative refractoriness may persist for an additional 15 or 20 seconds, in the sense that a subsequently elicited autonomic reaction is somewhat smaller in strength if it is elicited within 30–40 seconds after a preceeding elicited reaction. But by no stretch of the imagination can the conditioned fear response itself be stretched into the "unpleasant emotional state" called anxiety.

The most obvious reason for this mismatch between the time courses of conditioned fear and anxiety is that the classical conditioning paradigm involves a specific, intermittent conditioned stimulus, to which the autonomic reaction is conditioned. Even if conditioned fear reactions did not extinguish quickly, and even under experimental conditions contrived to prevent the development of fear management, there is no device within the classical conditioning domain by means of which the more or less *phasic* fear reaction can be transformed into a *tonic* state such as anxiety.[2]

Furthermore, the association of the unconditioned stimulus with a *specific* conditioned stimulus in classical conditioning concomitantly involves the possible association of "safety" with the *absence* of the conditioned stimulus. Seligman, Maier, and Solomon (1971) presented evidence to support the argument that subjects learn emotional responses in relation to the probability of shock when the

---

[2] Some writers, such as Konorski (1967), distinguish between the skeletal and emotional components of fear (or defensive) reactions to the same unconditioned stimulus on temporal grounds, the skeletal component being referred to as "phasic" and the slower emotional component as "tonic." There is no conflict involved in the present use of "phasic" for the fear reaction Konorski calls "tonic," since only relative durations are implied by these terms.

conditioned stimulus is present *and* in relation to the probability of shock when the conditioned stimulus is not present. The conventional classical fear conditioning procedure is one in which shock is never presented except when preceded by the conditioned stimulus. At the same time that the subject learns to fear the conditioned stimulus, because it presages the delivery of electric shock, it seems only reasonable to assume that he may learn to not fear the intertrial interval when no stimulus is present. Unsystematic observation of polygraphic autonomic records obtained during classical fear conditioning in human subjects tends to conform to this speculation, since a noticeable reduction in unelicited autonomic activity between trials does seem gradually to develop.

The root problem of the classical fear conditioning model, which renders it finally inadequate as an analytical key to the comprehension of anxiety, is that it is built upon the principle of *certainty;* without the opportunity of *controllability*, *certainty* results in *manageability*. If the conditioned fear response could control the occurrence of the unconditioned stimulus, persistent fear resembling anxiety might be established and adaptively maintained. Without controllability, however, only *uncertainty* is capable of generating a persistent anxiety state. Data in support of this conclusion have been provided recently by Masserman (1971) in a series of studies assessing the role of uncertainty in neurotigenesis in monkeys. Reviewing his earlier position regarding the etiology of neurotic behavior, which was based largely on the concept of biodynamic motivational conflict, Masserman posed the following question: "Are aberrations of behavior induced by conflicts of motivation or adaptation, or does the underlying neurotigenic anxiety arise from the organism's apprehension that impending events may exceed its powers of *prediction* and *control* [1971, p. 13, italics added]?"

After training his animals to vocalize for a prescribed period of time to turn on a light which was followed by food reinforcement, Masserman introduced delayed auditory feedback via the earphones the monkeys were wearing. Even though the response was still effective in producing the light and food, an anxiety reaction was generated by the delayed feedback intervention. When the animals adjusted to the delayed feedback, a return to normal feedback again resulted in an anxiety reaction. This experiment demonstrates that, even without altering controllability, the introduction of uncertainty via delayed feedback is a sufficient condition to produce anxiety.

Another experiment by Masserman may be even more illustrative of the effects of sequential or temporal uncertainty (coupled with uncontrollability) in the genesis of anxiety. The monkey was trained to work a series of five switches and a final lever to obtain food or to avoid shock. The five switches had to be operated in a particular sequence in order to make the final lever response instrumentally effective. After training, the required series or temporal pattern was unpredictably varied. Animals subjected to this type of unpredictability and resulting uncontrollability became highly emotionally disturbed, i.e., anxious, even to the point of refusing to feed or escape.

If Pavlov (1927) had decided to use the term "anxiety" to refer to the famous discovery of Shenger-Krestovnikova (1921), instead of "experimental neurosis," the role of uncertainty in the etiology of anxiety probably would have been fully recognized and analyzed long ago. The observable behavioral changes in a dog that was given successive presentations of a circle and a gradually less eccentric ellipse, following a history of conditioned differentiation of these stimuli by food reinforcement, would probably have been better described as anxiety than as neurosis in the first place, since these changes consisted of trembling, cowering, whimpering, and other dog-like signs of chronic anxiety. It is not insignificant that controllability was not at issue in Shenger-Krestovnikova's experiment, since it used the Pavlovian conditioning procedure. The food was presented in conjunction with the positive conditioned stimulus but not with the negative conditioned stimulus, regardless of what the dog did behaviorally. When the differentiation was established, as evidenced by salivation to the positive conditioned stimulus and not to the negative conditioned stimulus, the negative stimulus gradually was changed from trial to trial in the direction of resembling the positive stimulus. But, since the reinforcement was delivered following the positive conditioned stimulus regardless of whether the dog salivated, it must have been uncertainty that was responsible for the anxiety. The dog simply was denied its earlier opportunity to predict which stimulus would be followed by food and which would not.

It is also important to note that the earlier history of predictability is an essential aspect of genesis of the anxiety which was subsequently produced by unpredictability in Shenger-Krestovnikova's study. This must be so because an experiment in which a circle is reinforced with food and an indiscriminably different ellipse is not would not be likely to result in the development of experimentally produced anxiety, although the acquisition of the classical salivary response would probably not proceed normally. Since, to my knowledge, no experiment of exactly this type has been done, this observation must remain conjectural, albeit reasonable. It should be clear, in any case, that an alternative is needed for the classical fear-conditioning model, if we are to comprehend the manner in which "all anxiety reactions are probably learned (Freud, 1936; Mowrer, 1939)."

AN ALTERNATIVE AUTONOMIC
CONDITIONING MODEL

Previously, it was noted briefly that one of the principal factors underlying the ubiquitous tendency to employ the classical fear-conditioning model to explicate the concept of anxiety has been the pervasive belief that autonomic nervous system processes can only be modified classically. This view was first promulgated by S. Miller and Konorski (1928), in their landmark paper differentiating the two types of conditioning. It was soon embraced by American psychologists, most notably Skinner (1938), Schlosberg (1937), and Mowrer (1947). Even though this belief was based on almost no empirical data, the a priori notion that involuntary autonomic reactions are not instrumental in nature and, therefore, cannot be influenced by contingencies of reward and punishment was so appealing as to be veritably irresistable.

Actually, even though he was mistaken about the possibility of instrumental autonomic conditioning, Skinner laid the foundation for the anxiety-conditioning model proposed here, since it was his work that first emphasized *rate of response* as a significant dependent variable in the study of learning and *unsignaled* operant reinforcement as the means for modifying this measure. Influenced significantly by Skinner's definition of operant behavior, my students and I undertook in 1958 a program of research on instrumental conditioning of the galvanic skin response in humans (Kimmel, H. D., 1967). At first we used the simplest Skinnerian unsignaled operant reinforcement procedure, which basically involved waiting for unelicited responses to occur and following them as closely in time as possible with potentially reinforcing events. What was being conditioned in these studies was not a specific autonomic reaction to a specific stimulus, but the *rate* at which unelicited responses occur. In other words, the change brought about by the conditioning procedure was a change in what might be termed a *chronic* condition, with some subjects showing increases in chronic levels of autonomic activity and others showing decreases. However, since our attention at that time was concentrated on the effect of *reward* training on the rate of unelicited galvanic skin responses, the possible connection between this work and the etiology of chronic anxiety states was not even considered.

When instrumental reinforcement of unelicited autonomic responses is considered as an alternative to the classical fear-conditioning model, not only is the change that occurs capable of being conceptualized as *chronic* rather than *phasic*, it also tends to be both longer lasting than classically conditioned emotional responses and, possibly, more systemically pervasive. For example, DiCara and Miller (1968) rewarded unelicited changes in heart rate in rats with brief electric shocks to reward centers in the brain. Both learned increases and learned decreases in heart rate were retained over a 3-month period with no intervening formal practice. Even though the animals received no explicit additional training, the opportunity for extinction due to removal of reinforcement and presumed occurrence of responses was obviously present. One would expect a stimulus-elicited, classically conditioned autonomic response to extinguish under such conditions. DiCara and Weiss (1969) showed that rats trained to avoid or escape electrical shocks to the tail by increasing their heart rates, later showed poorer learning of shuttle-box avoidance than rats that had been trained to avoid or escape tail shock by decreasing their heart rates. On the assumption that the learned increase in heart rate is analogous to chronic anxiety, the results of this study suggest that this anxiety state interfered with the later learning of a stimulus-specific fear-motivated instrumental response. In addition, DiCara and Stone (1970) reported that rats trained to elevate their heart rates also had higher levels of endogenous norepinephrine, whereas rats trained to lower their heart rates had lower levels of norepinephrine. These findings are consonant with the notion that instrumentally learned elevations in autonomic activity level are analogous to elevations in chronic anxiety both in their obvious chronicity and in their endurance and pervasiveness.

When the results of the initial studies on the unelicited galvanic skin response, augmented by similar findings in other laboratories, using the galvanic skin response, heart rate, and the vasomotor reflex, appeared to establish that instrumental autonomic conditioning in humans is an empirically reliably phenomenon, it seemed reasonable to extend the scope of the work to include varieties of instrumental reinforcement other than simple response-contingent reward. Results from an increasing number of laboratories in the United States, Canada, and Japan showed that human subjects can learn to make anticipatory autonomic responses that prevent electric shock and, also, that response-contingent shock effectively suppresses both elicited and unelicited galvanic skin responses. To be sure, methodological complications arising from the use of yoked control designs and aversive stimuli in many of these studies left many questions not fully answered. But the overall conclusion from this work on instrumental autonomic conditioning using aversive stimulation is in general accord with the more unambiguously positive conclusion regarding the research with reward training.

Unsignalled Escape-and-Avoidance Conditioning of the Unelicited Galvanic Skin Response

In our effort to explicate the mechanism by which response-contingent reward has a reinforcing effect on the rate of occurrence of unelicited galvanic skin responses, we conducted one experiment in which a group of subjects was run completely in the dark and received a 25-minute acquisition period in which a brief light was contingent on unelicited responses, and another group was run with the light on and received brief terminations of it contingent on responses. Yoked controls were run for each group. We thoughtlessly used a circular red light in this study, instead of the dim white light we had used in previous studies, on the naive assumption that one light is as good as another. The results of this study (Kimmel, E., & Kimmel, H. D., 1968) proved how wrong this assumption was. The only group that showed an increase in rate of occurrence of unelicited responses during acquisition was the one whose responses turned the red light *off*. The group that received response-contingent red lights showed a *reduction* in response rate. Furthermore, these changes in chronic levels of autonomic activity persisted throughout the entire 15-minute period of extinction that followed training. In other words, an acquisition period of only 25 minutes' duration, in which the presence of a mild conditioned aversive stimulus, the red light, was made contingent on either responding or nonresponding, effectively produced either decreases or increases in chronic levels of autonomic activity (at least for the 15 minutes of extinction we used). Unfortunately, at that time we were still not thinking of our results in relation to anxiety and, therefore, did not pursue what now appear to be its obvious implications.

Only one other study has been published in which an unelicited autonomic response in humans has been conditioned instrumentally using escape from or avoidance of an aversive stimulus. In this study (Greene & Sutor, 1971) the unelicited galvanic skin response was conditioned on an escape-avoidance schedule. A discriminative stimulus (three horizontally arrayed dots) was employed to determine whether stimulus control of the escape-avoidance response could be attained. Reinforcement was escape from or avoidance of interruptions in music that was presented to the subject. During the presence of the three horizontal dots, the music played continuously as long as interresponse times were shorter than 30 seconds, i.e., a Sidman avoidance schedule was employed. If the subject failed to respond for 30 seconds, aversive interruptions of the music began to occur. Uninterrupted music could then only be restored by a galvanic skin response (i.e., escape), or by a scheduled change from the discriminative stimulus to a control stimulus, three vertically arrayed dots. When the vertical dots were present, some of the subjects were on extinction in the sense that their responses did not influence environmental events (which were either continuous music without interruptions, only interrupted music, or alternating periods of continuous and interrupted music), whereas some were on punishment, with interrupted music made contingent upon unelicited responses. All subjects were studied for 10 consecutive days.

All eight subjects in this experiment made more responses during the periods when interruptions could be avoided and escaped than during the various control periods. This difference increased from the first five to the last five daily sessions in seven of the eight subjects. The difference in response frequency during Sidman avoidance as compared with the control periods was greatest in the subjects who had received response-contingent punishment during the control periods. These subjects also showed the largest change from the first to the last five daily sessions. Examination of their response frequencies under the avoidance and punishment contingencies showed that the increased effect from the first to the last five sessions resulted *not* from a decrease during the punishment contingency but from an *increase* during the avoidance contingency. The intermixture of avoidance and punishment instrumental autonomic contingencies appears to have the effect of elevating avoidance responding, as if by some kind of contrast phenomenon.

The results of Greene and Sutor's (1971) study provide strong evidence that an unelicited autonomic response in humans can be brought under aversive control, via a Sidman avoidance schedule; that this control increases during 10 days of training; and that neutral stimuli may become effective signals for changes in scheduled consequences of responding. When the control stimulus is associated with response-contingent punishment, differentiation between the two schedules is greatest and increases the most with training. The significance of these findings for an alternative to the fear conditioning model of anxiety lies both in its verification of E. Kimmel and H. D. Kimmel's (1968) serendipitous finding of unsignalled escape and avoidance conditioning of an autonomic response in humans and in its demonstration that stimulus control may be superimposed on a basic schedule of aversive control. These two significant facts provide the foundation for a new model of the genesis of anxiety states and even for a possible differentiation between anxiety states that are "normal" and those that are not and between those more or less stimulus or situation bound (e.g., test anxiety) and those that appear to be more free floating.

Unelicited Emotion and Fortuitous Reinforcement

The proposed model is admittedly largely speculative and will require systematic empirical evaluation. However, on the assumption that the simple classical fear conditioning model is demonstrably inadequate, and given that sufficient evidence now is available suggesting that instrumental reinforcement via avoidance may be effective in establishing and maintaining elevated levels of chronic autonomic activation, a sufficient basis exists for such speculation.

Three basic assumptions are involved:

1. That exteroceptively unsignalled aversive anticipations are established, probably by association of *variable* internal stimuli with strong emotion-producing events; these anticipations are not necessarily ideational;

2. That these internal anticipations are capable of eliciting conditioned emotional reactions (i.e., involving acute autonomic changes), whether or not the individual actually has cognitive awareness of them; and

3. That adventitious instrumental reinforcement occurs when these emotional reactions are followed by substantial delay or complete absence of objective pain or insult.

Anxiety is a universal aspect of human existence. The model briefly outlined here suggests that adventitious reinforcement, by avoidance or delay of pain or insult, is likely to strengthen the tendency for "unelicited" emotional responses to occur, and that this should occur in all persons in varying degree. The fact that classically conditioned emotional reactions normally either extinguish or become manageable, and are themselves aversive, probably explains why the modal individual suffers only infrequent and usually mild anxiety states. The more invariant the stimuli initially associated with the original emotion-producing event, the more likely the conditioned emotional reaction will soon extinguish or, at least, become manageable. The greater the variability of the stimuli, the more likely that an instrumental strengthening effect may take hold (Kimmel, H. D., 1973).

Although the first assumption implies a classical conditioning process initially, it is also possible that *innate* "unelicited" emotional anticipations may be involved at this stage. These anticipations may be nothing more than the proprioceptive feedback associated with genuinely "unelicited" discharges of groups of neurons in the hypothalamus. Such feedback may be assumed to be innately aversive, or quickly learned to be aversive because of their normal association with unconditioned painful stimuli. It should also be noted that the classical conditioning process implied differs from ordinary classical conditioning in its emphasis on *variability* of internal conditioned stimuli, in contrast with the usual invariance of classical conditioned stimulus. It is possible, if not likely, that no more than a single pairing of each of many different internal stimuli with such aversive feedback is needed for this initial conditioning of anticipations to occur.

The finding of Greene and Sutor (1971), that alternation of signaled periods of Sidman avoidance with signaled periods of response-contingent punishment of unelicited autonomic responses tends to amplify autonomic unelicited responding during avoidance, may provide an additional key to distinguishing between the etiology of the mild and infrequent anxiety of the modal individual and that of the more intense and frequent anxiety states of a small number of people. Not only did Greene and Sutor's subjects show greater differences between response frequencies in the two conditions, they also showed more growth of these differences during the course of conditioning. This increase in degree of differential responding was not due to a reduction in responding in the punishment condition, but, rather, to an increase in responding in the avoidance condition, i.e., a *contrast* phenomenon. Since it is likely that emotional responses of the "unelicited" type described here are sometimes adventitiously followed closely in time by actual pain, the possibility of intermixed adventitious avoidance and punishment clearly exists. It is likely that the probability of adventitious reinforcement by avoidance and the probability of adventitious punishment of "unelicited" fear would not be totally independent (e.g., a person who experiences more frequent and/or intense pain may be more likely both to emotionally anticipate pain and, thus, gain adventitious avoidance when pain is absent, and occasionally to be punished soon after anticipating pain emotionally). In this case, at least, a hostile environment would be the ultimate villain.

Ordinarily, it would not be expected that periods of avoidance and punishment would be conveniently marked off by discriminative stimuli, as they were in Greene and Sutor's experiment. Under conditions of clear-cut stimulus differences, elevated autonomic activity during avoidance might result in adventitious reinforcement of skeletal behavior as well as autonomic activity, if the skeletal behavior is effective in altering the pattern of ongoing stimulation. This could be the way in which both phobic avoidance and certain compulsive behaviors originate. Without clear-cut stimulus differences which identify avoidance and nonavoidance periods, on the other hand, especially with occasional adventitious punishment of anticipatory fear, free-floating anxiety might develop. This conjecture implies also that the introduction of differentiating stimuli, or the identification of previously unidentified differentiating stimuli, might therapeutically "bind" the anxiety and increase the possibility of its ultimate management.

Systematic empirical evaluation of the proposed model is only in a preliminary stage in our laboratory. We are currently conducting an experiment in which two groups of subjects have been run, one in which unelicited galvanic skin responses are punished by contingent loss of money (indicated on a counter displayed to the subject), and the other in which an equivalent number of punishments are delivered at times of no unelicited responding. In addition to these two groups, a Sidman avoidance group will be run, in which loss of money can be postponed (or prevented entirely) by unelicited responses, along with another matched control receiving an equivalent number of punishments at times of nonresponding. Following the instrumental conditioning phase of this experiment, a classical fear-conditioning phase is introduced. This involves three preliminary presentations of an indifferent auditory stimulus; paired presentations of the auditory stimulus with electric shock; and, finally, extinction tests on the auditory stimulus alone. As should be apparent from the two-phase plan of this study, we are interested both in the establishment of aversive control of unelicited galvanic skin responses, both by direct punishment of nonresponding and by Sidman avoidance, and in the influence of the different instrumental reinforcement schedules on both reactivity to the indifferent auditory stimulus and acquisition of classical fear conditioning. It was expected that subjects who receive punishment for unelicited galvanic skin responses would be less reactive to the auditory stimulus and would show poorer acquisition of classical fear conditioning than subjects who are punished for nonresponding directly or via Sidman avoidance.

Preliminary results on 18 subjects, 9 in the punishment condition and 9 matched yoked controls, indicate that the two groups declined in response rate during the instrumental conditioning phase, but that no difference in group rates of decline was apparent. Nevertheless, the group that received response-contingent punishment during the instrumental phase subsequently made substantially smaller elicited responses to the auditory stimulus during its three initial unpaired presentations than did the yoked controls, who had received the punishment at times of nonresponding. This difference in magnitude of elicited galvanic skin response was statistically significant. During the first three classical conditioning trials that followed, the groups again appeared to differ, with the punished group making smaller conditioned responses than the yoked controls, and with an apparent difference in rate of increase in the size of conditioned responses, again favoring the yoked controls. Unfortunately, these differences between the groups during the beginning of fear conditioning fell short of being statistically significant, probably because of the small group size and large intraindividual variability after shock was introduced. Even on the basis of these meager results, however, it already seems clear that preliminary experimental variations in reinforcement contingencies are effective in generating differences in subsequent autonomic reactivity to neutral stimuli and, possibly, in the rate of acquisition of conditioned fear responses. It is expected that the Sidman avoidance group will be even more reactive to indifferent stimuli and will probably show even more rapid acquisition of conditioned fear. But these data remain to be collected.

As has already been acknowledged, the proposed instrumental conditioning model for the genesis of chronic anxiety states presently must be viewed as hardly more than a promising idea. It is offered in that spirit, and in the hope that others may be stimulated to join us in conducting empirical evaluations of some of its implications. It is our hope that the increased sophistication apparent in the definition and objective measurement of trait and state anxiety will soon be matched by rapid strides in the direction of increased comprehension of how anxiety is learned.

REFERENCES

Brown, J. S. *Motivation of behavior.* New York: McGraw-Hill, 1961.

DiCara, L. V., & Miller, N. E. Long term retention of instrumentally learned heart-rate changes in the curarized rat. *Communications in Behavioral Biology*, part A, 1968, 2, 19–23.

DiCara, L. V., & Stone, E. A. Effect of instrumental heart-rate training on rat cardiac and brain catecholamines. *Psychosomatic Medicine*, 1970, 32, 359–368.

DiCara, L. V., & Weiss, J. M. Heart-rate learning under curare and subsequent noncurarized avoidance learning. *Journal of Comparative and Physiological Psychology*, 1969, 69, 368–374.

Dollard, J., & Miller, N. E. *Personality and psychotherapy.* New York: McGraw-Hill, 1950.

Fitzgerald, R. D. Some effects of partial reinforcement with shock on classically conditioned heart-rate in dogs. *American Journal of Psychology*, 1966, 79, 242–249.

Freud, S. *The problem of anxiety.* New York: Norton, 1936.

Greene, W. A., & Sutor, L. T. Stimulus control of skin resistance responses on an escape-avoidance schedule. *Journal of the Experimental Analysis of Behavior*, 1971, 16, 269–274.

Kimble, G. A. *Hilgard and Marguis' conditioning and learning.* New York: Appleton-Century-Crofts, 1961.

Kimmel, E., & Kimmel, H. D. Instrumental conditioning of the GSR: Serendipitous escape and punishment training. *Journal of Experimental Psychology,* 1968, 77, 48-51.

Kimmel, H. D. Management of conditioned fear. *Psychological Reports,* 1963, 12, 313-314.

Kimmel, H. D. Instrumental inhibitory factors in classical conditioning. In W. F. Prokasy (Ed.), *Classical conditioning: A symposium.* New York: Appleton-Century-Crofts, 1965.

Kimmel, H. D. Inhibition of the unconditioned responses in classical conditioning. *Psychological Review,* 1966, 73, 232-240.

Kimmel, H. D. Instrumental conditioning of autonomically mediated behavior. *Psychological Bulletin,* 1967, 67, 337-345.

Kimmel, H. D. Pathological inhibition of emotional behavior. In H. D. Kimmel (Ed.), *Experimental psychopathology.* New York: Academic Press, 1971.

Kimmel, H. D. Reflex "habituability" as a basis for differentiating between classical and instrumental conditioning. *Conditional Reflex,* 1973, 8, 10-27.

Kimmel, H. D., & Lucas, M. E. Attempted maintenance of the classically conditioned GSR via response-contingent termination of the CS: Negative results. *Journal of Experimental Psychology,* 1973, 97, 278-280.

Konorski, J. *The integrative activity of the brain.* Chicago: University of Chicago Press, 1967.

Mandel, I. J., & Bridger, W. H. Is there classical conditioning without cognitive expectancy? *Psychophysiology,* 1973, 10, 87-90.

Masserman, J. The uncertainty principle in neurotigenesis. In H. D. Kimmel (Ed.), *Experimental psychopathology.* New York: Academic Press, 1971.

Miller, N. E. Studies of fear as a learnable drive: I. Fear as motivation and fear reduction as reinforcement in the learning of new responses. *Journal of Experimental Psychology,* 1948, 38, 89-101.

Miller, N. E. Learnable drives and rewards. In S. S. Stevens (Ed.), *Handbook of experimental psychology.* New York: Wiley, 1951.

Miller, S., & Konorski, J. On a particular type of conditioned reflex. *Proceedings of the Biological Society* (Polish Section). Paris, 1928, 99, 1155-1157.

Mowrer, O. H. A stimulus-response analysis of anxiety and its role as a reinforcing agent. *Psychological Review,* 1939, 46, 553-565.

Mowrer, O. H. Anxiety-reduction and learning. *Journal of Experimental Psychology,* 1940, 27, 497-516.

Mowrer, O. H. On the dual nature of learning: A reinterpretation of "conditioning" and "problem solving." *Harvard Educational Review,* 1947, 17, 102-148.

Overmeir, J. B., & Seligman, M. E. P. Effects of inescapable shock upon subsequent escape and avoidance responding. *Journal of Comparative and Physiological Psychology,* 1967, 63, 28-33.

Pavlov, I. P. *Conditioned reflexes* (Tr. by G. V. Anrep). London: Oxford University Press, 1927.

Schlosberg, H. The relationship between success and the laws of conditioning. *Psychological Review*, 1937, 44, 379–394.

Seligman, M. E. P., Maier, S. F., & Solomon, R. L. Unpredictable and uncontrollable aversive events. In F. R. Brush (Ed.), *Aversive conditioning and learning*. New York: Academic Press, 1971.

Shenger-Krestovnikova, N. R. Contributions to the question of differentiation of visual stimuli and the limits of differentiation by the visual analyzer of the dog. *Bulletin of the Lesgaft Institute of Petrograd*, 1921, 3, 1–43.

Skinner, B. F. *The behavior of organisms*. New York: Appleton-Century, 1938.

Skinner, B. F. *Science and human behavior*. New York: Macmillan, 1953.

Solomon, R. L., & Wynne, L. C. Traumatic avoidance learning: The principle of anxiety conservation and partial irreversibility. *Psychological Review*, 1954, 61, 353–385.

Spielberger, C. D. Conceptual and methodological issues in anxiety research. In C. D. Spielberger, (Ed.), *Anxiety: Current trends in theory and research*, Vol. 2. New York: Academic Press, 1972.

III

COPING WITH STRESS AND ANXIETY

9

MODERN TRENDS IN THE MANAGEMENT OF MORBID ANXIETY: COPING, STRESS IMMUNIZATION, AND EXTINCTION

Isaac Marks

Institute of Psychiatry
University of London
London, England

Anxiety is a normal feature of everyday life. When it is excessive in degree or duration, or occurs without obvious cause, we then speak of morbid anxiety. Such anxiety is one of the most common psychiatric symptoms, and its management is an important clinical problem. In some patients morbid anxiety is often one aspect of a more serious disorder such as schizophrenia or depression; in these cases, the main disorder is treated rather than the anxiety. In other patients, anxiety itself is the dominant problem, and the management of morbid anxiety is the chief matter of concern. The latter type of morbid anxiety is the subject of this report.

In handling clinical anxiety, a careful inquiry needs to be made of the patient's circumstance, to identify possible sources of apprehension. Where such precipitants are found they must be dealt with as conditions allow. Free and open discussion of problems is often sufficient to reduce morbid anxiety. This should be an integral aspect of good clinical care and need not be dwelled on further here.

Another way to relieve morbid anxiety is by the use of sedative drugs such as barbiturates and diazepam (Lader & Marks, 1971).

These drugs have an obvious palliative effect that can be helpful in tiding the patient over a temporary crisis. But the effect of sedatives is not lasting, and when the drug wears off the anxiety reasserts itself. Although the operative process that produces anxiety is damped down, the circumstances that give rise to the anxiety have not been changed. Furthermore, a proportion of anxious subjects become addicted to their sedative drugs, and others are able to reduce their anxiety only by taking such large doses that their everyday functioning is impaired. Whereas modified leucotomy is of lasting value in relieving general anxiety in some patients (Marks, Birley, & Gelder, 1966; Tan, Marks, & Marset, 1971), such methods are not justified except in a tiny proportion of the most extremely handicapped people.

The most effective methods for the lasting reduction of abnormal anxiety are psychological techniques of varying kinds. Many advances have been made in this sector in the last few years. With these techniques, anxiety is cued off or initiated by triggers in the environment, where the intensity of the anxiety state is disproportionate to the precipitating events (situational anxiety). This type of morbid anxiety is found in phobic and obsessive-compulsive disorders. In contrast, virtually no advance has been demonstrated in the psychological treatment of free-floating (nonsituational) anxiety. Unfortunately, this type of anxiety is the kind most often encountered in clinical practice.

In the history of fear-reducing methods, there has been a great deal of interplay between several theoretical schools and between the laboratory and common sense. Similar techniques have their origin in schools as diverse as learning theory, psychoanalysis, and existentialism. The fact that the same methods have often been generated by different theories would appear to owe at least as much to empirical trial and error and serendipity as to formal theory. Recently, however, there has been increasing controlled experimentation with treatments both in the clinic and the laboratory, with mutual enrichment. The techniques employed to reduce fear have come to be described, more or less, in the language of "learning theory," whatever their original pedigree.

Let us outline the approach to situational anxiety, examine the principles involved, and see how the application may be extended from situational to nonsituational anxiety.

SYSTEMATIC DESENSITIZATION

Of the many methods that have a significant effect in reducing morbid anxiety, most techniques expose the person to the stressful situation until he gets used to it. This process is variously called extinction, habituation, or deconditioning. The earliest and still the most often used method of this genre is systematic desensitization. With this technique the subject is taught to relax his muscles and, while relaxed, to imagine himself in a situation that is only minimally stressful; e.g., a bird phobic might be asked to imagine herself seeing a bird 100 yards away in a cage. The patient is asked to visualize the same scene several times until it occasions no anxiety, after which a slightly more stressful scene is imagined by the patient.

The original theoretical explanation for desensitization was that it acts by reciprocal inhibition (Wolpe, 1958). According to this theory, the potent ingredient in the procedure was the neutralization of anxiety during the imagining of phobic scenes by antagonistic responses such as muscular relaxation. Although the evidence is somewhat conflicting, a surge of articles in the last few years indicates that reciprocal inhibition occurs only exceptionally. Indeed, the effectiveness of desensitization is not generally impaired when muscular relaxation is omitted from the procedure.

In a study by Benjamin, Marks, and Huson (1972), 16 phobic outpatients were given a 50-minute preliminary session of relaxation training. Eight of these patients were then treated by six sessions of desensitization in fantasy, followed by six sessions of exposure in fantasy; the other eight patients had the reverse. In both conditions, patients visualized phobic images in a hierarchy, for 20 seconds at a time, with 50-second intervals between images. Each image in the hierarchy was visualized five consecutive times. Each session was 50 minutes long, given twice weekly. During desensitization, patients were relaxed before and after each image, and during exposure they looked at a neutral slide instead. Between phobic images, skin conductance activity was significantly lower during relaxation than during observation of the neutral slide. The patients, the therapist, and a "blind" assessor each rated the main phobia as significantly improved for both treatments together, and each treatment made a similar contribution to improvement during and after the treatment sessions, on measures of the main phobia, subjective anxiety, and heart rate.

CHANGE WITH SUCCESSIVE IMAGES

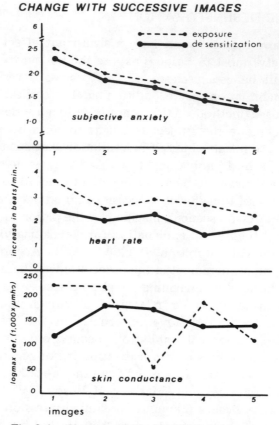

Fig. 9-1. Changes within sessions in eight out-patients treated by imagining phobic scenes up a hierarchy with relaxation (desensitization) and without (exposure). Each scene was imagined five times. The graph shows the mean change over the five scene presentations (pooled mean combining all hierarchy items, i.e., all sets of five images). Within-sessions subjective anxiety with each image decreased significantly—the decrease was as fast without as with relaxation. Physiological changes were also similar in both conditions. Improvement from start to end of treatment was equally fast with and without relaxation. (Reprinted by permission from S. Benjamin, I. M. Marks, & J. Huson, The role of active muscular desensitization. *Psychological Medicine*, 1972, 2, 381–390.)

Figure 9-1 shows the changes accompanying the presentation of phobic images in sets of five during each session. The graph depicts the mean decrement over all sets of images, pooling the hierarchy items. The trend was already obvious before crossover, before any interactional effects could have occurred. Although the relaxed group was significantly less aroused on a skin conductance criterion during treatment sessions, nevertheless this did not speed their improvement, which progressed at the same rate in the relaxed and nonrelaxed sessions. Relaxation training thus appeared redundant to the procedure of desensitization in fantasy.

When relaxation is left out of desensitization, the latter can be construed as a process of repeated brief exposure to phobic imagery, starting with items that are only slightly anxiety provoking and working up eventually to the most terrifying ones. There is now evidence that such graduation of approach is not essential for fear to decrease and that improvement occurs at a similar rate whether one goes up, down, or randomly across the hierarchy (Welch & Krapfl, 1970). Several studies have shown (e.g., Mathews, 1969) that during the presentation of phobic imagery, physiological arousal occurs to a similar degree whether or not relaxation is present.

Desensitization in fantasy is useful mainly for subjects with focal anxiety and is of little benefit for patients with a great deal of free-floating anxiety. Furthermore, because the method is slow, a search was made for other techniques of fear reduction. In the procedure known as "flooding," the patient is literally thrown into the deep end; he is confronted with the phobic situation—either in fantasy or in real life. For example, a bird phobic may be asked to imagine himself being in a room with several birds, and gradually approaching and touching them within a few minutes or an hour. The speed of anxiety reduction with this approach is more rapid than in desensitization. In this procedure, no emphasis is given to processes such as relaxation; and the element of exposure to the phobic object is obvious. Less obvious is the optimum pace at which exposure should proceed and what part subjective anxiety plays in improvement. Anxiety provocation itself may not be the crucial element for the reduction of avoidance behaviour during exposure. Exposure to the phobic situation seems more important (Marks, Marset, & Boulougouris, 1971; Watson, Gaind, & Marks, 1971; Watson & Marks, 1971).

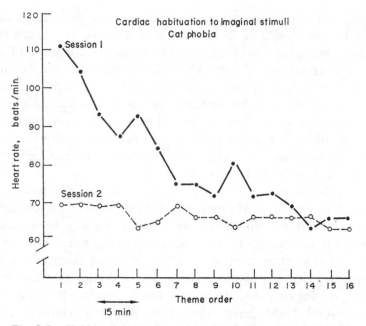

Fig. 9-2. Habituation to exposure in fantasy: A cat-phobic patient was flooded (exposed) in fantasy over two 2-hour sessions by the therapist describing her contact with cats in varying themes, each theme lasting 7.5 minutes. Tachycardia disappeared by the end of the first session and did not recur in session 2. (Reprinted by permission from J. P. Watson, R. Gaind, & I. M. Marks, Physiological habituation to continuous phobic stimulation. *Behaviour Research and Therapy*, 1972, **10**, 269–278.)

Contact with the real-life situation appears to be more effective than contact with imaginal scenes only. Evidence for this is still indirect, though direct tests are currently under investigation. The first datum in support of this idea is that trials of flooding in fantasy alone (Watson & Marks, 1971) have produced less improvement than those which have also incorporated flooding in real life (Marks et al., 1971; Stern & Marks, 1973; Watson, et al., 1971).

Other data come from single-case studies. Patients who have lost their anxiety to images of phobic objects during flooding in fantasy still show great anxiety when confronted with the real phobic situation. Figure 9-2 shows an example, taken from Watson et al. (1972), of a patient who was handicapped in her everyday activities by a severe phobia of cats. She was flooded in fantasy by being asked to imagine herself in contact with cats in a variety of ways, the scenes being presented as several themes, each of 7.5 minutes' duration. This patient showed tachycardia at the start of the first session. By the end of 2 hours this had diminished significantly from the first theme to the last ($p < .001$), independently of themes, so that by the end of the 2-hour session heart rate was normal. During the second 2-hour session of flooding in fantasy, there was no tachycardia.

Nevertheless, at the end of the second fantasy session the patient showed tachycardia as soon as she saw live cats 6 feet away (Fig. 9-3). As these were gradually brought nearer to her, and she was

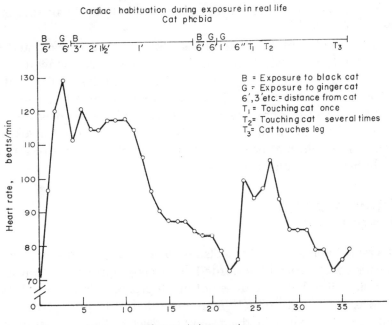

Fig. 9-3. Habituation to phobic images does not necessarily imply habituation to real-life phobic stimuli. Immediately following the fantasy flooding of session 2 in Fig. 9-2, live cats were brought near the patient. This resulted in recrudescence of tachycardia which subsided with continuing contact over the next 35 minutes. The real-life exposure continued for another hour (not shown), during which the patient fondled cats without tachycardia. Subjective anxiety also disappeared. (Reprinted by permission from J. P. Watson, R. Gaind, & I. M. Marks, Physiological habituation to continuous phobic stimulation. *Behaviour Research and Therapy*, 1972, **10**, 269–278.)

encouraged to play with them, her tachycardia disappeared. At the start of real-life exposure to a black cat 6 feet away for 1 minute, her heart rate increased from 70 to 96 after 30 seconds and to 120 after 60 seconds. The patient's heart rate did not return to normal during the minute's rest which followed and which preceded similar exposure to a ginger cat, during which the heart rate reached 120. After 15 minutes of progressive approach to the black cat as fast as she could tolerate, the patient was able to look at the cat one foot away. After this, looking at both cats 6 feet away evoked no tachycardia or subjective anxiety. Twenty-five minutes after the start of real-life exposure, the patient was able to touch the cats. By the end of 90 minutes' exposure in real life, there was no tachycardia despite the handling of cats over the preceding hour, heart rate being about 70/minute.

Outside treatment the patient also lost her fear of cats, and this improvement was maintained during a 3 months' follow-up. This patient's course is fairly typical. In general, fantasy treatment by exposure is now reserved for patients who are unable to tolerate the thought of real-life exposure at the beginning and so need preliminary improvement with fantasy treatment first, and for patients whose real-life phobic situations are particularly difficult to arrange, e.g., phobias of thunderstorms or sex.

OPERANT SHAPING AND MODELING

Operant-shaping procedures also reduce fear. With this method the subject is systematically rewarded for steady approach towards the phobic situation. When he does not make progress, praise is withheld; but moves in the right direction are rewarded. It is quite obvious that during operant treatment the therapist never shapes behaviour away from the phobic situation. An integral part of the procedure thus consists of graduated exposure.

The same applies to treatment by modeling (Bandura, Blanchard, & Ritter, 1969; Ritter, 1969). In the modeling procedure, the subject watches somebody deal with an anxiety-provoking situation either on film or in real life, the real life modeling being more effective. In an experiment by Bandura et al. (1969), the live model slowly approached a snake while being observed by a snake phobic. The snake phobic was then encouraged and cajoled into executing the same task. The procedure was thus, essentially, exposure in vivo after a model. A study by Meichenbaum (1971) showed that a coping model is better than a mastering model; i.e., it is more effective for the model first to show signs of anxiety and then to show the onlooker how he deals with his anxiety, step by step, rather than to appear fearless from the start.

Phobic anxiety can also be reduced by subjects rehearsing instructions to other phobics on how to overcome their fears (Hart, 1966). In this process the subject rehearses imagery concerning phobias. Other methods of reducing fear similarly involve exposure to distressing situations. Paradoxical intention (Frankl, 1960) is very similar to straight exposure in vivo. Frankl described an obsessive-compulsive patient with fears of contamination by dirt. This patient was asked first to watch the doctor dirtying his hands on the floor and then touch his face, and was then instructed to do the same. The idea is to tempt one's worst fears and see that the consequences do not materialize. This procedure is similar to modeling with exposure in vivo, which has proved so effective with obsessive-compulsive rituals (Hodgson, Rachman, & Marks, 1972; Rachman, Hodgson, & Marks, 1971).

USE OF DRUGS WITH PSYCHOLOGICAL TREATMENTS

Sedative drugs have been used to facilitate the contact of patients with their anxiety-producing situations. These have been given intravenously as methohexitone (Friedman & Lipsedge, 1971; Mawson, 1969) or orally with diazepam (Marks et al., 1972). There are many problems with regard to the best procedure for administering the drug (oral or intravenous), what class of drug to use, and how to time the exposure with reference to drug administration. Most drug effects seem to incorporate the element of exposure. Tricyclic drugs like imipramine (Klein, D. F., 1964; Klein, R., & Klein, D. F., 1971) for agoraphobia and school phobia have also been combined with firm insistence on contact with the phobic situation. Klein has suggested that there might be a synergistic action in which the antidepressants relieve the affective component of the disorder (e.g., nonsituational panics) and thus allow easier exposure to the distressing situation.

RELEVANT AND IRRELEVANT
FEAR DURING EXPOSURE

Although many of the newer methods of treatment can thus be seen as acting through a common mechanism, we are still unclear how best to apply them. We know that prolonged exposure in vivo for several hours at a time is usually a highly effective method of reducing fear with long-lasting effect (Stern & Marks, 1973). But we do not know whether this effect would be even greater were we to deliberately induce anxiety during exposure instead of simply allowing it to emerge as an inevitable and unfortunate byproduct of contact.

If anxiety is beneficial, a further question arises: Should the anxiety be relevant or irrelevant to the phobic situation? Watson & Marks (1971) showed that both relevant and irrelevant fear cues significantly reduce phobias, but these seem to act through different mechanisms. In this experiment, phobic patients were asked to imagine themselves in one of two kinds of frightening situations. The first was a phobic situation relevant to the patient; e.g., an agoraphobic was asked to imagine herself shopping in a crowded supermarket, feeling faint and dazed while people stared at her. The other condition involved an irrelevant fear that had nothing to do with the phobia; e.g., patients were asked to imagine themselves being chased by a tiger that had escaped from the local zoo. If flooding or exposure results in a specific extinction procedure, then only the relevant exposure in imagination should produce improvement. In fact the relevant and irrelevant fear cues produced an equal and significant amount of improvement (Fig. 9-4), which suggested that fear can be reduced by processes other than specific extinction.

Three findings from the study by Watson and Marks suggested that exposure to relevant and irrelevant fear cues in fantasy operate to reduce fear through different mechanisms. First, the amount of anxiety experienced *during* irrelevant fear induction correlated positively with outcome, but the anxiety experienced to relevant flooding did not. The amount of anxiety evident in a session can be regarded as an indirect index of catharsis; therefore, some justification exists for regarding the irrelevant fear treatment as an abreactive therapy. Since anxiety during relevant flooding did not correlate with outcome, relevant flooding does not seem to act through this mechanism.

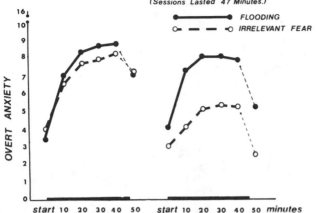

SESSIONAL ANXIETY II: *MEAN OVERT ANXIETY AT DIFFERENT TIMES DURING SESSIONS.*
(Sessions Lasted 47 Minutes.)

Fig. 9-4. Equal improvement with relevant and irrelevant fear imagery. Sixteen phobic patients had eight sessions of relevant flooding imagery followed by eight sessions of irrelevant fear imagery, or vice versa. Sessions were 50 minutes long. Patients improved equally with each treatment condition, both before and after cross-over. (Reprinted by permission from J. P. Watson & I. M. Marks, Relevant and irrelevant fear in flooding: A crossover study of phobic patients. *Behavior Therapy*, 1971, **2**, 275-293.)

Next, in the cross-over design, patients who first had the irrelevant fear ("tiger") treatment followed by relevant flooding experienced similar degrees of anxiety *during* both kinds of treatment sessions. In contrast, patients who first had relevant flooding followed by irrelevant fear treatment experienced less anxiety during the irrelevant fear sessions than in the relevant fear condition (Fig. 9-5). "Tiger" treatment did not reduce subsequent anxiety with the phobic stimulus, but relevant flooding did protect against subsequent excessive anxiety during irrelevant fear. This suggests that the relevant fear treatment teaches a more general coping set than does irrelevant fear, a finding that is the opposite to what one might have predicted.

The final discriminating prognostic factor was that the amount of anxiety patients had *before* treatment correlated positively with outcome to treatment with relevant flooding, but was unrelated to outcome with irrelevant fear treatment.

The finding of three differential prognostic items suggests that relevant and irrelevant treatment conditions produce equal

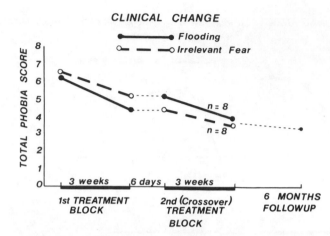

Fig. 9-5. Though patients improved equally with relevant and irrelevant fear imagery suggested by the therapist, other evidence indicated the two treatment conditions operated through different mechanisms. This is shown by the anxiety experienced by phobic patients during treatment sessions. The two treatment conditions produced equal anxiety during sessions in the first treatment block before cross-over, but in the second treatment block (after cross-over) subjects who previously had relevant flooding had less sessional anxiety during irrelevant fear treatment. (Reprinted by permission from J. P. Watson & I. M. Marks, Relevant and irrelevant fear in flooding: A crossover study of phobic patients. *Behavior Therapy*, 1971, 2, 275-293.)

improvement through different mechanisms, but these processes need not be mutually exclusive. If one combined both relevant and irrelevant stress experiences in phobic patients, the benefits possibly would be maximized.

Phobias are complicated sets of responses that consist of avoidance, physiological arousal in several dimensions, and subjective anxiety. Each component may vary according to the precise stimulus properties of the phobic situation at a given time. Furthermore, the various component responses might each be extinguishable independently, with only partial generalization from one to the other. It follows that the most wide-ranging improvement might be obtained by confronting the phobic with his frightening situation without allowing avoidance so that avoidance is extinguished, and also by deliberately inducing anxiety concerning the phobic object to extinguish subjective discomfort as well as avoidance. In addition, by inducing irrelevant anxiety and other unpleasant emotions, the patient can be taught how to cope with other unpleasant affects. Meichenbaum (1971) showed that phobic volunteers overcame their anxiety even better when desensitization was combined with deliberate attempts by the subject to manage the discomfort induced by electric shocks.

Perhaps the message is that the more the patient is exposed to discomfort and anxiety, the more he learns to tolerate, *provided he is agreeable to this procedure.* Obviously there must be limits to this approach, and much work is required to delineate the conditions under which it applies. Theoretically, under certain conditions the patient might be sensitized to anxiety instead of habituated.

EFFECT OF DURATION
OF EXPOSURE

Why should exposure to noxious stimuli lead to the development of phobias under certain circumstances and elimination of phobias under others? One important variable is duration. In general, long duration of exposure appears more effective than short periods, as was found in a study by Stern and Marks (1973). In a Latin-square design, 16 chronically agoraphobic outpatients had four sessions of long or short flooding in fantasy and in practice. Exposure in fantasy always preceded exposure in practice. During exposure in practice, patients went into their phobic situation (e.g., crowded bus or shop) near the top of the hierarchy and stayed there for the required time, first with the therapist, who subsequently faded from the scene. The fantasy sessions were given by tape recorder and produced minimal arousal with little improvement. In previous studies, which obtained significant arousal during phobic imagery and improvement from fantasy flooding, the instructions were delivered by a therapist facing the patient and speaking to him in a normal voice (Marks et al., 1971; Watson et al., 1971; Watson & Marks, 1971). Apparently, patients pay more attention to the normal voice of a nearby therapist than to a tape-recorded instruction using the same words.

In contrast to the fantasy sessions, 2 hours of exposure in practice reduced phobias significantly more than did four half-hour periods of the same procedure in one afternoon (Fig. 9-6). During long flooding in practice, heart rate and subjective anxiety decreased more over the

Composite Change Score Means (n=16)

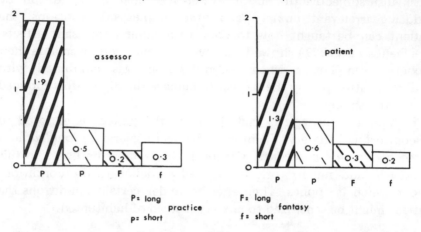

Fig. 9-6. Change in main phobia after treatment of 16 agoraphobics. Ratings by patient and by a "blind" assessor both showed that long exposure in practice (P) for 2 hours at a time was significantly superior to short exposure in practice (p) for four half-hour periods on the same afternoon ($p < .05$ and $p < .01$, respectively). Exposure in practice was significantly superior to exposure in fantasy (F = long, f = short). (Reprinted by permission from R. S. Stern & I. M. Marks, A comparison of brief and prolonged flooding in agoraphobics. *Archives of General Psychiatry*, 1973, 28, 269-276.)

second than the first hour of exposure to the real phobic situation. Though treatment was directed towards top hierarchy items, bottom items improved more. Implications for clinical practice are that exposure should proceed to the stage of prolonged real life confrontation as quickly as possible. The period of 2 hours may be a guideline for chronic patients such as the ones used in this study, whose phobias were all of more than 1 year's duration. For phobias of recent onset, shorter periods of exposure might still be effective. One wonders, however, how far the efficacy of long duration can be extrapolated—perhaps 4 hours are better than 2, 8 hours than 4, and so on, but the limits of this phenomenon remain to be defined experimentally.

Although very brief exposure with avoidance allowed may actually be sensitizing at times, several workers have found therapeutic effects from brief exposure with instructions by the therapist to escape from anxiety (Crowe, Marks, Agras, & Leitenberg, 1972; Everaerd, Rijken,

& Emmelkamp, 1972). Perhaps the fact of escape or avoidance is less important than whether it is initiated by the patient or by the therapist. The locus of control may decide whether escape/avoidance reinforces the phobia, and avoidance or escape initiated by the patient may have more damaging effects than that instructed by an external agent such as a therapist.

It is not clear why prolonged sessions are more potent than shorter ones. The duration of exposure as such may be less important than that of intervals between exposure. Incubation effects are important in the acquisition of fear in animals (Kamin, 1963) and may be important in the extinction of fear in humans. Cognitive rehearsal between periods of exposure might affect incubation processes, but clarification of this point needs further experimentation.

Another possibility is that prolonging sessions increases the chances that some other critical but unknown process may occur that facilitates improvement. A similar idea might lie behind the emphasis on reaching the point of emotional exhaustion during abreaction of war neuroses (Sargant, 1957).

The duration of optimum exposure may well vary from one person to another, and the optimum criterion for termination of a session is unknown. Perhaps this occurs when all components of the phobic response have subsided, i.e., subjective anxiety, attitude, and physiological arousal. Moreover, it might be more important for a patient to end a session on a good note of improvement rather than to simply have a prolonged session as such.

COPING SETS AND MATURATION

Patients commonly say that they have had experiences during which they were exposed to the phobic situation for an hour or more before they came to treatment, and yet were more anxious after that experience. Close enquiry generally reveals that during such exposure, patients were rehearsing internal avoidance responses throughout the exposure; e.g., they were saying to themselves, "I want to get out, I want it to end, help." During treatment, patients are taught a "coping set"—"I must stay here until I am used to it." Of course, variables like a "coping set" are difficult to investigate.

Clinical experience suggests that coping sets alone do not explain the failure of some patients to habituate even with very prolonged exposure in vivo to the situations that occasion them discomfort. The author has encountered a small minority of people who seemed to have a good prognosis for treatment of their phobias or obsessions with real-life exposure. They cooperated fully in treatment, carried out all therapeutic instructions faithfully, and gave no evidence of avoidance of their discomfiting situations, either externally or cognitively. Furthermore, their personalities were stable, and no excessive secondary gain could be discerned from their problem. Nevertheless, they failed to show any decrement of anxiety or rituals despite exposure for periods of up to 7 hours or longer. Clearly there are critical conditions for exposure to be effective of which we have little knowledge at present.

Motivational influences play a crucial role in deciding whether subjects will expose themselves to stressful situations inside and outside treatment. Subjects who will not cooperate in stressful treatments such as exposure in vivo are extremely difficult to treat. Group experiences might help certain patients to undergo exposure treatment. Hand, Lamontagne, and Marks (1974) showed that agoraphobics could be successfully exposed in vivo in groups of four to five patients at a time. Such exposure had greatest effects in the long run if the groups were structured to be socially cohesive, so that patients could share helpful experiences and encourage one another to perform difficult tasks of exposing themselves to stressful situations in everyday life.

In the study by Hand et al. (1974), 25 outpatients with chronic agoraphobia were treated in six groups of 4–5 patients each. Each patient had 12 hours of exposure in vivo, spread over 3 days of 1 week. Three groups were structured to increase social cohesion during exposure in vivo. This was enhanced by symptom-centred discussions before, during, and after treatment sessions. Three other groups were unstructured so that members were exposed with a minimum of group influence. The structured groups became significantly more cohesive than unstructured groups on five measures (together $p < .0001$, Fig. 9-7), though some cohesion developed spontaneously in all groups. Therapists found it easier to run the cohesive groups.

On behavioural tests and clinical scales, outcome of the main phobia for all groups was at least as good as in previous trials with individual patients. Shortly after treatment, the patients from structured and unstructured groups showed similar improvement.

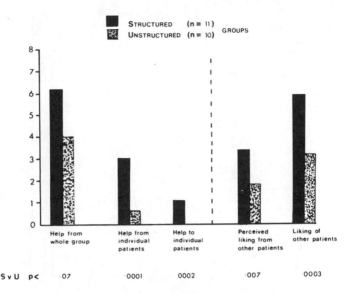

DURING TREATMENT SESSIONS

GROUP COHESION: PATIENT – PATIENT INTERACTION

Fig. 9-7. Increased group cohesion through structuring group experiences before, during, and after group exposure in vivo. Measures are ratings of interactions by patients with one another during treatment sessions. Significance of differences between structured (S) and unstructured (U) groups appear below each measure. (Reprinted by permission from I. Hand, Y. Lamontagne, & I. M. Marks, Group exposure [flooding] in vivo for agoraphobics. *British Journal of Psychiatry*, 1974, 124, 588–602.)

However, in a 3–6 months' followup the structured groups had become significantly better (Fig. 9-8, $p < .006$ to $< .07$ on varying raters). Social cohesion thus facilitated improvement in patients given group exposure in vivo.

Treatment also produced unexpected additional gains in social skills and assertion in patients who began with social anxieties. They became more able to talk about their problems, to look at other people in buses or trains, to ask strangers for directions in the street, and to eat in restaurants with other people. These situations all had to be dealt with as part of treatment exercises during exposure in vivo. Marital complications were frequent in patients before and after

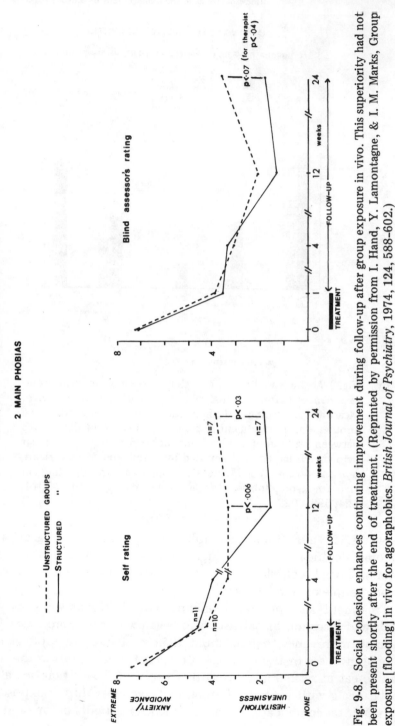

Fig. 9-8. Social cohesion enhances continuing improvement during follow-up after group exposure in vivo. This superiority had not been present shortly after the end of treatment. (Reprinted by permission from I. Hand, Y. Lamontagne, & I. M. Marks, Group exposure [flooding] in vivo for agoraphobics. *British Journal of Psychiatry*, 1974, 124, 588–602.)

treatment, but the group improved significantly in work, leisure, and social adjustments.

Another point to emerge from the study by Hand et al. (1974) was how weak a measure are behavioural-avoidance tests. Patients were sometimes able to perform well on an avoidance task during testing, even though they continued avoiding similar situations in everyday life. More dependable guides to progress were clinical scales that measured avoidance and anxiety in a variety of everyday situations over several days (Gelder & Marks, 1966; Watson & Marks, 1971). A behavioural-avoidance test by itself is inadequate as a measure of change in experiments on fear and must be combined with other ratings for meaningful conclusions to be drawn. Ideally it should be combined with measures of behaviour and subjective feelings during confrontation with the phobic situation in everyday life, and if possible with psychophysiological changes during such confrontation. Attitude measures are an additional guide to subjective feelings.

ABREACTION

The exposure hypothesis does not explain one important set of phenomena: the relief of fears and other problems after abreaction, not only of fear but also of anger, guilt, and other affects. Unfortunately, evidence in this area is nearly all anecdotal, and experimental data is badly needed. Clearly, relief of phobias after abreaction of anger does not neatly fit the exposure hypothesis. Though the analytic concept of defense against aggression might spring to mind here, this too fails to explain all the facts available. Perhaps we will find eventually that exposure to noxious stimuli can lead to improvement under many conditions, but that other mechanisms, so far unknown, can also be therapeutic. Science has its growing points where hypotheses do not quite fit all the facts, as is true here.

Concepts like coping are seductively appealing, but adequate tests of hypotheses about these variables are extremely difficult to devise. When is a patient's response a coping response and when is it not? The difficulties become clear when we try to devise an experiment to show that an *anti*coping set will not benefit the subject. If one gives an anxious patient an instruction that when he next panics he should deal with his anxiety by staying in the situation, breathing deeply to calm himself, counting slowly, and watching how long it takes for the panic to subside, this can be called coping. If one tries to give an *anti*coping set and instructs the patient when he next panics to rehearse escaping from the situation, screaming and the like, this paradoxical intention may serve as a distraction which can be equally helpful in keeping the patient in the situation. Even instructing the patient to leave his phobic situation as soon as he feels anxious can be therapeutic (Crowe, et al., 1972; Everaerd et al., 1972). Scientific advance depends on testable concepts; coping has to be made more precisely testable if it is to be of further value.

The same applies to the idea of stress immunization, although here it is a bit easier in that one might define the procedure as one in which the patient undergoes a stressful experience with the express intention of learning to live through other stresses in the future. Extinction, too, is a tantalizing but nebulous idea. If a patient's phobic experience is repeated and the patient does not respond to it, one can say that he extinguishes, habituates, or adapts to that stimulus. On the other hand, if his responses increase after repeated experience of the stimulus, we say that he sensitizes. Since apparently similar situations produce sensitization at times and extinction at other times, the mystery remains. The labels are useful in a purely descriptive and not in an explanatory sense.

The foregoing problems also arise in interpretation of the ingenious experiments of Meichenbaum (1971). He showed that subjects who give themselves positive self-statements to relax and deal with the situation reduce their fear. It has to be shown that negative self-statements are not therapeutic; it still has to be demonstrated that the content of the self-instruction is important. This experiment has not been done, but is obviously essential to elucidate the mechanism at work. If negative self-statements are also therapeutic, then improvement may have more to do with the set to grit one's teeth and bear it, or endure, or abandon oneself to the experience, than with the content of the self-instructions per se. Alternatively, simply talking to oneself might be therapeutic regardless of what one says.

Most of the work discussed so far has concerned situational anxiety. Free-floating nonsituational anxiety requires more controlled enquiry for meaningful principles of management to emerge. Bonn (1971) described the use of "chemical flooding" in anxiety states. Patients were given intravenous infusions of molar sodium lactate, and within a few minutes experienced anxiety-like phenomena which could continue for several hours, after which they felt better. The idea is interesting, but conclusions are difficult from his uncontrolled series. It is worthwhile undertaking controlled examination of the contributions of lactate versus saline infusions and lactate-induced anxiety versus psychologically induced flooding of patients with anxiety states in designs which allow long-term follow-up of effects. In anxiety states, much more work is needed on the possibilities of stress inoculation by psychological means and anxiety management training in the manner that has been used in phobias.

It is fascinating to speculate on the possible preventive contribution of present forms of fear reduction to normal living. Perhaps stress immunization techniques can be built into methods of child rearing so that the chances of morbid anxiety developing in later adult life are lessened. Anecdotal accounts of such educational methods were described in a tribe in Malaya 30 years ago (Stewart, 1935). This problem concerns the fields of child psychology, education, and sociology, which may have as much to offer psychiatry in the future as public health gave to medicine during the last two centuries. However, gazing into a crystal ball is much easier than the hard experimental work needed to provide the knowledge and resources that will be required for such an endeavour.

SUMMARY

A multivariate model is required to account for the various ways in which morbid anxiety can be managed. Drugs play a mainly palliative role at present. Several procedures can be regarded as extinction methods—desensitization and flooding in fantasy and in vivo, modeling, shaping, and cognitive rehearsal. In addition to specific processes of extinction, there are general ways of learning to deal with unpleasant affects which might be called coping or stress immunization, and, finally, the relief which is afforded by ventilation of affect—abreaction—which we ill understand today. Subjects often experience great relief simply by talking about their problems, a confessional effect that so far has not been subjected to scientific study, and which must be brought under experimental control if we are to understand it further. Cognitive and motivational variables affect outcome with all these methods.

REFERENCES

Bandura, A., Blanchard, E., & Ritter, B. Relative efficacy of desensitization and modeling approaches for inducing behavioral affective and attitudinal changes. *Journal of Personality and Social Psychology*, 1969, 13, 173-199.

Benjamin, S., Marks, I. M., & Huson, J. The role of active muscular desensitisation. *Psychological Medicine*, 1972, 2, 381-390.

Bonn, J. A. Paper presented at the 5th World Congress of Psychiatry, Mexico, Nov. 1971.

Crowe, M. J., Marks, I. M., Agras, W. S., & Leitenberg, H. Time-limited desensitisation, implosion and shaping for phobic patients: A crossover study. *Behaviour Research and Therapy*, 1972, 10, 319-328.

Everaerd, W. T., Rijken, H. M., & Emmelkamp, P. N. A comparison of "flooding" and successive approximation in the treatment of agoraphobia. *Behaviour Research and Therapy*, 1972, 11, 105-117.

Frankl, V. E. Paradoxical intention: A logotherapeutic technique. *American Journal of Psychotherapy*, 1960, 14, 520-535.

Friedman, D. E., & Lipsedge, M. Treatment of phobic anxiety and psychogenic impotence by systematic desensitisation employing methohexitone-induced relaxation. *British Journal of Psychiatry*, 1971, 18, 87-90.

Gelder, M. G., & Marks, I. M. Severe agoraphobia: A controlled prospective therapeutic trial. *British Journal of Psychiatry*, 1966, 112, 309-319.

Hand, I., Lamontagne, Y., & Marks, I. M. Groups exposure (flooding) in vivo for agoraphobics. *British Journal of Psychiatry*, 1974, 124, 588-602.

Hart, J. D. Fear reduction as a function of the assumption and success of a therapeutic role. Unpublished master's thesis, University of Wisconsin, 1966.

Hodgson, R., Rachman, S., & Marks, I. M. The treatment of chronic obsessive-compulsive neurosis: Followup and further findings. *Behaviour Research and Therapy*, 1972, 10, 181-189.

Kamin, L. J. Retention of an incompletely learned avoidance response: Some further analyses. *Journal of Comparative and Physiological Psychology*, 1963, 56, 713-718.

Klein, D. F. Delineation of two drug-responsive anxiety syndromes. *Psychopharmacologia*, 1964, 5, 397-408.

Klein, R., & Klein, D. F. Controlled imipramine treatment of school phobia. *Archives of General Psychiatry*, 1971, 25, 204-207.

Lader, M., & Marks, I. M. *Clinical anxiety*. London: Heinemann Medical, 1971.

Marks, I. M., Birley, J. L. T., & Gelder, M. G. Modified leucotomy in severe agoraphobia: a controlled serial inquiry. *British Journal of Psychiatry*, 1966, 112, 757-769.

Marks, I. M., Marset, P., & Boulougouris, J. Physiological accompaniments of neutral and phobic imagery. *Psychological Medicine*, 1971, 1, 299-307.

Marks, I. M., Viswanathan, R., & Lipsedge, M. S. Enhanced relief of phobias by flooding during waning diazepam effect. *British Journal of Psychiatry*, 1972, 121, 493-505.

Mathews, A. Reciprocal inhibition: Habituation or extinction? Paper presented at the Conference on Behaviour Modification, Dublin, Sept. 1969.

Mawson, A. Methohexitone assisted desensitisation. *Lancet I*, 1969, 1084-1086.

Meichenbaum, D. H. Cognitive factors in behaviour modification: What clients say to themselves. Paper presented at the Association for Advancement of Behavior Therapy, Washington, D.C., 1971.

Rachman, S., Hodgson, R., & Marks, I. M. The treatment of obsessive-compulsive neurosis. *Behaviour Research and Therapy*, 1971, 9, 237–247.

Ritter, B. Treatment of agoraphobia with contact desensitization. *Behaviour Research and Therapy*, 1969, 7, 41–45.

Sargant, W. *Battle for the mind.* London: William Heinemann Ltd., 1957.

Stern, R. S., & Marks, I. M. A comparison of brief and prolonged flooding in agoraphobics. *Archives of General Psychiatry*, 1973, 28, 269–276.

Stewart, K. Dream theory in Malaya. In C. Tart (Ed.), *Altered states of conscious.* New York: Wiley, 1969 (original article published 1935).

Tan, E., Marks, I. M., & Marset, P. Modified leucotomy in obsessive-compulsive neurosis. *British Journal of Psychiatry*, 1971, 118, 155–164.

Watson, J. P., Gaind, R., & Marks, I. M. Prolonged exposure: A rapid treatment for phobias. *British Medical Journal*, 1971, 1, 13–15.

Watson, J. P., Gaind, R., & Marks, I. M. Physiological habituation to continuous phobic stimulation. *Behaviour Research and Therapy*, 1972, 10, 269–278.

Watson, J. P., & Marks, I. M. Relevant and irrelevant fear in flooding: A crossover study of phobic patients. *Behavior Therapy*, 1971, 2, 275–293.

Welch, H. J., & Krapfl, J. E. Order of stimulus presentation in desensitisation. Paper presented at the Annual Meeting of Mid-West Psychological Association, Cincinnati, May 1970.

Wolpe, J. *Psychotherapy and reciprocal inhibition.* Palo Alto, Calif.: Stanford University Press, 1958.

10

A SELF-INSTRUCTIONAL APPROACH TO STRESS MANAGEMENT: A PROPOSAL FOR STRESS INOCULATION TRAINING

Donald Meichenbaum

University of Waterloo
Waterloo, Ontario, Canada

For a number of years we have been developing and assessing techniques designed to promote therapeutic gain by altering the cognitive processes of the anxious client. The present study represents an overview of this work. However, before embarking upon a discussion of the work conducted in our laboratory, it might be helpful to briefly consider two bodies of literature that have influenced our thinking to a marked extent. The first is the literature pertaining to cognitive variables in stress reactions. The second body of literature is more elusive and less well defined; we have been impressed by the fact that a number of psychotherapists and behavior therapists have suggested that alterations in the client's self-statements mediate therapeutic gain. Each of these literatures will be reviewed to provide a context for the discussion of our self-instructional approach to stress management.

The author is indebted to Roy Cameron for his editorial comments and to Myles Genest for his secretarial help. The studies reported in this paper were supported by grant 120 from the Ontario Mental Health Foundation.

COGNITIVE VARIABLES
IN STRESS REACTIONS

A major theme represented in previous conferences on stress (Appley & Trumbull, 1967; McGrath, 1970) has been the overriding influence of cognitive factors in the experience and control of stress. For example, McGrath introduced a conference on stress by noting that "the subject's emotional experience and to some extent physiological and performance measures are in part a function of the perceptions, expectations, or cognitive appraisals which the individual makes of the (stressing) situation [McGrath, 1970, p. 76]."

Major proponents of this viewpoint are Magda Arnold (1960, 1970) and Richard Lazarus (1966, 1968), who employed the concepts of appraisal and reappraisal to explain the nature of emotions and stress. Arnold (1970) conveys some of the complexities of the cognitive process of appraisal when she states:

> In interpreting a situation we do not merely know it is here and now . . . nor do we ascribe a vague cognitive "meaning" to it. We remember what has happened to us in the past, how this thing affected us and what we did about it. Then we imagine how it will affect us this time and estimate whether it will be harmful [p. 174].

In the same vein, R. Lazarus, Averill, and Opton (1970) argued that "each emotional reaction, regardless of its content, is a function of a particular kind of cognition or appraisal [p. 196]." One finds similar statements in the writings of Ax (1964), Glass and Singer (1972), Mandler (1962), Schachter (1966), and others. Each of these authors indicates that Ss react in widely different—and sometimes even opposite—ways to stimuli which are objectively "the same."

Three general research strategies have been employed in providing the empirical basis for such a cognitive view of stress reactions. (See R. Lazarus et al., 1970, for a more complete literature review.) The first research strategy attempts to directly manipulate S's cognitive processes. The second strategy employs a more indirect manipulation of cognitive processes by influencing the variables upon which cognitions are dependent (such as anticipation intervals preceding an aversive event: Epstein, 1972; Monat, Averill, & Lazarus, 1972; Nomikos, Opton, Averill, & Lazarus, 1968). The final strategy employs an individual-difference approach and studies *S*s who have been selected on the basis of dispositional characteristics (e.g., deniers and intellectualizers, avoiders and sensitizers: Andrew, 1967; Speisman, Lazarus, Mordkoff, & Davison, 1964). The latter research approach, which investigates the relationship between broad personality dimensions and stress reactions, has been seriously challenged by Endler and Hunt (1968); Mischel (1968); and, most recently, Averill, Olbrich, and Lazarus (1972), who stated: "Again and again, investigators have obtained what appears to be stable correlations between stress reactions and personality variables, only to have them disappear when tested in a slightly different setting [p. 29]."

The first strategy, that of directly modifying *S*'s cognitive processes, has most heuristic value for our present concerns. The nature of the manipulation in large part depends on the theoretical orientation of the investigator, with each investigator focusing on some particular aspect of the cognitive process. For some researchers *S*'s sense of control over the threatening situation seems most critical. Presumably a person will appraise a potentially aversive situation as less threatening if he perceives himself as having some measure of control over the aversive stimulus. Thus, a number of investigators (Bandler, Madaras, & Bem, 1968; Corah & Boffa, 1970; Glass & Singer, 1972; Hokanson, DeGood, Forrest, & Brittain, 1971; Staub, Tursky, & Schwartz, 1971) provided *S*s with the opportunity to self-administer or escape from an aversive event, or with the opportunity to decide when they wish to rest. In each case the perception of control appeared to reduce the negative effects of stress, whereas unpredictability and lack of control led to a sense of "learned helplessness" (Seligman, Maier, & Solomon, 1969; Thornton & Jacobs, 1971).

Another aspect of the cognitive process that has been manipulated is the cognitive (re)labeling process. The research by Schachter and his colleagues (Nisbett & Schachter, 1966; Schachter & Singer, 1962; Schachter & Wheeler, 1962) demonstrated that the specific emotion experienced by a person depends not only upon his state of physiological arousal, but also on the way in which *S interprets* or *labels* this state. They also found that this labeling process itself is influenced by what the person attributes as being the origin of this arousal. Some of the implications of differential self-attributions on stress reactions were investigated by Bem (1972), Davison and Valins (1969), Nisbett and Valins (1971), Ross, Rodin, & Zimbardo, (1969), Valins and Nisbett (1971), and Zimbardo (1969).

Perhaps the clearest demonstration of the direct manipulation of
S's cognitive processes are the studies by Richard Lazarus and his
colleagues, who found that under certain conditions information
about the nature of the stimulus may affects its assessment and in
turn its impact on people. Lazarus and his associates found that the
same potentially disturbing movie produces different degrees of
emotional disturbance depending on how it is interpreted (i.e., on
the kind of appraisal the person makes of it). They found that one
could "short-circuit" or reduce S's stress reaction, as measured by
physiological responses and verbal report, by providing information
that suggested that an operation that was part of a primitive
initiation ceremony which Ss watched on film did not produce harm
(Lazarus, R., & Alfert, 1964; Speisman et al., 1964) or that injury
suffered by someone on the film was enacted rather than real
(Lazarus, R., Opton, Nomikos, & Rankin, 1965). On the other hand,
the stress reaction was enhanced by information that emphasized the
harm inflicted by the observed operation (Speisman et al., 1964).

This brief literature review indicates a firm empirical foundation
for the role of cognitive factors in stress reactions. The direct
manipulation of S's sense of control, self-attributions, and emotional
appraisals is not only feasible, but also a strategy of great potential.
However, the full practical value and clinical potential of these
laboratory studies have not been assessed. In each of these studies S's
cognitive set and/or appraisal system were modified only within the
context of a brief laboratory experiment. The question arises as to
whether such cognitively directed procedures can be employed to
meaningfully alter S's cognitive behavior. That is, can one use the
general strategy of directly modifying S's cognitions to accomplish
long-range change and to significantly alter the stress reactions and
coping behaviors of clinical populations?

How might one proceed to significantly alter a client's cognitive
reactions to stress (i.e., his appraisal system, attributions, and sense
of control) in a clinical context? We began by conceptualizing such
cognitive events as specific sets of self-statements and/or self-instructions that the client could be trained to alter. Within this conceptual
framework, therapy consists of (a) identifying self-statements which
encourage the escalation of the stress reaction and (b) training the
client to substitute for these negative self-statements, positive (i.e.,
coping) self-instructions. The present study describes how the
techniques of behavior therapy, including modeling, imagery

practice, behavioral rehearsal, and anxiety relief conditioning, were each adapted for teaching self-instructional skills.

COGNITIVE FACTORS
IN BEHAVIOR THERAPY

An illustration of the potential of behavior therapy techniques in modifying the client's cognitions is indicated by the burgeoning literature on the treatment of phobics. The literature is now replete with studies documenting the efficacy of a myriad of therapy procedures designed to allevaite phobias. These procedures include systematic desensitization, flooding, modeling, operant conditioning, expectancy, and imagery manipulations (Bandura, 1969). A number of investigators made comments that converge to suggest that the alteration of the client's self-statement may represent a common mediator of the behavioral change brought about by many of these therapeutic techniques. For example, Lang (1969) suggested that systematic desensitization is

> designed to shape the response, "I am not afraid" (or a potentially competing response such as, "I am relaxed") in the presence of a graded set of discriminative stimuli. When well learned, the response could have the status of a "set" or self-instruction, which can then determine other mediated behavior [p. 187].

Similarly, Geer and Turtletaub (1967) hypothesized that self-statements (such as, "If the other client can do it, so can I.") may mediate the behavior change derived from a modeling procedure. Marks, Boulougouris, & Marset (1971) reported that following flooding, some clients spontaneously reported talking themselves out of feelings; others reported that they found it helpful to remind themselves that reality was never as bad as the horrors of fantasy; still others indicated that they had used self-challenging self-statements [e.g., "I'll show him." (the therapist)] to bolster their endurance during and after flooding. Davison (1968) and Valins and Ray (1967) provided further instances of self-instructions' being identified as a potential mediating mechanism of behavioral change. Thus, in each of these therapy procedures, there is the suggestion made that they operate by means of modifying the client's self-statements. If the hypothesis that the client's self-instructions mediate behavior change is valid, one would expect that explicit self-instructional training would enhance treatment effectiveness. Our work has consistently confirmed this hypothesis.

SELF-INSTRUCTIONAL PSYCHOTHERAPY

Our early research strategy was to adapt standard behavior therapy procedures to facilitate self-instructional training. Most recently, we have developed a new skills-oriented training procedure called stress inoculation treatment. In the following pages, our early research with adaptations of established behavior therapy techniques will be reviewed. Finally, our most recent research involving stress inoculation training will be described.

The first study (Meichenbaum, 1971) examined the use of *modeling* therapy to alter the self-statements or appraisal system of snake-phobic clients. The modeling study was designed to examine the differential efficacy of having models self-verbalize (i.e., model explicit self-statements that the client could use) versus the absence of any model verbalizations. A second factor included in the study was the modeling style: multiple models demonstrating coping behaviors (i.e., initially modeling fearful behaviors, then coping behavior, and finally mastery behavior) versus mastery models, demonstrating only fearless behavior throughout. The results clearly indicated that a coping model, who self-verbalizes throughout, facilitates greater behavioral change and more affective change as measured by self-report. The effectiveness of a model who verbalizes self-instructions along with self-reassuring and self-rewarding statements was indicated by the fact that five of the nine clients in the coping-verbalizing condition spontaneously overtly self-verbalized in the posttest assessment.

It may be instructive to illustrate the coping verbalizations that were modeled to alter the client's cognitions. Initially, the models commented on their anxiety and fear and the physiological accompaniments (sweaty palms, increased heart rate and breathing rate, tenseness, etc.). At the same time, the models attempted to cope with their fear by instructing themselves (*a*) to remain relaxed and calm by means of slow deep breaths, (*b*) to take one step at a time, and (*c*) to maintain a determination to forge ahead and handle the snake. The models were "psyching" themselves up to perform each task, and upon completion of that task, they emitted self-rewarding statements and positive affective expressions at having performed the task. One model bargained with the snake: "I'm going to make a deal with you. If you don't scare or hurt me, I won't scare or hurt you." It is interesting to note that two Ss who observed this series of coping verbalizing statements, upon return to the posttreatment assessment rooms, stated aloud (in essence): "You (referring to the snake) made a deal with her (referring to the model); I will make a similar deal. If you don't hurt me, I won't hurt you. I'm going to pick you up."

Perhaps more persuasive data that behavior therapy procedures can be used to modify clients' appraisal systems comes from our work with highly test anxious college students. Test anxious clients represent a population whose self-statements or cognitive processes evidently contribute to maladaptive behavior. By using a procedure of videotaping Ss while taking a test and then having Ss individually reconstruct their cognitions (i.e., using S's videotape as a Thematic Apperception Test), we were able to determine that high versus low test anxious persons say different things to themselves during an examination. Consider the situation in which other students hand in their exams early. For the high test-anxious individual, this event elicits worrying-type self-statements, e.g., "I can't get this problem. I'll never finish; how can that guy be done?" etc. This results in an increase in anxiety and further task-irrelevant and self-defeating thoughts. In comparison, the low test anxious student readily dismisses the other student's performance by saying to himself, "That guy who handed in his paper early must know nothing. I hope they score this exam on a curve." The same stimulus event (viz., other students handing in their examinations early) elicits different perceptions, attributions, and self-statements in high versus low anxious individuals.

The observations are consistent with the research by a variety of investigators (e.g., Liebert & Morris, 1967; Mandler & Watson, 1966; Wine, 1971) which has indicated that in evaluative situations high test anxious persons spend more of their time (a) worrying about their performance and about how well others are doing; (b) ruminating over alternatives; and (c) being preoccupied with such things as feelings of inadequacy, anticipation of punishment, loss of status or esteem, and heightened somatic and autonomic reactions. In other words, a worry component diverts attention away from the task and results in performance decrement. Thus, a treatment procedure aimed at controlling the "cognitive state" and attentional style of the high test anxious client should improve test performance.

Two studies have been conducted that use different training procedures to teach test anxious college students to talk to themselves differently, to control their attention. The first study (Meichenbaum, 1972) compared the relative efficacy of a cognitive modification treatment procedure with that of desensitization and waiting list control groups. The cognitive modification therapy attempted to make the test anxious clients aware of the negative self-statements (i.e., worrying behavior) they were emitting and to replace these thoughts with incompatible task-relevant self-instructions. The self-instructional training was conducted by means of *imagery rehearsal*, similar in format to desensitization. However, cognitive modification Ss were asked to visualize coping as well as mastery behaviors; viz., if they became anxious while imagining a scene they were to visualize themselves coping with this anxiety by means of slow deep breaths and self-instructions to relax and to be task relevant. The Ss were encouraged to use any personally generated self-statements that would facilitate their attending to the task and inhibit task-irrelevant thoughts. By use of such self-instructional imagery procedures, Ss provided themselves with a model for their own behavior, one that dealt with the anxiety they were likely to experience in reality.

The coping imagery procedure required S to visualize the experience of anxiety and ways in which to cope with and reduce such anxiety. It was designed to have the test anxious S view the anxiety he might experience following treatment as a discriminative stimulus i.e., a "signal" for employing the coping techniques of relaxation and self-instructions. The cognitive modification procedure required the client to explicitly rehearse by means of imagery the ways in which he would (a) appraise, label, and attribute the arousal he would experience; (b) control his thoughts and cope with his anxiety; and, more specifically, (c) self-instruct in evaluative situations.

The results of the study indicated that a cognitive modification treatment procedure was significantly more effective than standard desensitization in reducing test anxiety. The superiority of the cognitive modification treatment group was evident in an analog test situation, on self-report measures, and on grade point average. This improvement was maintained at a 1-month follow-up assessment. It is noteworthy that after treatment high test anxious Ss in the cognitive modification group did not significantly differ from low test anxious Ss on the performance and self-report measures.

Most interesting was the finding that only Ss in the cognitive modification treatment group reported a posttreatment increase in facilitative anxiety as assessed by the Alpert-Haber anxiety scale (1960). Following treatment, cognitive modification Ss labeled arousal as facilitative, as a cue to be task relevant, as a signal to improve their performance. The Ss were now saying that anxiety was helpful. This result is most impressive in light of other investigators' reports (Lang & Lazovik, 1963; Paul, 1966) that desensitization results in modified behavior, but a minimal decrease in self-reports of fear and anxiety. S. Johnson & Sechrest (1968), who conducted a desensitization study of test anxious Ss, failed to obtain changes in self-report on the Alpert-Haber scale, and they indicated that verbal behavior of reporting oneself as an anxious student is not dealt with directly by the desensitization procedures. The cognitive modification treatment demonstrated that the cognitions and appraisals that accompany arousal are modifiable.

Further evidence for the effectiveness of training high test anxious college students to self-instruct was provided by Wine (1971). Whereas Meichenbaum (1972) used a cognitive rehearsal self-instructional *imagery* procedure, Wine (1971) gave 6 hours of attentional training, which involved the modeling and behavioral rehearsal of self-instructions. The format of the self-instructional training was similar to one Meichenbaum and Goodman (1971) had developed to use with hyperactive impulsive school children. First, S is exposed to a self-verbalizing model and then given the opportunity to rehearse the attention-directing statements, initially aloud and subsequently covertly.

Subjects in Wine's self-instructional attention training group improved significantly both on performance measures and self-reports of facilitative anxiety relative to Ss in an "insight" group, who concentrated on the exploration of self-relevant verbalizations (viz., the thoughts they had in evaluative situations). Wine's results suggest that an "insight" procedure which concentrates only on making Ss aware of their anxiety-engendering self-statements *without* exploring and practising the use of incompatible self-instructions and behaviors is ineffective in reducing test anxiety and is likely to reinforce a deteriorative process.

Another clinical population for whom cognitive factors play an important role is speech anxious or interpersonally anxious individuals. The following example illustrates the relationship between the client's self-statements and his level of anxiety. The situation concerns the presentation of a public speech during which some members of the audience walk out of the room on two speakers, both of whom possess essentially the same speaking skills. This exodus elicits different self-statements from high versus low anxious speakers. The high speech anxious individual is more likely to say to himself: "I must be boring. How much longer do I have to speak? I know I never could give a speech," and so forth. These self-statements engender anxiety and become self-fulfilling prophecies. On the other hand, the low speech anxious S is more likely to view the audience's departure as a sign of their rudeness or to attribute their leaving to external considerations. He is more likely to say something like, "They must have a class to catch. Too bad they have to leave; they will miss a good talk." As with the test anxious individuals, the same stimulus event (e.g., two people walking out in the midst of the speech) elicits different perceptions, attributions, and self-statements in high versus low anxious individuals.

Hence, the goal of intervention is to make such "neurotic" patients aware of the self-statements which mediate maladaptive behaviors and to train them to produce incompatible self-statements and behaviors. This approach is not basically new: there is a long history of educational and semantic therapies that emphasize cognitive factors (e.g., Blumenthal, 1969; Coue, 1922; Ellis, 1963; Johnson, W., 1946; Kelly, 1955; Korzybski, 1933; Phillips, 1957). Typical of this view is Shaffer (1947), who defined therapy as a "learning process through which a person acquires the ability to speak to himself in appropriate ways so as to control his own conduct [p. 463]."

Thus, we conducted an experiment (Meichenbaum, Gilmore, & Fedoravicius, 1971) to assess the relative therapeutic value of a semantically based therapy versus the "proven" technique of desensitization in reducing speech anxiety. The self-instructional therapy was fashioned after the rational-emotive therapy approach of Albert Ellis (1963). The treatment approach emphasized the rationale that speech anxiety is the result of the self-verbalizations and internalized sentences emitted while thinking about the speech situation. The clients were informed that the goals of therapy were for each *S* to become aware of the self-statements he emitted in anxiety-evoking interpersonal situations. The therapy group discussed the specific self-verbalizations they emitted in speech and interpersonal situations and the irrational, self-defeating, and self-fulfilling aspects of such statements. In addition, they learned to produce both incompatible instructions and incompatible behaviors.

The major results indicated that the self-instructional semantic therapy approach was equally as effective as desensitization in reducing the behavioral and affective indicants of speech anxiety. However, a most interesting post hoc finding was that different types of clients received differential benefit from the semantic and desensitization treatment. Clients with high social distress who suffered anxiety in many varied situations benefited most from the semantic approach, which attends to and modifies the client's self-verbalizations. More recently, other investigators (Lazarus, A., 1971; Karst & Trexler, 1970) also reported successful treatment outcome with a similar rational-emotive-based treatment approach. Desensitization treatment appeared to be significantly more effective with *S*s whose speech anxiety was confined to formal speech situations. This latter finding is consistent with an increasing literature (Clarke, 1963; Gelder, Marks, Wolff, & Clarke, 1967; Lang & Lazovik, 1963; Lazarus, A., 1971; Marks & Gelder, 1965; Wolpe, 1964), which suggests that systematic desensitization works well with monosymptomatic phobias, and poorly with so-called free-floating anxiety states.

A SKILLS-TRAINING STRESS INOCULATION APPROACH

The research thus far reviewed indicates that developing the skill to employ a set of coping self-instructions has therapeutic benefit. A number of other investigators (D'Zurilla, 1969; D'Zurilla & Goldfried, 1971; Goldfried, 1971; Suinn & Richardson, 1971; Zeisset, 1968) also provided data to indicate that a skills-training approach followed by an opportunity for application practice or rehearsal is effective in reducing anxiety.

Our own research on the application of the behavior therapy procedure *anxiety relief conditioning* with phobics (Meichenbaum & Cameron, 1972a) has also indicated the importance of such a skills-training approach. The anxiety relief treatment procedure involves the client's pairing coping self-statements (e.g., "Relax", "Calm") with the offset of aversive stimulation (electric shock). Theoretically, according to Wolpe and Lazarus (1966), the verbal stimulus takes on counterconditioning anxiety relief qualities that generalize across situations. The notion is that the client will be able to reduce his anxiety level in virtually any situation by instructing himself to "relax," thus evoking the conditioned "relief" response. In fact, a number of investigators (Solyom, Kenny, & Ledwidge, 1969; Solyom & Miller, 1967; Thorpe, Schmidt, Brown, & Costell, 1964) presented data that purportedly demonstrate the therapeutic value of such anxiety relief techniques in alleviating phobic and obsessive behaviors.

Our research on the anxiety relief procedure with phobics indicated that such self-instructional anxiety relief conditioning is effective in reducing phobic behavior. Although the phobic client's exposure to the stressor of electric shock enhanced treatment efficacy, *the contingency of shock was found to be unimportant.* Hence, the plausibility of a counterconditioning explanation for treatment efficacy was called into question. Instead, the results indicated that the two important therapeutic elements were rehearsal of coping self-statements and practise using these self-instructions in an actual stress situation (viz., exposure to electric shock). The results suggested the possibility of teaching a phobic client general skills for coping with stress. Treatment would consist of the rehearsal of coping strategies and the testing of these strategies under stressful conditions (not necessarily related to the phobia). The ideal goal of treatment would be to "inoculate" the client against stress (i.e., to have him acquire skills which would enable him to deal with stress in general, and his phobias in particular).

Working within a skills-training framework, Meichenbaum and Cameron (1972b) developed a *stress inoculation* training procedure to treat *multiphobic* clients (i.e., phobic to both laboratory rats and harmless snakes). The stress inoculation training was designed to accomplish three goals. The first was to "eduate" the client about the nature of stressful or fearful reactions; the second, to have the client rehearse various coping behaviors; and, finally, to give the client an opportunity to practise his new coping skills in a stressful situation. The inoculation training was administered on an individual basis in six 1-hour sessions over a 4-week period.

The educational phase of the stress inoculation treatment began with a discussion of the nature of the client's fears. Discussion topics included how he felt and what he thought about when confronted by the phobic objects; and how he was currently coping with stressors in general and his phobic fears in particular. The therapist then went on to conceptualize the client's anxiety in terms of a Schachterian model of emotional arousal. That is, the therapist reflected that the client's fear reaction seemed to involve two major elements, namely, (a) his heightened arousal (e.g., increased heart rate, sweaty palms, rapid breathing, bodily tension, etc.), and (b) his set of anxiety-engendering avoidant thoughts and self-statements (e.g., disgust evoked by the phobic object, a sense of helplessness, panic thoughts of being overwhelmed by anxiety, a desire to flee, etc.). After laying this groundwork, the therapist noted that the stress reaction described by the client seemd to fit the theory that the cognitive set of self-statements a person emits while experiencing arousal is a prime determinant of his emotional behavior.

It should be noted that the Schachter and Singer theory of emotion was used for purposes of conceptualization only. Although the theory and the research on which it is based have been criticized (e.g., Averill & Opton, 1968; Fehr & Stern, 1970; Lazarus, R., 1968; Plutchik & Ax, 1967), the theory has an aura of face valicity that clients readily accept; and the logic of the treatment paradigm is more comprehensible to Ss in light of this conceptualization.

The therapist then indicated that treatment would be directed toward (a) helping the client control his physiological arousal and (b) substituting positive coping self-statements for the anxiety-engendering self-statements that habitually occupied his mind under stress conditions. This introduction provided the transition into the second (rehearsal) phase of treatment. The client was told that he would be taught a set of physical relaxation exercises which would provide the basis for reducing physiological arousal. It was also pointed out that if the client used these exercises in an anxiety-provoking situation, his concentration on doing something positive about his discomfort (i.e., relaxing) would in itself tend to eliminate the negative self-statements. The relaxation exercises, which began in session one and continued to session four, involved systematically tensing and relaxing various muscle groups as outlined by Paul (1966). Emphasis was also placed on the importance of breathing control. This emphasis was indicated by research conducted by Deane (1964, 1965), Wescott and Huttenlocher (1971), and Wood and Obrist (1964), which demonstrated that the amplitude and frequency of respiration has an effect on heart rate and the accompanying experience of anxiety.

The second aspect of coping training, which began in session two, involved practising self-statements which the client could use whenever confronted by stress, and especially in overcoming his fears. The first step in self-instructional training was for the client to view his phobic or stress reaction as a series of phases, rather than as one massive panic reaction. Four phases were suggested: preparing for a stressor; confronting or handling a stressor; possibly being over-whelmed by a stressor; and finally, reinforcing oneself for having coped. The inclusion of the third phase, of feeling overcome by anxiety and immobilized and socially embarrassed by one's fear, was indicated by previous research (Meichenbaum, 1973), which sug-gested that coping training (by means of modeling and imagery) with the possible eventuality of anxiety was more therapeutically effective than mastery-based treatments which did not consider future incapacities. A second factor was the clients' general concern that even though they had received coping training (i.e., relaxation and self-instructions), they might still be overcome by fear. Thus, practising ways of coping with his state helped to alleviate and "defuse" the client's dread of losing control, of being immobilized.

The client was encouraged to offer examples of self-statements he could emit during each phase. With some support, a package of self-statements emerged, similar to those listed in the list that follows. During sessions two, three, and four, clients practised self-instructing, initially aloud and subsequently covertly. This was done in conjunction with the relaxation and breathing exercises.

Examples of Coping Self-Statements That Stress Inoculation and Rehearsal Ss Practised

Stage of Preparing for a Stressor

What is it I have to do?
I can develop a plan to deal with it.
Just think about what I can do about it. That's better than getting anxious.
No negative self-statements, just think rationally.

Don't worry. Worry won't help anything.
Maybe what I think is anxiety is eagerness to confront it.

Stage of Confronting and Handling a Stressor

Just "psych" myself up. I can meet this challenge.
One step at a time; I can handle the situation.
Don't think about fear, just about what I have to do. Stay relevant.
This anxiety is what the doctor said I would feel. It's a reminder to use my coping exercises.
This tenseness can be an ally, a cue to cope.
Relax; I'm in control. Take a slow deep breath. Ah, good.

Stage of Coping with the Feeling of Being Overwhelmed

When fear comes just pause.
Keep focus on the present; what is it I have to do?
Let me label my fear from 0 to 10 and watch it change.
I was supposed to expect my fear to rise.
Don't try to eliminate fear totally; just keep it manageable.
I can convince myself to do it. I can reason my fear away.
It will be over shortly.
It's not the worst thing that can happen.
Just think about something else.
Do something that will prevent me from thinking about fear.
Just describe what is around me. That way I won't think about worrying.

Finally, Reinforcing Self-Statements

It worked; I was able to do it.
Wait until I tell my therapist about this.
It wasn't as bad as I expected.
I made more out of the fear than it was worth.
My damn ideas, that's the problem. When I control them, I control my fear.
It's getting better each time I use the procedure.
I'm really pleased with the progress I'm making.
I did it!

The self-statements encouraged the clients to (a) assess the reality of the situation; (b) control negative, self-defeating, anxiety-engendering ideation; (c) acknowledge use, and possibly relabel the anxiety they were experiencing; (d) "psych" themselves up to perform the task; (e) cope with the intense fear they might experience; and (f) reinforce themselves for having coped. The package of self-statements was derived from prior interviews with clinical and nonclinical populations, and from suggestions offered in the literature (e.g., Zane, 1972). It is interesting to note that over the course of training, clients gravitated to specific packages of self-statements, suggesting the possibility of tailoring self-instructions to a number of individual-difference dimensions.

Once S had become proficient in the relaxation exercises and the self-instructional techniques (i.e., usually by the end of session four) the therapist suggested that he should test out and practise his coping skills by actually employing them under stressful conditions. At this point, the therapist described the unpredictable shock situation. This situation was selected as the treatment stressor because several investigators (Elliott, 1966; Pervin, 1963; Skaggs, 1926) have shown that unpredictable (in terms of intensity and timing) shock represents a very stressful, anxiety-inducing situation. Indeed, Thornton and Jacobs (1971) have used unpredictable shock to induce a state of "learned helplessness" in human Ss. The nature of shock was explained to the Ss, and they were given an opportunity to experience various levels of shock so that a level that elicited emotional discomfort could be ascertained. All Ss regarded the unpredictable shock situation as threatening, but highly challenging.

The third phase of training (rehearsal under stress) began with session five and continued in session six. Clients were told:

> Sometime in the next two or three minutes, maybe in a few seconds, maybe after three minutes, maybe somewhere in between, you will receive a shock. Just exactly how intense and exactly when you receive the shock depends on a random, predetermined schedule. Try to cope with the anxiety and tenseness elicited by this situation by means of the coping techniques you have learned.

In each practice session the client received ten 1-second shocks which ranged in intensity from .5 MA to 3 MA. There was an intertrial interval of 1 minute.

Immediately before the shock trials began, the therapist modeled how to use the coping skills to deal with the stressor. His modeling was followed by the client's rehearsing the coping strategies, initially self-instructing aloud, and then covertly. Following this preparation, the client began shock trials. We observed that clients "tried on" various packages of self-statements during these practice trials. Some would brace themselves and self-instruct in a reassuring manner, while others instructed themselves to attend to their breathing (which was under their control) and to just endure the shock (over which they had no control). Session six ended in this, as in all treatment groups, with a discussion about how the client could apply the skills he had acquired to overcoming his presenting fears.

In retrospect we wonder whether a different type of stressor might have been more desirable. The limitation of the shock stressor lay in the fact that it did not permit the client to practise the full range of self-statements which he had rehearsed. An obvious possibility would be to use ego-threatening (e.g., stress-inducing films) as well as pain-threatening stressors.

In summary, stress inoculation training involved discussing the nature of emotion and stress reactions, rehearsing coping skills, and testing these skills under actual stress conditions. A variety of therapeutic techniques were woven into the stress inoculation training. These included didactic teaching, modeling, discussion, reinforcement, and self-instructional and behavioral rehearsal techniques. Obviously, then, the present stress inoculation therapy regimen is complex and multifaceted. Only future research can determine which are the necessary and/or sufficient conditions for promoting change. For the present we deemed it best to bring the full clinical armamentarium to bear in the cause of translating the phobic client's sense of "learned helplessness" into "learned resourcefulness."

The relative therapeutic efficacy of the stress inoculation training procedure in reducing multiple phobias was determined relative to (a) a systematic desensitization treatment group, (b) a self-instructional rehearsal group, and (c) a waiting list assessment control group. The inclusion of the desensitization group provided an interesting treatment comparison, a comparison between an imagery-based treatment and the self-instructionally based treatment of stress inoculation. Half the multiphobic Ss in the desensitization group were desensitized only to rats, while the other half were desensitized only to snakes, thus providing the means to assess the degree of treatment generalization that results from desensitization as compared with stress inoculation. The multiphobic Ss in the self-instructional rehearsal group were treated exactly as Ss in the stress inoculation group, except that they had no opportunity to practise their skills under shock conditions. Whereas the stress inoculation Ss received exposure to shock in treatment sessions five and six, rehearsal Ss simply received further practice in relaxation and self-instruction. Hence, a comparison between this rehearsal group and the stress inoculation group indicates the therapeutic gain derived from practicing the coping techniques in a stressful situation. The inclusion of the waiting list assessment control group provides an index of the improvement which might result from repeated assessments (pre-post-follow-up) and the promise of treatment in the future.

The results proved most exciting. The stress inoculation training was the most effective treatment in reducing avoidance behavior and in fostering treatment generalization. The systematic desensitization treatment proved effective in reducing fear *only* to the desensitized object. When the desensitized S was confronted with the nondesensitized object, *minimal* treatment generalization was evident. In contrast, the two self-instructionally based treatment procedures (i.e., stress inoculation and self-instructional rehearsal) yielded treatment generalization.

The relative efficacy of the respective treatments was indicated by the percentage of Ss in each condition who were able to perform the terminal approach behavior of handling the phobic objects outside of their cages for 1 minute at both the posttest and follow-up assessments. The respective rates for the treated animal were 83% for stress inoculation, 50% for desensitization, 16% for self-instructional rehearsal, and 0% for waiting list control groups. The rates for the generalization phobic object were 83% for stress inoculation, 50% for self-instructional rehearsal, 0% for desensitization, and 0% for waiting list control.

The finding that the desensitization group showed minimal generalization (to the nondesensitized object) is consistent with the findings of Bandura, Blanchard, and Ritter (1969), Meyer and Gelder (1963), and Wolpe (1958, 1961), who indicated that desensitization seems to alleviate only those phobias that are being treated, without mitigating other coexisting phobias. As Wolpe (1961) states, "Unless different hierarchies have *unmistakable common features* desensitization to one hierarchy does not in the least diminish the reactivity to another (untreated) hierarchy [p. 201, emphasis added]."

Within the Wolpeian desensitization framework, the degree of treatment generalization is viewed as a function of the stimulus gradient or the number of identical elements that occur across situations or hierarchies. Within a self-instructional stress inoculation framework, the degree of treatment generalization is a function of the common set of responses, mainly self-instructional, that are emitted across situations. In other words, the degree of consistency of behavior across situations (or treatment generalization) is a function of the likelihood that the same set of *covert* discriminative stimuli or self-statements will be elicited. Thus, training clients to emit a set of self-instructional coping responses that are appropriate across stress-inducing situations will likely enhance treatment generalization. As Lang (1968) has noted, "the absence of programs for shaping cognitive sets and attitudes may contribute to the not infrequent failure of transfer of treatment effects [p. 94]."

The stress inoculation training provided a useful way of altering the phobic client's cognitive set, or what he says to himself. Typical of most phobic patients, our *S*s reported that prior to training they felt that they could do nothing about their debilitating fears; their pretreatment condition seemed to be one of "learned helplessness." The stress inoculation paradigm was designed specifically to modify this attitude by training coping skills. This approach is consistent with a burgeoning literature on both animals (Mowrer & Viek, 1948; Richter, 1959; Seligman et al., 1969) and humans (Glass & Singer, 1972; Hokanson et al., 1971) that having some instrumental response at one's disposal and being able to perceive the relationship between one's action and the termination of an aversive stimulus breaks this pattern of hopelessness. R. Lazarus (1966) and Rotter (1966) have also hypothesized (from somewhat different vantage points) that the availability of coping responses will reduce stress-related responding. Following stress inoculation, *S*'s perception of his condition had changed from "learned helplessness" to "*learned resourcefulness.*" It was quite common for clients in the stress inoculation group to report spontaneously that they had successfully applied their new coping skills in other stressful situations, including final exams and during dental visits. One client even taught the procedure to his pregnant wife. This change in attitude seemed to have larger ramifications in affecting one's self-concept by encouraging clients to initiate confrontations with real-life problems.

Given the increasing demand for people to deal with stress, the possibility of using stress inoculation training for prophylactic purposes is most exciting. The notion of providing the S with a prospective defense against anxiety is in some respect analogous to immunization against attitude change (McGuire, 1964; Tannenbaum, 1967) and, of course, medical inoculation against biological disease. The general underlying principle in these two analogous situations is that a person's resistance is enhanced by exposure to a stimulus which is strong enough to arouse the defenses without being so powerful as to overcome them. An examination of the way in which this principle is applied by both social psychologists and physicians may suggest methods for refining and improving stress inoculation. For instance, it may prove helpful to expose S to a variety of graded stressors (e.g., cold pressor test, stress inducing films, fear inducing imagery, deprivation conditions, fatigue, etc.). Presumably, the more varied and extensive the application training, the greater the likelihood S will develop a general learning set, a general way of talking to himself in order to cope. Cognitive coping modeling films can also be used to facilitate learning.

Several investigators (Henderson, Montgomery, & Williams, 1972; Poser, 1970) have pointed to the potential of preventive intervention approaches, especially with high risk populations. The possibility of explicitly teaching even nonclinical populations to cognitively cope by such diverse techniques as information seeking, anticipatory problem solving, imagery rehearsal, task organization, altering attributions and self-labels, shifting attention, using abstraction and relaxation, etc., seems to hold much promise. An explicit training program that would teach coping skills and then provide application training in handling a variety of stressors is in marked contrast to the haphazard and chance manner in which people now learn to cope with stress. The research on stress seems to indicate the necessary skills required to cope, and the armamentarium of broad spectrum behavior therapy seems to provide a promising means for teaching such skills.

Finally, one may note that the proposed stress inoculation approach is consistent with the findings of a number of stress researchers that the resistance of people to meet adverse life events may be enhanced by previous exposure to stressful stimuli of increasing magnitude. For example, the research by Egbert, Battit, Welch, & Bartlett (1964), Janis (1958), and Moran (1963) indicated that providing surgical patients with preparatory communications stimulates the "work of worrying" which results in high stress tolerance when the crisis is at hand. Janis (1958) suggests that such *emotional inoculation* arouses vigilance and helps to build up a self-concept of being able to cope with anticipating threat and danger. In an entirely different context, Epstein (1967) also found evidence for the importance of graded preexposure to stress. Epstein, who compared the anxiety levels of experienced and inexperienced parachutists, found that novice parachutists tend toward an all-or-none variety of controlling levels of anxiety; whereas experienced parachutists use compensatory responses that are modulated and involve inhibiting reactions implemented at low intensities of anxieties. Epstein indicates that the ability to tolerate stress is acquired not through previous security, but through *inoculations* with increasing amounts of stress.

Such naturalistic and experimental studies suggest that persons learn to cope with stressors by means of a graded set of preexposures to stress or by means of naturally occurring inoculations (e.g., facing life crises). From such inoculations we haphazardly develop response skills to employ in stress-inducing situations. The proposed stress inoculation training program takes what seems to be a haphazard chance sequence, which only some portion of our population successfully masters, and systematizes it for widespread application. Surely, the potential of the stress inoculation technique has yet to be tested. The finding of its therapeutic value with multiphobic clients is, at best, an encouraging first step. The possibility of assessing its efficacy with such populations as soldiers, novice parachutists, etc., who have to confront well-defined stressors, provides promising future avenues for research.

SUMMARY

A review of the stress literature indicates the important role of cognitive processes in the experience and control of stress (e.g., research by Glass and Singer (1972), R. Lazarus (1966), Schachter (1966), and others). Although such laboratory-based experimental studies indicated that by directly modifying S's cognitive state one can reduce S's stress reaction, they did not move beyond the stage of demonstration. To assess the clinical potential and long-term effects of directly modifying the client's cognitive state (viz., his self-attribution, appraisal system, sense of control), these cognitive events were translated into specific sets of self-statements the client could rehearse. The techniques of behavior therapy (e.g., modeling, imagery rehearsal, anxiety relief conditioning) and semantic therapy were successfully employed in changing the cognitions or self-statements, as well as reducing the maladaptive behavior of phobics and high test anxious and speech anxious persons. These studies indicate that the most successful and most promising approach in affecting S's stress behavior is a stress inoculation skills training procedure. The stress inoculation training involves (a) a Schachterian elucidation of stress reactions, (b) training and rehearsal of relaxation and self-instructional coping skills, and (c) exercising these new coping skills under actual stress conditions. The implications of a skills-oriented stress inoculation procedure are discussed.

REFERENCES

Alpert, R., & Haber, R. Anxiety in academic achievement situations. *Journal of Abnormal and Social Psychology*, 1960, 61, 207-215.

Andrew, J. Coping styles, stress relevant learning and recovery from surgery. Unpublished doctoral dissertation, University of California, Los Angeles, 1967.

Appley, M., & Trumball, I. (Eds.) *Conference on psychological stress.* New York: Appleton-Century-Crofts, 1967.

Arnold, M. B. *Emotion and personality.* New York: Columbia University Press, 1960. 2 vols.

Arnold, M. Perennial problems in the field of emotion. In M. Arnold (Ed.), *The Loyola symposium: Feelings and emotion.* New York: Academic Press, 1970.

Averill, J., Olbrich, E., & Lazarus, R. Personality correlates of differential responsiveness to direct and vicarious threat. *Journal of Personality and Social Psychology*, 1972, 21, 25-29.

Averill, J., & Opton, E. Psychophysiological assessment: Rationale and problems. In P. McReynolds (Ed.), *Advances in psychological assessment.* Vol. 1. Palo Alto, Calif.: Science and Behavior Books, 1968.

Ax , A. Goals and method of psychophysiology. *Psychophysiology*, 1964, 1, 8-25.

Bandler, R., Madaras, G., & Bem, D. Self-observation as a source of pain perception. *Journal of Personality and Social Psychology*, 1968, 9, 205-209.

Bandura, A. *Principles of behavior modification.* New York: Holt, Rinehart, & Winston, 1969.

Bandura, A., Blanchard, E., & Ritter, B. The relative efficacy of desensitization and modeling treatment approaches for inducing affective, behavioral, and attitudinal changes. *Journal of Personality and Social Psychology*, 1969, 13, 173-199.

Bem, D. Self-perception theory. In L. Berkowitz (Ed.), *Advances in experimental social psychology*. Vol. 6. New York: Academic Press, 1972.

Blumenthal, A. The base of objectivist psychotherapy. *The objectivist*. New York, 1969.

Clarke, D. The treatment of monosymptomatic phobia by systematic desensitization. *Behaviour Research and Therapy*, 1963, 1, 63-68.

Corah, N., & Boffa, J. Perceived control, self-observation, and response to aversive stimulation. *Journal of Personality and Social Psychology*, 1970, 16, 1-4.

Coue, E. *The practice of autosuggestion*. New York: Doubleday, 1922.

Davison, G. Systematic desensitization as a counterconditioning process. *Journal of Abnormal Psychology*, 1968, 73, 91-99.

Davison, G., & Valins, S. Maintenance of self-attributed and drug attributed behavior change. *Journal of Personality and Social Psychology*, 1969, 11, 28-33.

Deane, G. Human heart rate responses during experimentally induced anxiety: A followup with controlled respiration. *Journal of Experimental Psychology*, 1964, 67, 193-195.

Deane, G. Cardiac rate as function of changes in respiration. *Psychological Reports*, 1965, 16, 41-42.

D'Zurilla, T. Reducing heterosexual anxiety. In J. Krumboltz & G. Thoresen (Eds.), *Behavior counseling: Cases and techniques*. New York: Holt, Rinehart, & Winston, 1969.

D'Zurilla, T., & Goldfried, M. Problem solving and behavior modification. *Journal of Abnormal Psychology*, 1971, 78, 107-126.

Egbert, L., Battit, G., Welch, C., & Bartlett, M. Reduction of post operative pain by encouragement and instruction of patients. *New England Journal of Medicine*, 1964, 270, 825-827.

Elliott, R. Effects of uncertainty about the nature and advent of a noxious stimulus (shock) upon heart rate. *Journal of Personality and Social Psychology*, 1966, 3, 353-356.

Ellis, A. *Reason and emotion in psychotherapy*. New York: Lyle-Stuart, 1963.

Endler, N., & Hunt, J. McV. S-R inventories of hostility and comparisons of the proportions of variance from persons, responses, and situations for hostility and anxiousness. *Journal of Personality and Social Psychology*, 1968, 9, 309-315.

Epstein, S. Toward a unified theory of anxiety. In B. Maher (Ed.), *Progress in experimental personality research*, Vol. 4. New York: Academic Press, 1967.

Epstein, S. The nature of anxiety with emphasis upon its relationship to expectancy. In C. D. Spielberger (Ed.), *Anxiety: Current trends in theory and research*. New York: Academic Press, 1972.

Fehr, R., & Stern, J. Peripheral physiological variables and emotion: the James-Lange theory revisited. *Psychological Bulletin*, 1970, 74, 411-424.

Geer, J., & Turtletaub, A. Fear reduction following observation of a model. *Journal of Personality and Social Psychology*, 1967, 6, 327-331.

Gelder, M., Marks, I., Wolff, H., & Clarke, M. Desensitization and psychotherapy in the treatment of phobic states: A controlled inquiry. *British Journal of Psychiatry*, 1967, 113, 53-73.

Glass, D., & Singer, J. Behavioral aftereffects of unpredictable and uncontrollable aversive events. *American Scientist*, 1972, 60, 457-465.

Glass, D., & Singer, J. *Urban stress: Experiments in noise and social stressors.* New York: Academic Press, 1972.

Goldfried, M. Systematic desensitization as training in self-control. *Journal of Consulting and Clinical Psychology*, 1971, 37, 228-325.

Henderson, A., Montgomery, I., & Williams, C. Psychological immunization: A proposal for preventive psychiatry. *Lancet*, 1972, 13, 1111-1112.

Hokanson, J., DeGood, D., Forrest, N., & Brittain, T. Availability of avoidance behaviors in modulating vascular-stress responses. *Journal of Personality and Social Psychology*, 1971, 19, 60-68.

Janis, I. *Psychological stress: Psychoanalytic and behavioral studies of surgical patients.* New York: Wiley, 1958.

Johnson, W. *People in quandries.* New York: Harper, 1946.

Johnson, S., & Sechrest, C. Comparison of desensitization and progressive relaxation in training test anxiety. *Journal of Consulting and Clinical Psychology*, 1968, 32, 280-286.

Karst, T., & Trexler, L. Initial study using fixed-role and rationale-emotive therapy in treating public speaking anxiety. *Journal of Consulting and Clinical Psychology*, 1970, 34, 360-366.

Kelly, G. *The psychology of personal constructs.* New York: Norton, 1955. 2 vols.

Korzybski, A. *Science and sanity.* Lancaster, Pa.: Lancaster Press, 1933.

Lang, P. Fear reduction and fear behavior: Problems in treating a construct. In J. Shlien (Ed.), *Research in psychotherapy.* Vol. 3. Washington, D.C.: American Psychological Association, 1968.

Lang, P. The mechanics of desensitization and the laboratory study of human fear. In C. Franks (Ed.), *Assessment and status of the behavior therapies.* New York: McGraw-Hill, 1969.

Lang, P., & Lazovik, A. Experimental desensitization of a phobia. *Journal of Abnormal and Social Psychology*, 1963, 66, 519-525.

Lazarus, A. *Behavior therapy and beyond.* New York: McGraw-Hill, 1971.

Lazarus, R. *Psychological stress and the coping process.* New York: McGraw-Hill, 1966.

Lazarus, R. Emotions and adaptation: Conceptual and empirical relations. In W. Arnold (Ed.), *Nebraska Symposium on Motivation*, Lincoln: University of Nebraska Press, 1968, 16, 175-270.

Lazarus, R., & Alfert, E. The short-circuiting of threat by experimentally altering cognitive appraisal. *Journal of Abnormal and Social Psychology*, 1964, 69, 195-205.

Lazarus, R., Averill, J., & Opton, E. Towards a cognitive theory of emotion. In M. Arnold (Ed.), *Feeling and emotions.* New York: Academic Press, 1970.

Lazarus, R., Opton, E., Nomikos, M., & Rankin, N. The principle of short-circuiting of threat: Further evidence. *Journal of Personality*, 1965, 33, 622-635.

Liebert, R., & Morris, L. Cognitive and emotional components of test anxiety: A distinction and some initial data. *Psychological Reports*, 1967, 20, 975-978.

Mandler, G. Emotion. In R. Brown (Ed.), *New directions in psychology*. New York: Holt, Rinehart, & Winston, 1962.

Mandler, G., & Watson, D. Anxiety and the interruption of behavior. In C. Spielberger (Ed.), *Anxiety and behavior*. New York: Academic Press, 1966.

Marks, I., Boulougouris, J., & Marset, P. Flooding versus desensitization in the treatment of phobic patients. *British Journal of Psychiatry*, 1971, 119, 353-375.

Marks, I., & Gelder, M. A controlled retrospective study of behavior therapy in phobic patients. *British Journal of Psychiatry*, 1965, 111, 561-573.

McGuire, W. Inducing resistance to persuasion: some contemporary approaches. In L. Berkowitz (Ed.), *Advances in social psychology*. Vol. 1. New York: Academic Press, 1964.

McGrath, J. (Ed.) *Social and psychological factors in stress*. New York: Holt, Rinehart, & Winston, 1970.

Meichenbaum, D. An examination of model characteristics in reducing avoidance behavior. *Journal of Personality and Social Psychology*, 1971, 17, 298-307.

Meichenbaum, D. Cognitive modification of test anxious college students. *Journal of Consulting and Clinical Psychology*, 1972, 39, 370-380.

Meichenbaum, D. Cognitive factors in behavior modification: Modifying what clients say to themselves. In R. Rubin (Ed.), *Advances in behavior therapy*, Vol. 4. New York: Academic Press, 1973.

Meichenbaum, D., & Cameron, R. An examination of cognitive and contingency variables in anxiety relief procedures. Unpublished manuscript, University of Waterloo, Ontario, 1972a.

Meichenbaum, D., & Cameron, R. Stress inoculation: A skills training approach to anxiety management. Unpublished manuscript, University of Waterloo, Ontario, 1972b.

Meichenbaum, D., Gilmore, J., & Fedoravicius, A. Group insight vs. group desensitization in treating speech anxiety. *Journal of Consulting and Clinical Psychology*, 1971, 36, 410-421.

Meichenbaum, D., & Goodman, J. Training impulsive children to talk to themselves: A means of developing self-control. *Journal of Abnormal Psychology*, 1971, 77, 115-126.

Meyer, V., & Gelder, M. Behavior therapy and phobic disorders. *British Journal of Psychiatry*, 1963, 109, 19-28.

Mischel, W. *Personality and assessment*. New York: Wiley, 1968.

Monat, A., Averill, J., & Lazarus, R. Anticipatory stress and coping reactions under various conditions of uncertainty. *Journal of Personality and Social Psychology*, 1972, 24, 237-253.

Moran, P. Experimental study of pediatric admissions. Unpublished manuscript. New Haven, Yale School of Nursing, 1963.

Mowrer, O., & Viek, P. An experimental analogue of fear from a sense of helplessness. *Journal of Abnormal and Social Psychology*, 1948, 43, 193-200.

Nisbett, R., & Schachter, S. Cognitive manipulation of pain. *Journal of Experimental and Social Psychology*, 1966, 2, 227-236.

Nisbett, R., & Valins, S. *Perceiving causes of one's own behavior*. Morristown, N.J.: General Learning Press, 1971.

Nomikos, M., Opton, E., Averill, J., & Lazarus, R. Surprise and suspense in the production of stress reaction. *Journal of Personality and Social Psychology*, 1968, 8, 204-208.

Paul, G. *Insight vs. desensitization in psychotherapy: An experiment in anxiety reduction*. Stanford, Calif.: Stanford University Press, 1966.

Pervin, L. The need to predict and control under conditions of threat. *Journal of Personality*, 1963, 31, 570-585.

Phillips, E. *Psychotherapy: A modern theory and practise*. Englewood Cliffs, N.J.: Prentice-Hall, 1957.

Plutchik, R., & Ax, A. A critique of "Determinant of Emotional States" by Schachter and Singer (1962), *Psychophysiology*, 1967, 4, 79-82.

Poser, E. Toward a theory of "behavioral prophylaxis", *Journal of Behavior Therapy and Experimental Psychiatry*, 1970, 1, 39-43.

Richter, C. The phenomenon of unexplained sudden death in animals and man. In H. Feifel (Ed.), *The meaning of death*. New York: McGraw-Hill, 1959.

Ross, L., Rodin, J., & Zimbardo, P. Toward an attribution therapy: The reduction of fear through induced cognitive-emotional misattribution. *Journal of Personality and Social Psychology*, 1969, 12, 279-288.

Rotter, J. Generalized expectancies for internal versus external control of reinforcement. *Psychological Monographs*, 1966, 80(1 Whole No. 609).

Schachter, S. The interaction of cognitive and physiological determinants of emotional state. In C. Spielberger (Ed.), *Anxiety and behavior*. New York: Academic Press, 1966.

Schachter, S., & Singer, J. Cognitive, social, and physiological determinants of emotional state. *Psychological Review*, 1962, 69, 379-399.

Schachter, S., & Wheeler, L. Epinephrine, chloropromazine, and amusement. *Journal of Abnormal and Social Psychology*, 1962, 65, 121-128.

Seligman, M., Maier, S., & Solomon, R. Unpredictable and uncontrollable aversive events. In F. Brush (Ed.), *Aversive conditioning and learning*. New York: Academic Press, 1969.

Shaffer, L. The problem of psychotherapy. *American Psychologist*, 1947, 2, 459-467.

Skaggs, E. Changes in pulse, breathing and steadiness under conditions of startledness and excited expectancy. *Journal of Comparative and Physiological Psychology*, 1926, 6, 303-318.

Solyom, L., Kenny, F., & Ledwidge, B. Evaluation of new treatment paradigm for phobias. *Canadian Psychiatric Association Journal*, 1969, 14, 3-9.

Solyom, L., & Miller, S. Reciprocal inhibition by aversion relief in the treatment of phobias. *Behaviour Research and Therapy*, 1967, 5, 313-324.

Speisman, J., Lazarus, R., Mordkoff, A., & Davison, L. Experimental reduction of stress based on ego defense theory. *Journal of Abnormal and Social Psychology*, 1964, 68, 367-380.

Staub, E., Tursky, B., & Schwartz, G. Self-control and predictability: Their effects on reactions to aversive stimulation. *Journal of Personality and Social Psychology*, 1971, 18, 157–167.

Suinn, R., & Richardson, F. Anxiety management training: A non-specific behavior therapy program for anxiety control. *Behavior Therapy*, 1971, 2, 498–510.

Tannenbaum, P. The congruity principle revisited: Studies in the reduction, induction, and generalization of persuasion. In L. Berkowitz (Ed.), *Advances in social psychology*. Vol. 3. New York: Academic Press, 1967.

Thornton, J., & Jacobs, P. Learned helplessness in human subjects. *Journal of Experimental Psychology*, 1971, 87, 367–372.

Thorpe, J., Schmidt, E., Brown, P., & Costell, D. Aversion-relief therapy: A new method for general application. *Behaviour Research and Therapy*, 1964, 2, 71–82.

Valins, S., & Nisbett, R. *Attribution processes in the development and treatment of emotional disorders*. Morristown, N. J.: General Learning Press, 1971.

Valins, S., & Ray, A. Effects of cognitive desensitization on avoidance behavior. *Journal of Personality and Social Psychology*, 1967, 7, 345–356.

Wescott, H., & Huttenlocher, J. Cardiac conditioning: The effects and implication of controlled and uncontrolled respiration. *Journal of Experimental Psychology*, 1961, 61, 353–359.

Wine, J. Investigations of attentional interpretation of test anxiety. Unpublished doctoral dissertation, University of Waterloo, Ontario, 1971.

Wolpe, J. *Psychotherapy by reciprocal inhibition*. Stanford, Calif.: Stanford University Press, 1958.

Wolpe, J. The systematic desensitization treatment of neuroses. *Journal of Nervous and Mental Disease*, 1961, 132, 189–203.

Wolpe, J. Discussion of experimental studies in desensitization. In J. Wolpe, A. Salter, & L. Reyna (Eds.), *The conditioning therapies*. New York: Holt, Rinehart, & Winston, 1964.

Wolpe, J., & Lazarus, R. *Behavior therapy techniques*. New York: Pergamon Press, 1966.

Wood, D., & Obrist, P. Effects of controlled and uncontrolled respiration in the conditioned heart rate in humans. *Journal of Experimental Psychology*, 1964, 69, 221–229.

Zane, M. Fighting fear by group confrontation. *Medical World News*. Feb. 1972, 76–80.

Zeisset, R. Desensitization and relaxation in the modification of psychiatric patients' interview behavior. *Journal of Abnormal Psychology*, 1968, 73, 18–24.

Zimbardo, P. *The cognitive control of motivation*. Glenview, Ill.: Scott, Foresman, 1969.

APPENDIX A

ABSTRACTS OF PAPERS PRESENTED AT THE CONFERENCE

HOW SUBJECTS RESPOND TO TWO STATE AND TRAIT ANXIETY QUESTIONNAIRES

Monique DeBonis

Centre National de la Recherche Scientifique
Paris, France

This study investigated the role of test instructions and wording of items on the responses given to trait and state anxiety questionnaires. To characterize these effects, 74 psychiatric patients were given anxiety questionnaires, each containing 37 items, in a counterbalanced order. The content of the items was identical for both tests, the only difference being with respect to, the wording of the test instructions ("in general" for the trait form and "within the previous eight days" for the state form). Each item, printed on a card, had to be sorted by the subject into one of five pigeonholes that corresponded to a magnitude scale from zero (entirely false or never) to 4 (entirely true or always). The subjects were tested within 5 days following their hospitalization at a time when the state anxiety is presumably highest.

The role of test instructions and wording was evaluated: (*a*) by comparing the responses given by the same subjects to each item of the trait form with its homologue in the state form and (*b*) by analyzing the utilization of the available response range (0 to 4) for the 37 trait questions and the 37 state questions. The differences between "trait" and "state" responses to the same content items were quantified using analysis of variance for paired samples.

Of the 37 item comparisons, 10 reached an acceptable level of statistical significance. For some of the items, the score was higher for the state form, whereas for other items, the reverse was true. A similar statistical analysis was applied on pseudofactorial scores (i.e., mean scores for responses to items loaded on each of the four rotated factors, which had been identified in a previous study). These four pseudofactorial scores corresponded respectively to free-floating anxiety, somatic anxiety, tension, and specific fears. The trait-state difference was statistically significant for two of them: somatic anxiety and specific fears. It appeared that patients manifest higher than usual somatic anxiety levels; conversely, they reported specific fears of lesser intensity.

These analyses show a significant and complex interaction between wording and content of items. The difference on somatic anxiety was related to the wording of the item in eliciting responses in terms of trait and state. The difference on specific fears may be better interpreted in terms of response sets. It should be noted that the discrepancy between actual fears and usual fears cannot be attributed to patients' underestimating their fears of rats, spiders, or snakes in contrast to their real-life worries, because the same phenomenon was observed in a sample of normal subjects.

To evaluate the differences in the utilization of the response range, trait data and state data were separately analyzed. The matrix: Questions by response levels was factored, using the correspondence analysis method, and the results revealed distinct patterns for trait and state. For the trait data, response levels were well spaced and ordered on the first axis. Each level is well differentiated from another. For the state data, the zero category was widely separated from levels 1, 2, 3, and 4. On the second axis, intermediate levels 1, 2, and 3 are distinguished from extreme ones (0 and 4) for the trait, but not for the state.

The five-response system was more justified in the case of trait-anxiety than for the state-anxiety (Figs. A-1 and A-2).

These findings emphasize the fact that test instructions and wording of items have complex influences. These variables may interact with semantic content of items and induce different utilization of the response scale.

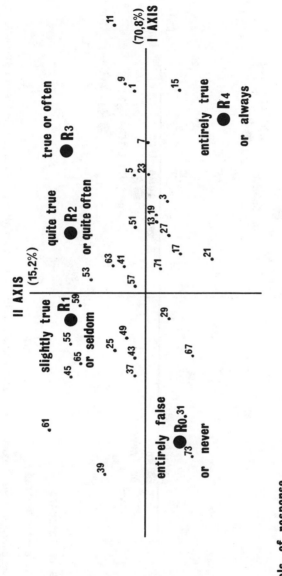

Fig. A-1. Correspondence analysis, Anxiety Trait Questionnaire: Simultaneous plotting of items and levels of responses.

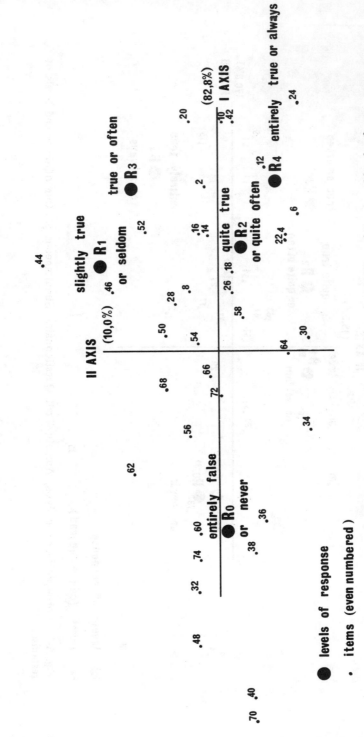

Fig. A-2. Correspondence analysis, Anxiety State Questionnaire: Simultaneous plotting of items and levels of responses.

● levels of response

• items (even numbered)

DEBILITATING ANXIETY, FACILITATING ANXIETY, AND GENERAL ANXIETY

J. A. Feij

Department of Psychology
Vrije Universiteit
Amsterdam, The Netherlands

In this report some preliminary results are presented of an investigation into the meaning of several anxiety scales. A large battery of personality questionnaires was given to 83 male and 50 female psychology freshmen. Factor analysis (normal varimax rotation) on the scores yielded the classical two higher order factors:

Factor I. Emotional stability versus neuroticism, or general anxiety. High loadings (ranging from .57 to .81) had, among others: Neuroticism subscale of the ABV, constructed by Wilde (1963) after the model of Eysenck's MPI; 16 PF–C (ego strength); O (guilt proneness); L (paranoid tendency); Q3 (self-sentiment); and Q4 (ergic tension). The last five scales are source traits of anxiety, according to Cattell. The O and L scales had negative loadings.

Factor II. Introversion versus extraversion. High loadings (from −.60 to −.75) were the ABV-Extraversion Scale, 16 PF–F (surgency: enthusiastic, happy-go-lucky), 16 PF–H (parmia: adventurous, thick skinned), and impulsiveness. Four more factors were obtained, which are not relevant here.

Fear of failure was measured with the PMT, (Hermans, 1967) by means of two subscales: one measuring debilitating, the other measuring facilitating anxiety. These concepts are similar to the negative (AAT−) and positive (AAT+) achievement anxiety concepts of Alpert and Haber (1960). The AAT− is highly correlated with the Test Anxiety Questionnaire of Mandler and Sarason (1952). In our study, debilitating anxiety loaded relatively high on factor I (emotional stability: −.53) *and* on factor II (introversion: .57). Facilitating anxiety, however, only loaded on factor II (introversion: −.47).

Debilitating anxiety showed its highest correlations with questionnaires measuring "audience anxiety" ($r = .63$) and "audience sensitivity" ($r = .56$). Facilitating anxiety was not related to general anxiety scores at all. Its highest correlations were with impulsiveness ($r = .39$) and 16 PF-H ($r_s = .32$). The results suggested that negative achievement anxiety (fear of failure, debilitating anxiety) was related to other measures of specific anxiety, (e.g., speech anxiety) and also to general anxiety. Furthermore, negative achievement anxiety appears to measure "dysthymia" and to be related to both anxiety and introversion. Schalling, Rissler, and Edman (1970) reported a similar finding with respect to "anticipation" and "thrill" subscales of their "Situational Unpleasantness" scale. Thus, the concept of "introverted anxiety" seems to be a valid one, characterized by anticipation of failure or other kinds of (ego) threat.

The importance of "modeling" was stressed both by Sarason and Meichenbaum. It is possible that fear of failure is a learned fear that reflects disturbed self-confidence, and that may be the basis of a general anxiety disposition. It seems clear that parents are among the most important models for the child who has to learn to cope with ambiguous and problem situations. Hermans, Ter Laak, and Maes (1972), for instance, found that parents of children with high debilitating anxiety scores showed fewer reactions when the child expressed insecurity during problem solving, produced more negative and fewer positive tension releases, and withheld more reinforcements after correct solutions.

A significant negative correlation was found in this study between facilitating and debilitating anxiety ($r = −.33; p < .01$). It is possible that their common variance is a consequence of their opposite relationship to the introversion-extraversion dimension. Facilitating anxiety was found to be related to impulsiveness (debilitating anxiety was not) and 16 PF-H (adventurousness). These results suggest that "facilitating anxiety" is not really anxiety at all and might be partially related to concepts like "optimal arousal level," "arousal tolerance," or even "need for arousal" as used by Zuckerman (1971).

Zuckerman (1971) describes subjects with high scores on his "Sensation Seeking Scale" as characterized by an "impulsive, dominant type of extraversion." A Sensation Seeking Scale was not available, and we could only indirectly test our hypothesis that there is some conceptual correspondence between "facilitating anxiety" and "optimal level of arousal or stimulation" (actually this correspondence already follows from the definition of facilitating anxiety).

To confirm this hypothesis, a stronger orienting response (galvanic skin response, GSR) on the first (novel) presentation of a series of simple visual stimuli in high sensation seekers would be expected. We would predict a positive relationship between facilitating anxiety scores and GSR amplitude to the first of a series of stimuli. In our study, this relation was found, but only in Ss with low general anxiety and neuroticism scores ($N = 21; r_s = .38; p < .05$) but not in high anxious Ss ($r_s = -.09$). It is possible that in the latter group the meaning of a GSR as either an orienting response (OR) or a defensive response (DR) is confused.

Finally, in the present study we found evidence that Ss with high debilitating anxiety scores had higher skin conductance levels during stress (mental arithmetic) than Ss with low scores. This was in line a report of Kissel and Littig (1962). However, high general anxiety scores also seemed to have some relationship with high skin conductance levels.

REFERENCES

Alpert, R., & Haber, R. N. Anxiety in academic achievement situations. *Journal of Abnormal and Social Psychology*, 1960, 61, 207–215.

Hermans, H. J. M. *Motivatie en prestatie*. Amsterdam: Swets & Zeitlinger, 1967.

Hermans, H. J. M., Ter Laak, J. J., & Maes, P. C. Achievement motivation and fear of failure in family and school. *Developmental Psychology*, 1972, 6, 520–528.

Kissel, E., & Littig, L. W. Test anxiety and skin conductance. *Journal of Abnormal and Social Psychology*, 1962, 65, 276–278.

Mandler, G., & Sarason, S. B. A study of anxiety and learning. *Journal of Abnormal and Social Psychology*, 1952, 47, 166–173.

Schalling, D., Rissler, A., & Edman, G. Pain tolerance, personality and autonomic indices. Differential consequences of noxious electrical stimulation. University of Stockholm Report, 1970.

Wilde, G. J. S. *Neurotische labiliteit gemeten volgens de vragenlijst methode.* Amsterdam: Van Rossen, 1963.

Zuckerman, M. Sensation seeking and habituation of the electrodermal orienting response. Paper presented at the meetings of Society for Psychophysiological Research. St. Louis, Oct. 1971.

THE FIRST FACTOR OF THE MINNESOTA MULTIPHASIC PERSONALITY INVENTORY: A ROSE BY ANY OTHER NAME

C. Raymond Millimet

Department of Psychology
University of Nebraska at Omaha
Omaha, Nebraska, United States

In an attempt to develop an instrument for selecting persons who exhibit differential recall of threatening stimuli, 10 subscales of the Minnesota Multiphasic Personality Inventory (MMPI) believed to be related to defensive style were pooled to form a composite scale. To eliminate the possibility of confounding scale content with sex, three separate item-analyses were performed on men and women college students, resulting in a 63-item scale for men and a 59-item scale for women (Millimet, 1970). Each form possesses very high reliability estimates: a test-retest coefficient of .95 over a 2-month period; and a K–R 20 and Spearman-Brown internal consistency coefficient of .91 and .90, respectively.

The 10 scales which formed the composite scale and the newly derived scale were intercorrelated and factor analyzed. The first factor was marked by the new scale, which exhibited a factor loading of .98. However, the Welsh (1956) Anxiety Scale, the Taylor (1953) Manifest Anxiety Scale (MAS), and the MMPI Psychasthenia Scale also exhibited loadings in the mid-90's on the first factor. The strong anxiety component associated with the dimension believed to be solely defensive style could not be denied. Previous research had already noted a strong relationship between trait anxiety scales and the Byrne (1964) Repression-Sensitization (R–S) Scale. In an attempt to capture the commonality of the two personality dimensions, the new scale was called the Manifest Anxiety-Defensiveness (MAD) Scale (Milliment, 1970).

Curiously, Byrne (1964) referred to the high correlation between anxiety and defensiveness as a "disturbing finding." In part, Byrne's view stemmed from his belief that the use of extreme defensive style would result in predominantly maladaptive behavior, i.e., a curvilinear relationship between R–S and personal adjustment. However, considerable research has reflected a strong linear relationship between tendency toward sensitization and maladjustment (Millimet, 1972). Because Byrne associated extreme defensive style with unrealistic behavior and failed to accept the relationship between trait anxiety and defensiveness, he was forced to argue for maladjustment at both poles of the R–S dimension.

Contrary to Byrne's arguments, the defensive capability of the person with low trait anxiety does not stem from a process of denying or distorting reality, or removing aspects of reality from conscious awareness, or even shifting attention away from the source of threat. Rather, the low trait anxiety individual successfully defends against an increase in state anxiety which tends to accompany threatening events. The maintenance of low state anxiety arises from a high threshold for perceiving threat to self-esteem. This aspect of personality generally results in correctly labeling most environmental events as irrelevant to the self-system, freeing the person to concentrate on the positive qualities of himself and the reality of the situation. On the other hand, the person with high trait anxiety possesses a low threshold for perceiving threat to self-esteem, leading him to the generally erroneous conclusion that most environmental events pose a serious threat to him. As his state anxiety mounts, the high trait anxiety individual is compelled to experience and ruminate about the negative qualities of himself, which seriously disrupts his daily activities.

In this regard, Millimet and Gardner (1972b) examined the effect of psychological stress on the arousal of state anxiety in low and high trait anxiety college students. The results showed that both trait anxiety groups experienced equally low state anxiety in a nonstress condition. Upon introducing a highly threatening intellectual assessment procedure, both anxiety groups exhibited a significant increase in state anxiety. However, the low trait anxiety subjects continued to experience positive affect, whereas the high trait anxiety subjects reported negative affect. The difference in affect between the two groups following the onset of the stress condition was highly significant. In another study, Millimet and Gardner (1972a) showed that persons with low trait anxiety possess high self esteem, whereas persons with high trait anxiety possess low self-esteem.

Such theorizing and empirical evidence suggests that in addition to the assessment of trait anxiety and defensive style, measures associated with the first factor of the MMPI are also related to personal adjustment. In this regard, Millimet (1970) showed that psychiatric patients possessed significantly higher trait anxiety than a college student sample. It was hypothesized that psychiatric patients are forced to resort to extreme symptomatology such as delusions, hallucinations, and behavioral withdrawal, in an attempt to defend against mounting state anxiety and distress for which they do not have effective lower order defensive capabilities. Further analysis showed that the patients with extremely high scores on the MAD scale exhibited an average MMPI profile of 87"246F'. These patients were viewed as possessing behavioral signs consistent with poor prognosis. As the average MMPI profile for the low trait anxiety psychiatric patients possessed no scale equal to or greater than the 70th T score, it was hypothesized that low scoring patients are less disturbed than high scoring patients and should have a favorable prognosis. In a college population, Millimet (1972) showed that using the Rotter Incomplete Sentences Blank as a measure of adjustment significantly identified low and high trait anxiety students as adjusted and maladjusted, respectively. Moreover, Millimet and Cohen (1973) found that high trait anxiety college students described their opposites with great envy and appreciation for their general success in life, referring to them as "self-assured," "relaxed," "carefree," and "having no problems." On the other hand, low trait anxiety students described their opposites in negative terms: "lacking self-confidence," "extremely sensitive," "indecisive," "worried," and "unstable."

REFERENCES

Byrne, D. Repression-sensitization as a dimension of personality. In B. A. Maher (Ed.), *Progress in experimental personality research*. New York: Academic Press, 1964.

Millimet, C. R. Manifest Anxiety-Defensiveness Scale: First Factor of the MMPI revisited. *Psychological Reports*, 1970, 27, 603–616.

Millimet, C. R. Support for a maladjustment interpretation of the anxiety-defensiveness dimension. *Journal of Personality Assessment*, 1972, 36, 39–44.

Millimet, C. R., & Cohen, H. J. Repression-sensitization: A reflection of test-taking set or personal adjustment? *Journal of Personality Assessment*, 1973, 37, 255–259.

Millimet, C. R., & Gardner, D. F. Induction of threat to self-esteem and the arousal and resolution of affect. *Journal of Experimental Social Psychology*, 1972, 8, 467–481. (a)

Millimet, C. R., & Gardner, D. F. Trait-state anxiety and psychological stress. *Journal of Clinical Psychology*, 1972, 28, 145–148. (b)

Taylor, J. A. A personality scale of manifest anxiety. *Journal of Abnormal and Social Psychology*, 1953, 48, 285–290.

Welsh, G. S. Factor dimensions A and R. In G. S. Welsh & W. G. Dahlstrom (Eds.), *Basic readings on the MMPI in psychology and medicine*. Minneapolis: University of Minnesota Press, 1956.

TYPES OF ANXIETY AND TYPES OF STRESSORS AS RELATED TO PERSONALITY

Daisy S. Schalling

Department of Psychology
Karolinska Institute
Stockholm, Sweden

Some recent anxiety studies in our laboratory have been based on the assumptions that there are systematic individual differences, not only in the *degree of anxiety* (intensity and/or frequency), but also in the *type of anxiety* and in the *type of stressors* (situations that evoke anxiety), and that these differences are related to personality dimensions. Degree of anxiety was assumed to be high in persons who were high in *Neuroticism* (Eysenck, 1967). Type of anxiety, however, may, to some extent, depend on whether the individual is high or low in *Extraversion*. Further, it was assumed that the self-reported sensitivity to different types of stressors is related to these personality dimensions.

In the following, the main results of two anxiety studies will be briefly reported. The first study was made on a group of

These investigations have been supported by grants from the Swedish Medical Research Council (21X-5473) and from the Swedish Council for Social Science Research (588/72). Thanks are due to my students, especially Gunnar Edman, Karin Lagerberg-Aberg, Birgitta Tobisson, Margareta Eriksson-Skold, and Ulla Pettersson, who participated in the studies reported.

nonpsychotic, temporarily drug-free psychiatric inpatients and rehabilitation clients ($N = 37$; for details, see Schalling, Cronholm, Asberg & Espmark, 1973a). The second study was made on a group of students ($N = 70$).

In the first study, both state and trait anxiety measures were used (cf. Spielberger, 1972). A modification of the clinical anxiety rating scale by Buss was applied as *state anxiety* measure. It comprises a number of common indicators of anxiety, rated on a 5-point scale on the basis of a clinical interview concerning symptoms during the last few days. The interjudge reliability (intraclass correlation coefficient) for three raters was quite high (Schalling et al., 1973a). The items were a priori subdivided into two groups, assumed to reflect two types of anxiety. One was called *Somatic Anxiety* and included Autonomic disburbances, Somatic complaints, Distractibility and Disquietude (vague diffuse feelings of uneasiness, distress, inner tenseness, and panic). The other was called *Psychic Anxiety* and included Muscular tension and Worry (anxiousness, apprehensions attached to a cognitive content, ruminations, and worrying in advance). This grouping is thus not equivalent to a division into physiological and psychological items, and the terms Somatic and Psychic Anxiety may be misleading. They were retained, however, in adherence to the tradition by Buss and other writers. Cluster analysis and component analysis on the present data on the whole supported the grouping of items (Schalling, Cronholm & Asberg, 1973b).

On the basis of the content in the Buss Somatic and Psychic Anxiety items, but influenced also by clinical experience and various factors found in factor analyses of anxiety inventories like MAS, we have constructed a *trait anxiety inventory, the Multi-Component Anxiety (MCA) scale.* In the present version, there are two subscales, one consisting of items corresponding to the Somatic Anxiety concept, the other of items corresponding to the Psychic Anxiety concept, as described. Reliability of the scale (Kuder-Richardson) was .94. (For details, see Schalling et al., 1973b).

In various studies, we have obtained significant intercorrelations between the Somatic and Psychic Anxiety measures, both for state and trait, as might be expected. However, they have proved to be differentially related to external criteria, thus supporting the theoretical interest of treating them as separate constructs, at least for certain purposes. For example, independent Rorschach ratings of amount of anxiety were significantly related to both Psychic and

Somatic Anxiety scores, whereas the correlations with Rorschach ratings of coping with anxiety in terms of undercontrol-versus-over-control indicated that Somatic Anxiety is associated with under-control and "free-floating" anxiety (Schalling et al., 1973b).

Psychic and Somatic Anxiety measures have shown an interesting pattern of relationships with *personality variables.* In the personality measures used in our studies are included the Eysenck Personality Inventory (EPI) and the Marke Nyman Personality Inventory (MNT), the latter having the advantage of comprising separate measures related to the two main components of extraversion, impulsiveness (Solidity), and sociability (Stability), which in our studies consistently have shown different relationships to external criteria (Schalling, 1970).

Among the results obtained in the study on psychiatric patients, the state and trait anxiety measures were significantly correlated (p < .001) which may be expected in a group of mainly acute cases. It is in line with the assumptions that both Psychic Anxiety and Somatic Anxiety were significantly correlated with Neuroticism, both for state and trait measures (p < .001). The pattern of relations between the anxiety measures, and Extraversion or impulsiveness (Solidity) is of special interest. Psychic Anxiety trait scores were *negatively* correlated with EPI Extraversion (p < .01); i.e., introvert patients reported higher Psychic Anxiety than did extravert patients. In contrast, Somatic Anxiety scores [both state (p < .05) and trait (p < .001)] were *positively* correlated with impulsiveness (as estimated by Solidity). Thus, more impulsive patients tended to report higher Somatic Anxiety than did less impulsive patients, whereas they did not differ in Psychic Anxiety. Further, the proportion of Somatic Anxiety to total anxiety scores was higher in the more impulsive than in the less impulsive patients. Sociability (as estimated by Stability) was not significantly related to the anxiety measures in this group.

These results may be interpreted to indicate an association between degree of anxiety and *autonomic arousal,* and between type of anxiety and *cortical arousal,* on the assumption that high Neuroticism is assocaited with high Autonomic arousal (Eysenck, 1967) and that high extraversion-impulsiveness is associated with low cortical arousal (Schalling, 1970). The findings may have implications for differential treatment of anxious psychiatric patients, especially for pharmacological treatment. Sedative drugs given to anxious impulsive patients may have negative effects by further lowering the already suboptimal cortical arousal and thereby possibly further increasing the vague uneasiness and autonomic symptoms associated with Somatic Anxiety, whereas a certain amount of sedation may be beneficial for more introvert patients, dampening the cortical excitation and thereby helping them to relax from the excessive ruminations and worry associated with the Psychic Anxiety predominating in these cases. It should be pointed out that this analysis pertains to the formal quality of the anxiety, disregarding the idiosyncratic conflicts and problems that may be experienced as the core content of the anxiety.

The second study concerned relations between sensitivity to different *types of stressors* or anxiety-provoking situations as related to personality variables. Subjects were asked to rate, on a 9-point scale, the degree of unpleasantness (from highly pleasant to highly unpleasant) they would experience in finding themselves in a series of concrete situations described in an inventory, the *Situational Unpleasantness Sensitivity Scale* (Schalling, 1970). The situations were selected a priori on the basis of content, but controlled later by item analyses and factor analyses. The latest version of the inventory comprises seven scales: *Criticism* (negative evaluation, e.g., being scolded by your boss, hearing that people are talking about you behind your back), *Anticipation* (e.g., waiting to be tested for a drivers's license), *Aggression* (e.g., seeing a man shot down on TV, seeing a fight in the street), *Pain-Medical* (e.g., taking a blood sample), *Pain* (e.g., having your finger hurt by a thorny bush), *Thrill* (e.g., sailing in a small boat in a storm), and *Boredom* (e.g., working on an assembly line).

Among the results, Neuroticism and trait-anxiety measures were associated with high unpleasantness in situations involving critical evaluation ($p < .01$) and anticipation ($p < .01$) but not with situations involving physical pain. These findings support the hypotheses by Spielberger (1972). However, Neuroticism and Somatic Anxiety were associated with unpleasantness in Pain-Medical situations ($p < .01$; $p < .05$), in which presumably the physical pain aspect is less important than other aspects. Unpleasantness in thrilling adventurous situations was positively related to the anxiety measures ($p < .05$), but negatively to impulsiveness ($p < .01$) and Extraversion ($p < .01$), which is in line with the personality model described by Schalling (1970). Finally, extravert subjects reported less unpleasant feelings than introverts in anticipatory situations ($p <$ .01), which is in line with physiological studies from our laboratory (Schalling, 1972).

REFERENCES

Eysenck, H. J. *The biological bases of personality*. Springfield, Ill.: Charles C Thomas, 1967.

Schalling, D. Contributions to the validation of some personality concepts. Reports from the Psychological Laboratories, The University of Stockholm, Suppl. 1, 1970.

Schalling, D. Spontaneous fluctuations in skin conductance in different experimental situations as related to psychopathy. Paper presented at the Symposium for the Society for Psychophysiological Research, Boston, November, 1972.

Schalling, D., Cronholm, B., Asberg, M., & Espmark, S. Ratings of psychic and somatic anxiety indicants. *Acta psychiatrica Scandinavica*, 1973, 49, 353–368. (a)

Schalling, D., Cronholm, B., & Asberg, M. Components of state and trait anxiety as related to personality and arousal. In L. Levi (Ed.), *Emotions—Their parameters and measurement*. New York: Raven Press, 1975.

Spielberger, C. D. Conceptual and methodological issues in anxiety research. In C. D. Spielberger (Ed.), *Anxiety: Current trends in theory and research*, Vol. 2. New York: Academic Press, 1972.

PREFERENCE FOR SIGNALED SHOCK: EFFECT OF SAFETY SIGNAL OR PREPARATORY RESPONSE?

Otello Desiderato and Jane Arabian

Department of Psychology, Connecticut College
New London, Connecticut, United States

It is generally accepted that uncertainty about the time of occurrence of aversive or traumatic events contributes to the stressfulness of contemporary life. Data from animal studies indicate that exposure to unsignaled, inescapable electric shock produces more gastric ulcers and other psychosomatic disorders than does exposure to the same shock which is preceded by a warning stimulus (Weiss, 1970). Both human (Lanzetta & Driscoll, 1966) and animal subjects (Badia, Culbertson, & Lewis, 1971), given the choice, will act to provide themselves with a warning stimulus that signals the onset of the painful event. It has been frequently observed that rats prefer to spend more time in the signaled, rather than the unsignaled-shock side of a shuttle box (Lockard, 1963; Perkins, Seymann, Levis, & Spencer, 1966).

The preference for signaled shock has given rise to two different interpretations: (*a*) The *preparatory response (PR) hypothesis*, which contends that the signal evokes some type of preparatory process, either peripheral or central, which serves to attenuate the effect of the shock stimulus (Kimmel, 1965) and (*b*) the *safety-signal (SS)* hypothesis, which views signal offset as the crucial factor, since it is the absence of the signal that permits the subject to discriminate a shock-free, or "safe," period from a danger period (Lockard, 1963; Seligman, 1968). According to the safety-signal hypothesis, signaled shock is less stressful not because S is given time to "prepare," but because it can rest, or relax, during periods that are reliably free of danger.

Since the same signal necessarily serves both as a warning stimulus and as a cue setting off periods of safety from periods of danger, the usual signaled-shock paradigm does not permit an easy assessment of the SS and PR hypotheses. In our laboratory, we have used two discrete stimuli: a light to identify relatively long (10-minute) periods of "danger" (during which shock probability was > 0 and in the absence of which S was entirely "safe"), and a tone which functioned as a reliable predictor of shock 5 seconds later. Thus, the *absence* of the light can serve as a SS, while the *onset* of the tone can serve to evoke a PR.

Figure A-3 shows three paradigms we have used to vary independently the safety signal and preparatory response properties of experimental conditions. In each paradigm, a 20-minute session is divided into equal periods of light and darkness. Paradigm S/P ensures a total of 10 minutes of safety (S) in the absence of the light, but also contains the stimulus for a preparatory response (P), since the 5-second tone always precedes a shock. We assumed that 5 seconds would be sufficient time for a perparatory response to develop, and that the light stimulus itself would not act as a safety signal since it is correlated with the signaled-shock phase of the paradigm.

In paradigm NS/NP, light offset is not a reliable safety signal; in addition, since the tone occurs independently of shock, tone onset should not be expected to evoke a preparatory response. Finally, in paradigm S/NP, light offset is a reliable predictor of safety; however, tone onset, again a poor predictor of shock, should remain an ineffective elicitor of a preparatory response.

Our basic procedure was to confine rats for 20-minute periods on each (discriminably different) side of a shuttle box, with one paradigm in effect on one side, another paradigm on the other. On the assumption that the rat would attempt to avoid the more aversive side, a 10-minute preference test was then given, during which the partition separating the two sides was removed; and the amount of

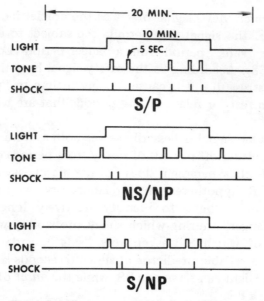

Fig. A-3. Three experimental conditions (in rats), employing various combinations of safety (S) and preparatory response (P), including no safety periods (NS) and no preparatory signals (NP).

time the rat spent on the "preferred" side was recorded. During each 10-minute test, neither tones nor shocks were presented. This procedure was followed twice a day on each of 10 days. On one of the two daily tests, the light was on continuously for the entire duration of the test period; on the second test, it remained off.

To observe the effect of providing the subjects with both safety-signal and preparatory response opportunities, one group of eight rats was exposed to conditions S/P on one side, and NS/NP on the other side, of the shuttle box. These animals quickly demonstrated a preference for the S/P side, spending an average of 72% of the time on the side that provided *both* a safety signal and a signal for a preparatory response. This finding corresponds to the results of single-stimulus paradigms which, as noted above, inherently contain both SS and PR possibilities.

To then assess the effect of removing the signal for a preparatory response, a second group of eight rats was exposed to S/NP conditions on one side, and NS/NP on the other. Subjects in this group spent 82% of the time on the S/NP side. Removal of the opportunity for making a preparatory response enhanced, rather than diminished, the attractiveness of the S/NP side. This result suggested to us that the warning tone might actually have been aversive.

In a more direct test of the aversiveness of the warning signal, a third group of eight rats was exposed to the S/P paradigm on one side and the S/NP paradigm on the other side of the shuttle box. It will be noted that, for this group, "safe" periods were provided on both sides, but the tone served as a reliable warning stimulus on only one side of the shuttle box. Animals in this group *avoided* the warning stimulus side, spending 88% of the time on the S/NP side.

These results confirm the importance of safety periods in affecting preference behavior in situations in which shock is unavoidable. That predictable periods of safety also contribute to stress reduction is supported by the finding that, only in the last group (S/P vs. S/NP), for which *both* sides of the shuttle box provided the safety signal, did the number of boluses show a systematic decrease across the 10 experimental days. Finally, it would appear that a warning stimulus that signals the imminent onset of pain is not a condition animals seek to maintain; rather, they seek to avoid it, as one should predict on the basis of the known fear-inducing and behavior-disrupting properties of such stimuli.

REFERENCES

Badia, P., Culbertson, S., & Lewis, P. The relative aversiveness of signalled vs. unsignalled avoidance. *Journal of the Experimental Analysis of Behavior*, 1971, 16, 113–121.

Kimmel, H. D. Instrumental factors in classical conditioning. In W. Prokasy (Ed.), *Classical conditioning*. New York: Appleton-Century-Crofts, 1965.

Lanzetta, J. T., & Driscoll, J. M. Preference for information about an uncertain but unavoidable outcome. *Journal of Personality and Social Psychology*, 1966, 3, 96–102.

Lockard, J. S. Choice of a warning signal or no warning signal in an unavoidable shock situation. *Journal of Comparative and Physiological Psychology*, 1963, 56, 526–530.

Perkins, C. C., Jr., Seymann, R., Levis, D. J., & Spencer, R. Factors affecting preference for signal shock over shock-signal. *Journal of Experimental Psychology*, 1966, 72, 190–196.

Seligman, M. E. P. Chronic fear produced by unpredictable shock. *Journal of Comparative and Physiological Psychology*, 1968, 66, 402–411.

Weiss, J. M. Somatic effects of predictable and unpredictable shock. *Psychosomatic Medicine*, 1970, 32, 397–408.

SOME STUDIES OF ORIENTING AND DEFENSIVE RESPONSES

Robert D. Hare

Department of Psychology
University of British Columbia
Vancouver, British Columbia, Canada

According to recent integrations of Western and Soviet theory and research, the orienting response (OR) to novel stimulation should include heart rate (HR) deceleration and cephalic vasolidation, while the defensive response (DR) to noxious or intense stimulation should include HR acceleration and cephalic vasoconstriction. There is some evidence (e.g., Graham & Clifton, 1966) that the appropriate changes in HR do in fact occur in situations that logically call for orienting or defensive behavior. Similarly, HR deceleration and acceleration appear to be associated with sensory intake and sensory rejection, respectively (Lacey, 1967). However, even though Sokolov (1963) emphasized the importance of cephalic vasomotor activity in differentiating between orienting and defensive responses, the expected differences have generally not been found.

Elsewhere (Hare, 1972) I have suggested that one of the reasons for the failure to obtain the cardiovascular patterns putatively associated with the OR and the DR is the routine use of undifferentiated group data. By analyzing some earlier data, we found that some Ss did in fact respond to slides of homicide victims with both HR deceleration and cephalic vasodilation, whereas others responded to the same slides with both HR acceleration and cephalic vasoconstriction. Presumably the former pattern reflected the elicitation of an OR in Ss who found the slides interesting, and the latter was part of a DR in Ss who found the slides aversive. An additional reason for the frequent failure to observe the cardiovascular patterns supposedly associated with the OR and the DR may be the use of stimuli (e.g., tones, shocks) that are inappropriate for their intended purpose. Since these stimuli are usually of shorter duration than the latencies of the physiological responses they elicit, it is difficult to see how these responses could influence reception of the stimuli that produced them.

On the other hand, when visual stimulation with intense connotations is used, the physiological changes produced by the initial contact with the stimulus could, by their continued presence, facilitate intake or rejection of the stimulus. We found, for example, that when Ss are shown colored slides of things they greatly fear (e.g., spiders) the predicted DR pattern is elicited; an OR pattern is elicited in other Ss unafraid of spiders (Hare, 1973). These findings are nicely supported by some data recently collected (Hare, R. D., & Blevings, G. An attempt to condition orienting and defensive responses. Unpublished manuscript, 1973). Nine female Ss afraid of spiders (P) and nine unafraid of spiders (N) were shown a series of colored slides of spiders (s) and "neutral" objects and scenes (n), each 5 seconds in duration. As Figs. A-4 and A-5 indicate, Group P responded to the spider slides with marked HR acceleration and cephalic vasoconstriction, i.e., with the cardiovascular components of a DR. On the other hand, these same Ss gave an OR (HR deceleration and cephalic vasodilation) to the neutral slides.

From an adaptive point of view it could be argued that orienting and defensive responses would be particularly useful when they are anticipatory in nature, thus preparing the person for the impending stimulation. As part of the study just referred to (Hare & Blevings, previously cited unpublished manuscript) we therefore included a classical conditioning paradigm. The conditioned stimuli (CS) were two tones, each 11 seconds long and easily discriminable. One tone was always followed by a 5-second presentation of a spider slide, whereas the other tone was always followed by a 5-second slide of an ordinary object or scene ("neutral" slide). The tone-slide combinations were presented in random order, 12 times each, with the

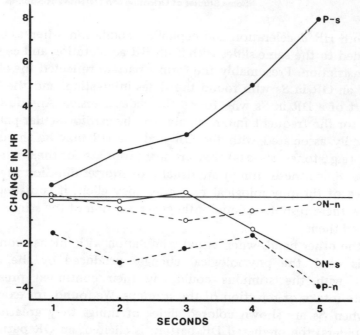

Fig. A-4. Mean second-by-second changes (bpm) in HR given by Ss afraid of spiders (P) and Ss unafraid of them (N) to slides of spiders (s) and of neutral scenes (n).

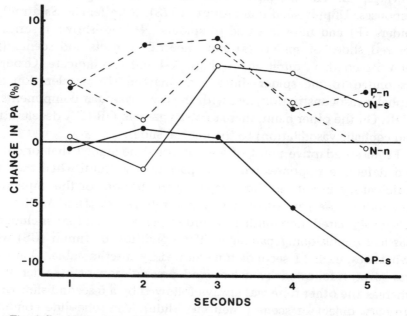

Fig. A-5. Mean second-by-second change (percent) in cephalic pulse amplitude (PA). Legend as for Fig. A-4.

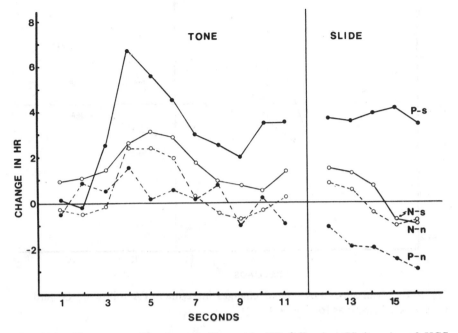

Fig. A-6. Mean second-by-second changes in HR following CS (tone) and UCS (slide) onset. Legend as for Fig. A-4.

intertrial interval varying between 25 and 35 seconds. Figure A-6 shows the mean second-by-second HR response (as deviations from the mean rate of the 5 beats prior to tone onset) of each group to the tones preceding each slide, and to the slides themselves. It is evident that the two groups of Ss differed markedly in their anticipatory HR responses, with Group P showing a strong accelerative component to the CS followed by spider slides. Further, only this group showed any real differentiation of response to the slides, continued accelera-tion (above prestimulus level) to the spider slides and deceleration to the neutral slides. The expected group differences in anticipatory cephalic vasomotor response were not significant. However, as Fig. A-7 suggests, the generally larger anticipatory vasoconstriction (a decrease in pulse amplitude) to the tones preceding spider slides than to those preceding neutral slides suggests that cephalic vasomotor activity may be capable of being conditioned.

The conditioned HR acceleration shown by Group P was generally associated with concomitant increases in palmar skin conductance, respiration rate and amplitude, muscle tension (EMG activity from

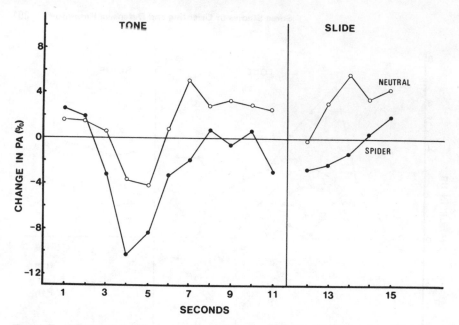

Fig. A-7. Mean second-by-second changes in œphalic PA following CS and UCS onset. Legend as for Fig. A-4.

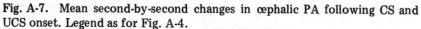

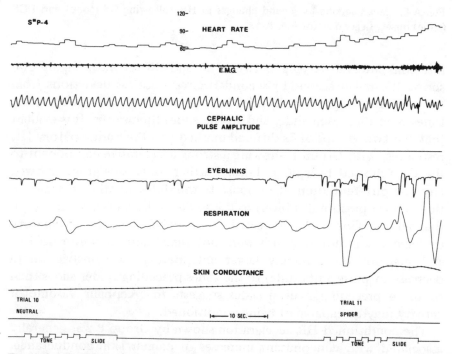

Fig. A-8. Portion of the polygraph record of one *S* in Group P, showing combined somatic and autonomic responses to the tone preceding a spider slide.

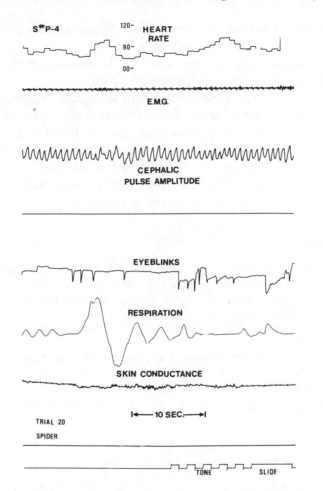

Fig. A-9. A later portion of the record shown in Fig. A-8 illustrating that large anticipatory increases in HR can occur without increases in EMG and respiratory activity. The skin conductance channel was inoperative at this point.

the chin), and blink rate, as well as cognitive and behavioral attempts to deal with the forthcoming aversive stimulation. A particularly good example of this complex anticipatory response is shown in Fig. A-8, in which part of the polygraph record of one S in Group P is reproduced. It should be noted, however, that the association between somatic and autonomic activity illustrated by this record did not always occur. Figure A-9 shows that on a later trial this same S gave a large anticipatory increase in HR even though no appreciable increase in EMG activity occurred, and despite the fact that there was a reduction in respiratory activity.

It is not known why the HR and cephalic vasomotor components of the OR and DR occurred in response to the slides presented alone and not in response to signals preceding the slides. In particular, Ss who feared spiders gave more or less the same anticipatory cephalic vasomotor responses as did those who did not fear them. However, cephalic vasomotor activity is a difficult variable to work with, and it is possible that subsequent research will find that such activity occurring prior to an anticipated event will be in accordance with the theoretical properties of orienting and defensive responses.

REFERENCES

Graham, F. K., & Clifton, R. C. Heart-rate change as a component of the orienting response. *Psychological Bulletin*, 1966, 65, 305–320.

Hare, R. D. Cardiovascular components of orienting and defensive responses. *Psychophysiology*, 1972, 9, 606–614.

Hare, R. D. Orienting and defensive responses to visual stimuli. *Psychophysiology*, 1973, 10, 453–464.

Lacey, J. Somatic response patterning and stress: Some revisions of activation theory. In M. Appley & R. Trumbell (Eds.), *Psychological stress: Issues in research*. New York: Appleton-Century-Crofts, 1967.

Sokolov, E. *Perception and the conditioned reflex*. New York: MacMillan, 1963.

AROUSAL AND RECALL

Steven Schwartz

Department of Psychology
Northern Illinois University
De Kalb, Illinois, United States

To investigate the effects of arousal on subsequent recall, four experiments were conducted. The focus of these experiments was a decision theory analysis of arousal's effect on two retrieval strategies: filtering and pigeonholing.

Borrowing principles generally associated with perception, Broadbent (1971) described filtering as occurring when one adopts a "stimulus set" choosing items on the basis of some common feature (e.g., a particular sound) and ignoring those items in the store without this feature. Pigeonholing, on the other hand, occurs when one adopts a "response set" selecting from a large list of items (e.g., a list of mixed words) those constituting a subvocabulary (e.g., the names of colors). If an operating characteristic is derived relating the probability of a correct response to the probability of an incorrect response (false alarm), pigeonholing produces an increase in the number of correct responses as the false alarm rate increases, whereas filtering produces a change in the number of correct responses with a constant false alarm rate. In decision theory terms, filtering is mirrored by changes in d' and pigeonholing by changes in β.

If arousal affects one retrieval strategy but not the other, contradictory effects would be expected depending on the strategy employed. Moreover, the changes in arousal's effect with time reported in some studies may have been due to arousal's dissipation with time. These hypotheses were assessed in experiments I and II in which subjects were required to recall parts of visually presented word lists. On any particular trial, the words were either unrelated, phonemically related, or sematically related. Arousal improved recall for phonemic lists, but not for semantic lists. To the extent that memory for phonemic lists involves filtering and memory for semantically related words involves pigeonholing, arousal facilitated the former but not the latter. These effects were reversed with delay (semantic were superior), probably due to the dissipation of arousal with time. In a third experiment, subjects were asked to remember the names of characters in short stories. Probe names were suggested, and the subjects were asked to indicate if the name was correct and to give a confidence rating in their judgment. Arousal during the story presentation made for improved recall, by increasing the efficiency of filtering as reflected by changes in d'.

Although these findings indicate that arousal affects filtering, earlier research (Broadbent & Gregory, 1965) found that in vigilance experiments, arousal affected pigeonholing by reducing the number of "not sure" responses. That is, subjects were more certain that a signal was presented or more certain that no signal was presented than were unaroused subjects. Such a mechanism may produce contradictory effects on pigeonholing. Specifically, when conditions favor cautious responding, a change in the number of "not sure" responses may improve performance; when conditions favor risky responding, arousal may impede performance. The experiments described thus far were not designed to assess such a differential effect on pigeonholing. At the very least it is necessary to know, in advance, when subjects will adopt a risky criterion and when they will adopt a conservative one, so that the discrepant effects of arousal may be parcelled out. The procedure of experiment III is easily modified for this purpose. Ingleby (1969) using the procedure of experiment III, found that although d' was actually greater for rare names, recall for common character names was superior because subjects employed a riskier criterion for common names. Experiment IV, therefore, replicated three, using both rare and common names. It was hypothesized that arousal would affect pigeonholing by producing a decrease in the separation of criteria for the two name types. In other words, it was expected that β for rare names would decrease, but β for common names would increase, thus reducing the advantage of common names.

In experiment IV, subjects heard short stories, in each of which half the characters' names were judged common and half rare. At the conclusion of each story, subjects were given probe names and required to decide whether the names were correct or incorrect and to give a confidence rating in their judgment. As predicted β decreased for rare but increased for common names. The Noise-by-Name interaction was significant and indicated that although β was lower for common names in the no-noise condition, β did not differ for the two types of names in the noise conditions.

White-noise-induced arousal led to an increase in β for common names and a decrease in β for rare, supporting the hypothesis that arousal improves pigeonholing when conditions favor cautious responding, but impairs pigeonholing when a risky criterion is likely to be employed. Interestingly, the convergence in criteria did not result in equal hit rates for the two types of names. Even in noise, common names were significantly better recalled than were rare names. Since β did not differ it made sense to look at d'. Rare and common names did not differ in sensitivity and no-noise but there was a significant increase in d' for common names in noise. Thus, the superiority of common names in noise was due to their higher value of d' whereas their superiority in no-noise was due to their lower value of β. Arousal, as in the first three experiments, affected filtering in experiment IV. Its effect was to make filtering more important than pigeonholing as a retrieval strategy.

The failure to find an increase in filtering for rare names in experiment IV may have been due to inherent differences in discriminability. Thus, although the signal-to-noise ratio was quite good, it is possible that given the large dynamic range of speech, some loss of acoustic information occurred due to masking. Such masking may have affected common and rare names differentially because common names possessed phonemic characteristics resistent to masking or because rare names were masked more easily.

Arousal it seems will lead to improved recall when conditions favor cautious responding only if the material may also be recalled by filtering. The observed effect of arousal will be the result of the interaction of a number of factors including the level of arousal (which dissipates with delay), and the criterion adopted and the potential for filtering, both of which are related to the type of material to be recalled.

REFERENCES

Broadbent, D. E. *Decision and stress.* New York: Academic Press, 1971.

Broadbent, D. E., & Gregory, M. Effects of noise and of signal rate upon vigilance analyzed by means of decision theory. *Human Factors*, 1965, 7, 155–162.

Ingleby, J. D. Decision making processes in human perception and memory. Unpublished doctoral dissertation, University of Cambridge, 1969.

SOCIETAL STRESS AND THE QUALITY OF LIFE

T. N. Bhargava

Center for Urban Regionalism
Kent State University
Kent, Ohio, United States

The primary purpose of this study is to provide a systems approach for investigating psychosocial implications of environmental alterations on a society and its quality of life. These alterations trigger a chain of compensatory changes, much like a nuclear reaction in physics, in the human ecosystem and its pattern of behavior. A manageable summary description of the process involved in the dynamics of the environmental system is shown in Fig. A-10.

In terms of the impact of this process on society, we consider environmental stress to be stress that interferes with the satisfaction of basic needs or that disturbs or threatens to disturb the stable equilibrium of society; society's reaction to this stress constitutes a strain on itself, affecting the behavior patterns of people. Figure A-11 gives a summary form.

There are several variables of which the quality of life, QL, is a function, and clearly there are all sorts of ways to describe it. It is a

This research received partial support from the Office of Graduate School and Research, Kent State University.

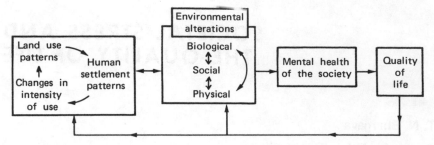

Fig. A-10.   The impact of environmental alterations on society.

nebulous concept, and varies from region to region, culture to culture, and so on, thus defying attempts to precisely define it. However, it seems entirely possible to find ways to get at least an idea of the relative level of the quality of life for comparative and predictive purposes. For example, let H = Health, mental and physiological; A = Academics, education and research; P = Population, density and demography; P = Physical system, spatial patterns; I = Institutional, community and family; N = Norms, social, order, and law; E = Employment, quantity and quality; S = Support systems, life and resources; S = Standard of living, absolute and relative. Then $QL = f(H,A,P,P,I,N,E,S,S)$.

To obtain an index of the quality of life of a society vis-a-vis the stress impinging on it, we assume that a society is a unique entity consisting of the aggregate of its members. Next, we proceed as if we were to investigate the condition of one's mental health, and, through the total history, identify those factors that have a direct and significant bearing on it. Finally, we make use of the fact that anxiety and stress are a part of all mental illness.

This method can appropriately be called the diagnostic approach, similar to the process of simulation. Throughout this, we, as model builders, remain conscious of the fact that the process we are

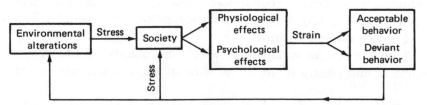

Fig. A-11.   Stress and strain originating in environmental alterations.

attempting to recreate has functioned for a long time. We only hope to capture the essential features and produce in miniature a sequence of outcomes that strongly resemble the original.

Most measures of mental health are based on incidence of some specific emotional disorders and statistics of the same; for example, data on suicides, mental institutions, psychiatrists, and the like. We consider these to be indicative of the relative level of anxiety of a society and accordingly call these indexes of anxiety level, AL. The question of stress, however, is a different matter. Stress is indicated by the incidence of the use of various devices that enable one to cope with the stress and strain reaction to the stress and is measured by the stress load, SL.

In either case, interacting effects of anxiety level and stress load with total environmental diversity may now be expressed by means of a diagram (Fig. A-12). We have simplified the represented interactions for the sake of analytical manageability; in reality, these interactions may indeed be more complex. In Fig. A-12, the dark arrows indicate the interactions, and the dotted-line arrows represent the analytical steps in the simulation process.

An estimate of the total stress on society may then be obtained by means of suitable overall general indicators that reflect it. For example, one may say that an undue amount of stress on a person usually results in deviation from the normal sleep pattern; this lack of the required amount of sleep, in turn, results in an inability to completely follow the person's usual activity pattern. Thus, resort is made to various aids for nonmedical reasons, mostly in the form of drugs, tobacco, and alcohol—called stress relief devices (SRDs)—to try to cope with stress. Our rationale for studying SRDs rather than measuring the actual prevalence of stress is perhaps best explained by the following analogy: the man-environment

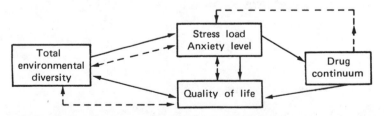

Fig. A-12. Interacting effects of anxiety level and stress load with total environmental diversity. Dark arrows indicate interactions, dotted lines the analytical steps.

interaction of two objects, as in physics. We know that when two objects rub together friction may be the result. In our model this friction is the stress. Man then needs a buffer agent to reduce the possible friction involved in his confrontation with this environment. The use of SRDs is one important buffer now prevalent in our society. The consumption of SRDs becomes a more meaningful statistic when it is related not as an absolute, but rather as a scale illustrating the various nonmedical reasons for taking SRDs. A sample of a few points in the drug continuum might be described as follows:

Carrying on	Making it	Getting high	Escaping	Terminal

The knowledge needed to study this continuum is both theoretical and statistical. For example, in assigning a value for each point one needs to know first the effect produced by the use of an SRD. Statistical data may then enable one to estimate the consumption of this SRD by the society for each point of the continuum. In implementing this continuum, it is our aim to approximately locate critical cut-off points, such as the point at which drug use is no longer analogous to a buffer agent, and, in the drug continuum, passes from a coping tool to, say, a suicidal tool. Once this is devised as a valid way of defining and demarcating different states of the society's mental health, microstudies can be undertaken for full and further investigations.

REFERENCES

Bhargava, T. N., Doyle, P. H., & Wenninger, E. P. Envirodynamics and mental health. Environmental Studies Series, No. 1, Center for Urban Regionalism, Kent State University, 1972.

SOCIETY, STRESS, AND SUICIDE

Herbert H. Krauss and Beatrice J. Krauss

Department of Psychology
Hunter College of the City University of New York
New York, New York, United States

Stimulated by Freud's intuitions about the nature of man, psychologically oriented theorists have sought the key to suicidal phenomena in the intrapsychic development, structure, and economy of the personality of the individual (e.g., Freud, 1956). In marked contrast, sociologists, following the path blazed by Durkheim (e.g., Durkheim, 1951), have attempted to relate the incidence of suicide to the operation of such societally determined variables as the extent to which a person is integrated within his culture. For almost 70 years and for rather artificial reasons, there has been little effort directed toward integrating psychological and sociological thinking into a unified theory of suicide (e.g., Krauss, Robinson, & Cauthen, 1972). Recently, however, social scientists have come to believe that a comprehensive theory of suicide, a theory that encompasses both the psychological and sociological traditions, will be necessary before a workable understanding of suicide is possible (Krauss, 1966; Krauss & Krauss, 1968; Maris, 1969). To date, perhaps the most fruitful approach toward developing such a theory of suicide has been suggested by Naroll (1969).

Naroll's (1969) formulation has its roots in the frustration-aggression hypothesis articulated by Dollard, Doob, Miller, Mowrer, and Sears (1939). These researchers identified various institutions or agencies that produce relatively constant interaction patterns associated with interpersonal frustration, e.g., divorce freedom. Further, they demonstrated cross-culturally that the rate of suicide of a society varies directly with the number of such institutions present in that society, a finding confirmed and expanded somewhat by Krauss (1966) and Krauss and Krauss (1968). Those subsequent investigations suggested that institutions that produce interpersonal frustration, termed thwarting-disorientation situations (TDS) by Naroll (1969), are infrequently directly responsible for suicidal behavior. Instead they seem to increase the "stress level" of a society, producing suicide in those people, who, for whatever reason (e.g., psychopathological condition), are most vulnerable to stress.

In sum, the rate of suicide within a society was found to be a function of the level of interpersonal stress present in that society, and that the level of stress present in a society affects differentially various subgroups within that society.

Many important issues remain to be resolved with respect to the relationship between societal stress and its manifestations in individuals. Are TDS linked causally to other conditions considered pathological—heart disease, rate of homicide, and so on? How do stress-producing institutions originate and perpetuate themselves within a society? By what mechanisms is stress transmitted to the culture bearers of a society? These and other questions must be put to the scrutiny of research.

REFERENCES

Dollard, J., Doob, L. W., Miller, N. E., Mowrer, O. H., & Sears, R. R. *Frustration and aggression.* New Haven: Yale University Press, 1939.

Durkheim, E. *Suicide.* Glencoe, Ill.: Free Press, 1951.

Freud, S. Mourning and melancholia. In *Collected Papers of Sigmund Freud,* Vol. 4. London: Hogarth, 1956.

Krauss, H. H. A cross-cultural theory of suicide. Unpublished doctoral dissertation, Northwestern University, 1966.

Krauss, H. H., & Krauss, B. J. Cross-cultural study of the thwarting-disorientation theory of suicide. *Journal of Abnormal Psychology,* 1968, 73, 353–357.

Krauss, H. H., Robinson, I. E., & Cauthen, N. R. Toward a comprehensive theory of suicide. In S. Dinitz & H. Goldman (Eds.), *Research in comprehensive psychiatry.* Columbus, Ohio: Ohio State University Press, 1972.

Maris, R. W. The sociology of suicide prevention: Policy implications of differences between suicidal patients and completed suicides. *Social Problems*, 1969, 17, 132-249.

Naroll, R. Cultural determinants and the concept of the sick society. In S. C. Plog & R. B. Edgerton (Eds.), *Changing perspectives in mental illness.* New York: Holt, Rinehart, & Winston, 1969.

SOCIAL STRESS AND MORTALITY: A SOCIOLOGICAL APPROACH

Miles E. Simpson

Department of Sociology
Texas Technical University
Lubbock, Texas, United States

This study argues that the study of social stress requires a microlevel empirical effort, and that new indicators of social stress are needed. A large literature has accumulated on the topic of the impact stress and its social sources. Recent efforts have emphasized family structure, stress-producing occupations, and a number of environmental factors; little attention, however, has been paid to "macroenvironments": cities, regions, and nations. Here, we will propose that the standard metropolitan statistical area (SMSA) represents an economic and cultural environment that produces different levels of stress. Furthermore, the National Institute of Health's Mortality Statistics provide indicators of others yet to be explored.

Sociologists during the 1940–1950's launched a major research effort into the study of the moral integration of American cities (Angell, 1947; Porterfield, 1949). With crimes of violence and suicide as their indicators of stress, these pioneers not only found major differences between cities, but the indicators were also related to other variables, e.g., welfare effort. Despite the early promise, these efforts appeared to collapse about 1950, due to the ecological correlation problem and the extensive data analyses required without the aid of high speed computers. This approach should now be renewed with new stress indicators, a systems approach and a major analytical tool not available to these pioneers—the computer.

Previous investigations of the forces behind social stress employed mainly crime and suicide as indicators of stress. The classic empirical study was carried out by Durkheim (1898) who did a major multivariate study of European rates of suicide. Durkheim asserted that suicide, a rare event, was primarily a product of social, not individual, forces. After examining suicide rates for Catholic and Protestant countries, among different occupations, between the sexes, and between different age groups, Durkheim concluded that the social integration of the individual is critical to suicide.

The copious literature on the impact of social stress and a variety of illnesses cannot be summarized here, but a number of good summaries appear elsewhere. In general, a large number of stressful social conditions such as divorce, occupational and geographic mobility, and overcrowding appear to be related to hypertensive disease. Some argue that the linkage between disease is based on aspiration-achievement and relative deprivation, whereas others contend that it is due to uncertainty or anomie, or to overloading that results from hyperactivity and the development of inappropriate coping responses (King, 1972). Regardless of the mechanism that best fits the particular disease, social stress is an important "causal agent" in many diseases.

Previous studies have focused on individuals, be they mobile, or divorced, "inconsistent" or "nonequilibrated" in terms of their social attributes; but epidemiologists have done little work on the contextual factors that might provide new sources of strain. This is mainly due to the fact that the environment has been a constraint, not a variable. We should look at variations in mortality rates in more macroenvironments (SMSAs), and compare variations in stress indexes with variations in different macroenvironments. Smaller environments may also be important to look at, in particular, home and work; but the SMSA provides a unit that varies along important cultural and structural dimensions. The results of a pilot study that I am presently completing showed a strong set of intercorrelations between death rates for hypertensive heart disease, other hypertensive diseases, cirrhosis of the liver, and ulcers. A regional breakdown of my sample of SMSAs over 100M indicated, in each region—the Northeastern states, and Midwest, the Mountain and Pacific states—that the rates for these stress-related diseases were intercorrelated.

Betz (1972) has shown that cities and their SMSA differ considerably in terms of income inequality. This inequality can be predicted on the basis of the SMSA's economic diversity, its educational level, and its percentage of black and other minority groups. Other studies have shown that differences in crime rates are related to natural log city size. Porterfield (1960) has shown that SMSA murder and suicide rates (not correlated at the SMSA level) are both correlated with SMSA auto death rates. Earlier researchers found that measures of moral "integration," which included welfare organizations, medical facilities, and the education of the population, were negatively related to crime rates. For homicide rates, the north-south cultural dimension is important (Gastil, 1971) in that SMSAs differ in terms of ethnic and racial heterogeneity. Age and sex ratios also vary by SMSA. More importantly, some SMSAs have undergone major changes in population, some growing rapidly, others remaining the same size but experiencing changes in the age pyramid, and others declining in size. Wechsler (1961) links suicide death rates to rapid population changes.

Economic changes, including expansion of industries and general changes in the "occupational structure," could have disruptive effects on interpersonal relationship. Some cities are marked by recent changes in residence patterns (Bay area, California) and others by their stable neighborhoods (Baltimore, Maryland, and Portland, Oregon). In all, there are many important dimensions by which cities can be differentiated; any one of these dimensions could have significant causal import for social stress.

REFERENCES

Angell, R. C. The social integration of American cities of more than 100,000 population. *American Sociological Review*, 1947, 12, 335–341.

Betz, M. D. The city as a system, generations income equality. *Social Forces*, 1972, 5, 192–198.

Durkheim, E. *Suicide*. New York: Free Press, 1962 (First published, 1898).

Gastil, R. D. Homicide and a regional culture of violence. *American Sociological Review*, 1971, 36, 412–426.

King, S. H. Social-psychological factors in illness. In H. E. Freeman, S. Levine, & L. G. Reeder (Eds.), *Handbook of medical sociology.* Englewood Cliffs, N.J.: Prentice-Hall, 1972.

Marks, R. V. Social stress and cardiovascular strain. Factors involving social and demographic characteristics. *The Milbank Memorial Fund Quarterly,* 1967, 155, 51-108.

Porterfield, A. L. Indices of suicides and homicide by states and cities: Some southern-nonsouthern contrasts with implications for research. *American Sociological Review,* 1959, 14, 481-490.

Porterfield, A. L. Traffic fatalities, suicide and homicide. *American Sociological Review,* 1960, 25, 817-901.

Saxon, Graham, & Reeder, L. G. Social factors in chronic illness. In H. E. Freedman, S. Levine, & L. G. Reeder (Eds.), *Handbook of medical sociology.* Englewood Cliffs, N.J.: Prentice-Hall, 1972.

Smith, T. Factors involving sociocultural incongruity and change. *The Milbank Memorial Fund Quarterly,* 1967, 45, 23-40.

Wechsler, H. Community growth, depressive disorders, and suicide. *The American Journal of Sociology,* 1961, 67, 9-17.

ANXIETY, DEATH, AND THE HEALTH CARE PROFESSIONAL

Lynwood L. Swanson

Department of Pastoral Care
Wilmington Medical Center
Wilmington, Delaware, United States

Utilizing data obtained from experimental sources, i.e., patients, family and hospital staff, we have endeavored to present a practical study of the death drama. Six stages or acts, each embracing the extremities of human reaction, seem to be apparent: Shock, Emotion, Negotiation, Cognition, Commitment, and Completion.

The initial experience of the patient (and/or family) to a terminal diagnosis is that of shock. The patient may react with either denial or panic. The latter, a totally destructive reaction, is less common than that of denial. We direct our interest to both the intellectual and emotional facets of this reaction. Since a patient may give intellectual acceptance to the information and simultaneously deny such on an emotional level, it is important to probe both aspects, to avoid an unhealthy prolongation of this stage.

In the emotional phase of the process, catharsis, or the healthy and overt expression of the patient's feelings, is to be encouraged. It should be noted that this is often hindered by family or staff who do not wish to witness the emotional experience of the patient.

A third and important act of the drama is that of negotiation. The patient often sees two alternatives: he may "sell out," or he may bargain for a miracle. The latter is a more healthy choice. The staff must not permit itself to become a functional part, but should remain a sympathetic listener.

With the increased awareness and acceptance of the situation as it is, the patient now confronts two opposing possibilities. He may, with the assistance of family and staff, choose to retain a realistic hope, to find meaning within the death drama. If left alone and avoided, he may lapse into despair.

In the stage we term "commitment," the patient will either emotionally or intellectually affirm and live the process of death, or he may choose the posture of despair. A positive level of fulfillment in death can be achieved if, throughout the process, the patient is permitted to retain the integrity and dignity that are his right in death as well as in life.

STRESS AND ANXIETY IN MODERN LIFE: A FANTASY

Peter Vroegop

Marine Keuringscentrum
Noodweg, Hilversum, The Netherlands

It seems to be accepted that there is a specific relation between stress and anxiety, on the one hand, and modern life, on the other. Therapeutic techniques, most recently those belonging to behavior therapy, and research findings on psychosomatic medicine might be thought of as reflecting the relation between stress and anxiety, and modern life. The abuse of drugs, the increase in psychosomatic disease and crime, and many people suffering from anxiety are all facts to be mentioned in this respect.

What then, in modern life, is there that could explain these facts? Traits, inherited or not, learning processes, and psychosocial stressors of all kinds seem to have explanatory value. We might formulate the question of the causes of stress and anxiety in another way. Not: what causes stress and anxiety, but rather: what is *not* there? For example, let us imagine that there were no women, only men in the world, but that in ancient, prehistorical times there were women. What would happen? There would be an inexplicable feeling of discomfort in man for which all kinds of solutions would be invented.

Psychologists might seek and find many correlations between this peculiar feeling of discomfort and other personality and psychosocial data. Behavior therapists might develop all kinds of techniques to reduce the unwanted feelings, and the anxiety caused by handling these feelings and the accompanying symptoms. They might ask themselves why so many people did not come to them for help although they had techniques that were effective. Most people, however, would have a vague notion, not easy to express verbally, and perhaps more unconscious than conscious, that these techniques did not bring the real solution. Psychologists would say to themselves: "People need their symptoms." The people themselves would have a vague feeling that there was, in their symptoms, a kind of last awareness of a fuller way of being human, and that without the symptom they would lose this inner connection with a real, though unknown, aspect of life. Formulated in another way, they would feel, probably more unconsciously than consciously, that the anxiety they experienced was a form of knowledge about things lying outside the horizon of consciousness. But because they could not explain the origin and the logic of these vague feelings, rational science would speak about these people as patients who did not understand themselves, and that would be true. Psychologists who would say that these feelings had nothing to do with reality, and that these people needed to be cured, would be right too.

Other people might have strange dreams or obsessive thoughts about a nonexisting being, and some of them might enter psychiatric hospitals. They would undoubtedly be treated with tranquilizers for their restlessness, even though a better explanation might be obtained from analysis of the content of their dreams. The most intuitive, natural-thinking people would least accept the developed therapeutic techniques because they would feel these techniques dealt only with symptoms, not the cause of symptoms. Many sophisticated psychologists would say that the symptom *is* the disease. Others might feel a little bit discontented with this view, concluding that something else must be wrong. However, they would be unable to deliver scientific data to support this feeling, except perhaps to insist that man is a whole, not a bundle of symptoms, and would risk being labeled "ethical," "humanistic," or "mystical."

Some people might be attracted by old myths, which would speak about feelings and emotions they could not understand anymore, but which would have an inexplicable attraction on them. The idea, however, that these myths were an expression of an earlier, real way of life would lie far beyond the scope of science.

This situation, I think, is akin to ours, although there are women, of course. Perhaps we miss something else and do not accept that we miss it. We do not know it, or, deeply, we know but do not accept something we had in earlier days. Understanding man as being involved in a process of evolution also raises the possibility that he possesses a slowly developing new ability, a new need, or something like that? What is it? Would an analysis of the symptoms and their content indicate the direction? I think this might be the case.

We, as psychologists, have to study, to mull over and analyze, what leads people to use drugs, what they seek, not what they try to escape, so that we may help them to adjust to situations in which they are not happy. We should understand symptoms as a form of significant, though aberrant behavior. As psychologists, we often look at our patients and clients in the wrong way. We look for mechanisms and correlations, and we run the risk of missing the real causes of human problems. It is our task to understand people, what is going on in them, not only to make distinctions between normal and abnormal behavior and invent techniques to cure the abnormal. Our task might be much broader than we are inclined to view it.

PROGRAM FOR THE ADVANCED STUDY INSTITUTE ON STRESS AND ANXIETY IN MODERN LIFE

GOALS AND SPONSORSHIP OF THE INSTITUTE

The goals of the Advanced Study Institute were to provide an opportunity for the dissemination of current knowledge about stress and anxiety, to facilitate the exchange of information among behavioral and medical scientists who were presently working in these areas, and to stimulate research on these topics. The Scientific Affairs Division of the North Atlantic Treaty Organization provided the primary support for the institute. Irwin G. Sarason and Charles D. Spielberger were the scientific directors, and the host country arrangements coordinator was J. C. Brengelmann.

The institute was held in Murnau-am-Staffelsee, West Germany, June 10–16, 1973. The general format consisted of lecture-seminar presentations designed to facilitate give-and-take critical discussions of theory and research on stress and anxiety. At the beginning of each session, an assigned lecturer presented a comprehensive paper and this was followed by a question-and-answer period and extensive discussion.

The titles of the ten major lectures that were presented at the institute are listed in the next section. The chapters in this volume are based on these lectures as revised by the authors. In addition, participants at the institute made brief presentations describing their own work. Abstracts of some of these brief papers are also included in this volume.

LECTURERS AND TITLES OF PAPERS PRESENTED AT THE INSTITUTE

Psycho-Social Stresses in Human Communication and Psychosomatic Disease
> J. Bastianns and J. J. Groen
> Rijksunsiversiteit Leiden
> Leiden, The Netherlands

Anxiety and the Natural History of Neuroses
> Hans J. Eysenck
> Institute of Psychiatry, University of London
> London, England

Conditioned Fear and Anxiety
> H. D. Kimmel
> University of South Florida
> Tampa, Florida, United States

The Nature of Clinical Anxiety in Modern Society
> Malcolm H. Lader
> Institute of Psychiatry, University of London
> London, England

Coping, Stress Immunization, and Extinction in the Reduction of Morbid Anxiety
> Isaac Marks
> Institute of Psychiatry, University of London
> London, England

Modifying What Clients Say to Themselves
> Donald Meichenbaum
> University of Waterloo
> Waterloo, Ontario, Canada

Problems in the Removal of Different Kinds of Anxiety
> R. W. Ramsay
> Universiteit van Amsterdam
> Amsterdam, The Netherlands

Test Anxiety: An Experimental Approach
   Irwin G. Sarason
   University of Washington
   Seattle, Washington, United States
Anxiety: State-Trait-Process
   Charles D. Spielberger
   University of South Florida
   Tampa, Florida, United States

INSTITUTE PARTICIPANTS

S. Achilles, West Germany
W. D. Anton, Florida, United States
P. F. Ashler, Florida, United States
T. N. Bhargava, Ohio, United States
J. Block, California, United States
G. E. Chandler, Connecticut, United States
M. DeBonis, France
J. de Lange, The Netherlands
O. Desiderato, Connecticut, United States
N. S. Endler, Canada
J. A. Feij, The Netherlands
J. P. Fields, Kentucky, United States
W. Fritz, West Germany
J. L. Greaner, Florida, United States
E. Gries, West Germany
K. Haaseth, Norway
R. D. Hare, Canada
R. M. Kaplan, California, United States
S. Karson, Michigan, United States
E. Kimmel, Florida, United States
H. H. Krauss, New York, United States
H. L. Lange, Illinois, United States
V. Lattanzo, Italy
A. Liakos, Greece
N. Mai, West Germany
K. A. McCormick, Wisconsin, United States
C. R. Millimet, Nebraska, United States

M. J. Misch, California, United States
P. Moxnes, Norway
J. S. Nunes, Portugal
B. Olsen, Denmark
J. F. Orlebeke, The Netherlands
A. Paschalis, Greece
H. E. Peplau, New Jersey, United States
C. A. Perlmutter, Wisconsin, United States
M. S. Perlmutter, Wisconsin, United States
S. Proctor, Wisconsin, United States
R. E. Pruett, Illinois, United States
D. Revenstorf, West Germany
P. G. Salmon, Illinois, United States
D. S. Schalling, Sweden
G. R. Schiff, North Carolina United States
S. Schwartz, Illinois, United States
S. Sharma, India
M. E. Simpson, Texas, United States
L. L. Swanson, Delaware, United States
M. A. van Kalmthout, The Netherlands
M. von Cotta-Schonberg, Denmark
P. Vroegop, The Netherlands
J. E. Williams, North Carolina United States

AUTHOR INDEX

Numbers in italics refer to the pages on which the complete references are cited.

SUBJECT INDEX